Food

justice, joy and daily bread

Introduction by Michael Schut

with Diane Ackerman
Dan Barker
Jake Batsell
Wendell Berry
Jennifer Bogo
Marcia Bunge
Mike Connelly
Alan Durning
Tewolde Egziabher
M.F.K. Fisher
Carol Flinders
Brian Halweil
Ben Jacques
Derrick Jensen
Elizabeth Johnson
Miriam Therese MacGillis
George McGovern
Anuradha Mittal

Donella Meadows
Thomas Moore
Jim Mulligan
Gary Paul Nabhan
Marion Nestle
Redefining Progress
John Robbins
Pattiann Rogers
Bernard Rollin
John Ryan
Eric Schlosser
Vandana Shiva
Joel Sisolak
Marilyn Snell
Gary Snyder
David Suzuki
Anthony Trewavas
Norman Wirzba

edited and compiled by Michael Schut
published in cooperation with Earth Ministry

Living the Good News
a division of Church Publishing Incorporated
600 Grant Street, Suite 400
Denver, CO 80203

Living the Good News
a division of Church Publishing Incorporated
Editorial Offices:
600 Grant Street, Suite 400
Denver, CO 80203

Photography: Regan MacStravic
Illustrations: Victoria Hummel

Printed in the United States of America.

The scripture quotations used within are from *The Holy Bible, New International Version.* © 1973, 1978, 1984 by International Bible Society. Used by permission of Zondervan Bible Publishers.

Because this is an anthology of articles from many sources, the style of punctuation and documentation varies.

ISBN 978-1889108-90-2
ISBN 1-889108-90-1

Acknowledgements

Any book is the result of the combined efforts and wisdom of many people. This seems true even for books written by only one person, for that individual is an expression of all those who have influenced her or his life. The writing embodies the wisdom garnered from the community. This is even more the case, then, for an anthology such as this, combining the work of not only all the authors and the communities which have influenced them, but the input and wisdom from many members of my community. This book is all the richer and fuller for it, and I am grateful.

I am a staff member at Earth Ministry, an ecumenical, Christian, environmental nonprofit organization. For literally making the work of Earth Ministry possible, thank you to all our donors! Special thanks to The Greenville Foundation (Sonoma, CA), The Northwest Fund for the Environment (Seattle, WA), and The Dudley Foundation (Bellingham, WA) for their generous support of this project. These foundations were able to see beyond the perceived boundary typically drawn between environmental and religious concerns.

We are also grateful for the financial support of the Evangelical Lutheran Church in America (Danielle Welliever and the World Hunger Coordinating Committee) and the Reformed Church in America (John Paarlberg and the Office of Social Witness and Worship).

In 1997, Earth Ministry published *Food, Faith, and Sustainability*, an anthology of eight essays and a five-week curriculum. This book is a significant expansion of that previous version. Those mentioned here include people who helped on *Food, Faith, and Sustainability* as well as *Food and Faith*.

This is the second book Earth Ministry has published with Living the Good News. Living the Good News originally saw the value in publishing *Simpler Living, Compassionate Life* and we are grateful for their interest in publishing this book with us as well. Thank you especially to Kathy Coffey, James Creasey, and Liz Riggleman for your enthusiasm, wisdom in navigating the publishing world and patience. Thank you, Kathy, for serving as editor, and for your good humor. Thank you to the rest of the staff at Living the Good News for your support. We at Earth Ministry believe strongly in our mission and the resources we produce; your support and involvement with us has spread that work to thousands of individuals and hundreds of churches.

My deepest thanks to Rev. Jim Mulligan, Earth Ministry's Executive Director. Jim and I have worked together for seven years, on many projects. The word unique is overused, but Jim is a unique "boss." Thank you, Jim, for serving as my primary dialogue partner on *Food and Faith*, for helping my own writing become more clear, for reading the essays, providing ideas for essays and for sharing your wisdom and insights to help shape this book.

The rest of Earth Ministry's staff also played important roles. In various brainstorming sessions, all the staff provided input on *Food and Faith's* content. Pete Dorman and Yvonne Wilhelmsen were always available for administrative and marketing support. Tanya Barnett's deep concerns for the issues raised in this book have been inspiring to me; she has also served as a dialogue partner. Rev. Nancy Wright and volunteer extraordinaire Ruth Mulligan were supportive of this project throughout.

Scott Warner and John Hoerster provided professional, friendly, and pro-bono legal advice as we developed *Food and Faith*. Their expertise and thorough attention to detail were invaluable to us lay-folk!

Other former staff and current volunteers helped make this book's precursor—*Food, Faith, and Sustainability*—more readable and user-friendly: Phebe Gustafson, Sheryl Wiser, Jeanette Carlson, Ruth Mulligan, Carol Sue Janes, Mark Musick, and Victoria Campbell. Earth Ministry board member Joel Sisolak helped edit and refine the introductory essay.

Cecile Andrews graciously offered her "Study Circles" ideas and principles, an approach to learning that we follow closely.

The majority of the content of this book comes from the hard work, perceptive thinking and deep care that all the included authors bring to their life and work. They are leaders in their fields of expertise. I have personally benefited from many of their writings a great deal. I hope their inclusion here helps many others.

Thanks to the many publishers for permission to reprint the essays contained herein. To all those who used the original *Food, Faith, and Sustainability* curriculum and sent in written evaluations or spoke with me in person, your comments and encouragement were always appreciated and helped in forming *Food and Faith*.

Thank you to my mother and father, Wayne and Joyce Schut, and my grandparents, Henry and Wilma Van Roekel and Henry and Hazel Schut—for living out and teaching me about the value of community, neighborliness and taking care of the soil. Thank you to my dear friends Jeanine and Larry Diller Murphy for their prayers and financial support of *Food and Faith*. I am grateful to my church, New Creation Community, for their prayers.

Michael Schut
September, 2002

If we no longer believe that the Earth is sacred, or that we are blessed by the bounty around us, or that we have a caretaking responsibility given to us by the Creator...then it does not really matter to most folks how much ecological and cultural damage is done by the way we eat.

—Gary Paul Nabhan

If we are to live and eat compassionately, with care, then the most fundamental shift we must make is a spiritual one. The essence of that shift is to live as if the Earth "is the Lord's," not a treasure chest for human plunder. Put differently, we must remember and act as if our home is a sacred place, and that God is not only transcendent but also immanent, very near.

—Michael Schut

Table of Contents

Study Guide by Michael Schut

Introduction

Our hope lies in that minority of people whose lives are less
defined by economics than by beauty and the love which
attends it.

—Wes Jackson

We can [not] live harmlessly or strictly at our own
expense; we depend upon other creatures and survive
by their deaths. To live, we must daily break the
body and shed the blood of creation. The point is,
when we do this knowingly, lovingly, skillfully,
reverently, it is a sacrament; when we do it
ignorantly, greedily, clumsily, destructively, it
is a desecration…in such desecration, we
condemn ourselves to spiritual and moral
loneliness, and others to want.

—Wendell Berry

Overview

by Michael Schut

Food and Faith is both an anthology of essays and a community building Study Guide, similar to Earth Ministry's previous book, *Simpler Living, Compassionate Life*. The theme of the sacramentality of food, developed in the introduction, brings coherence to *Food and Faith's* various topics, beginning with two common food-related themes: the celebration of food and the joy it brings to life (Section 1), and the connections between diet and good health (Section 2). Section 3 evokes the ways in which food nourishes spirituality. Section 4 helps establish a Christian ecological ethic, showing the inherent connections between caring for people and caring for Earth and its creatures.

"The Family Farm" (Section 5) explores the challenges farmers face in the global food system. The industrialization of agriculture encouraged by that global system then becomes a theme running through the next three sections. "Economics as if Creation Mattered" (Section 6) explores the ecological and social costs hidden within our current agricultural system, and introduces practical political steps individuals and communities can take to support a more sustainable food economy. Sections 7 and 8 focus on industrial agriculture's impacts on farm and slaughterhouse workers, the treatment of farm animals, and its support for genetically modified organisms.

"Addressing Hunger—Political and Economic Perspectives" (Section 9) highlights what it will take to confront hunger in our time. The final essays in Section 10 present simple, encouraging stories of promising directions related to food choices and agriculture today.

Food and Faith brings together a rich collection of "voices." Whether reading it on your own or with a group, you are invited into the conversation. When reading *Food and Faith*, you are encouraged to also explore the Study Guide, which includes questions for reflection and suggested action steps. The Study Guide is designed to help create a community of support as you explore the sometimes challenging realities described by this book.

We're glad you joined us for this exploration of food and faith!

[This book has been published in cooperation with Earth Ministry. Please see p. 284 for more information about this ecumenical, Christian, environmental, nonprofit organization.]

Food As Sacramental

by Michael Schut

Michael Schut has served on Earth Ministry's staff for seven years. He is the editor of the award-winning *Simpler Living, Compassionate Life: A Christian Perspective*, also published by Living the Good News. Earth Ministry helps connect Christian faith with care and justice for all creation. Michael's work with them includes teaching, speaking and writing on topics of voluntary simplicity, economic justice, food choices and sustainability, and environment and faith. Michael has a B.S. in Biology from Wheaton College and an M.S. in Environmental Studies from the University of Oregon. He likes to backpack, climb, play tennis, sing and play guitar, and eat ice cream.

∞

A Pilgrimage: Coming Home to Eat

I grew up in southeastern Minnesota. Mom and Dad grew up on farms where they learned to garden and to work hard. As adults they planted huge gardens every spring and had no qualms about working their children hard. Picking green beans—knee-high, bushy plants with large green leaves meant (it seemed) to conceal the skinny green beans growing at backbreaking levels—was the worst. My sisters, Lynn and Katrina, and I felt those rows upon rows of green beans were interminable. Had my parents forgotten they were no longer farming? Had they missed the fact that there were only five of us to feed? Were they unaware of child labor laws? In contrast, tomatoes—sporting large, red fruit against green vegetation—seemed well worth the effort.

Describing tomatoes as "well worth the effort," however, is a bit like saying Yosemite or the Grand Canyon are "worth seeing." Southeastern Minnesota is prime tomato country, featuring that wonderful combination of summer heat, humidity and rich soil that each year miraculously turns little seeds into the richest of fare.

As early August rolled around, Mom or Dad gave periodic "tomato progress reports." We knew when those first few blushes of red appeared, and when we might expect to taste the first of that year's crop. The occasion of harvesting the first ripe tomato was a significant calendar marker: Katrina's birthday is in January, Mom's in February, mine in May, Lynn and Dad's are in June, tomatoes ripen in August. That first tomato was both highly anticipated and anxiety provoking: though all five of us were raised to be generous, we also definitely wanted to get our one-fifth share. Among other genetic similarities, each one of us cherished fresh garden tomatoes as a favorite food. Even when there were enough for breakfast, lunch and dinner, I remember furtively watching the tomato platter as it was passed, challenging my sisters if they exceeded their fair share of the best slices. I know I was also under their surveillance.

I now live in Seattle, Washington where I tend a small backyard garden. I grow tomatoes, though they never really taste as sweet, rich, or complex as the ones from home. I usually make it back to Minnesota during August for the tomato harvest. It's a comforting time to be at home. I feel nurtured not only through being "back home" around Mom and Dad, but through their garden's bounty.

My August trips in some ways resemble a pilgrimage. Pilgrims travel to kindle their connections to a sacred place and thus to nurture their relationship with the divine. Their journeys bring them, if not to a physical home, then to a "home within," a restful, familiar, healing place that reminds them of who they are. The sacred site to which I return is connected to my roots. My body remembers the feel of the garden underfoot, the aroma of mom's cooking, the crickets at night, the wall of heat and the colors and tastes of garden-fresh meals.

Those tomatoes become not only food for my physical self, but a symbol of the ways in which we as a family seek to care for each other and a reminder of the connections between us. So it is not difficult to remember that, no matter my parents' gardening skills, our sustenance ultimately depends on the Earth's fertility: a gift. From there a simple prayer of gratitude seems the most natural thing. In a way the tomato becomes sacramental, not in the formal sense as part of the liturgical rites of the Church, but as a "sign or symbol of a spiritual reality" (to quote Webster).

Food As Sacramental

Seeing the tomato, a common food in many meals, as potentially sacramental is not a stretch when recalling Jesus' last meal with his friends. At dinner, Jesus took bread and wine, the commonly available, everyday elements of a meal in that time and place. He then broke the bread and poured the wine both to remind his disciples of his life and teachings and to serve as an invitation to follow his acts of love and compassion. It is not accidental that Christ chose a meal for the setting and bread and wine as the symbols for instituting what has become the most central of Christian sacraments. The settings and elements of everyday meals carry within them a kind of "sacramental power."

This book invites you to explore and celebrate food's sacramentality. In doing so, the book looks beyond the food itself to examine how it grew, was processed and made its way to our table. Wendell Berry summarizes this perspective beautifully:

> We can [not] live harmlessly or strictly at our own expense; we
> depend upon other creatures and survive by their deaths. To live, we
> must daily break the body and shed the blood of creation. The point
> is, when we do this knowingly, lovingly, skillfully, reverently, it is a
> sacrament; when we do it ignorantly, greedily, clumsily, destructively,
> it is a desecration…in such desecration, we condemn ourselves to
> spiritual and moral loneliness, and others to want.[1]

"When we do this knowingly, lovingly, skillfully, reverently, *it is a sacrament.*" Berry is suggesting that we can be blessed with sacramental moments when we "break the body and shed the blood of creation" in a certain way: more knowingly than ignorantly, more lovingly than greedily, more skillfully than clumsily, more reverently than destructively.

In suggesting that food can be sacramental, this book recognizes that, in the Christian tradition, the Church *formally* celebrates seven sacraments. (Protestants generally have two sacraments, Communion and Baptism. Catholics have these two plus five others: Confirmation, Reconciliation, the Sacrament of the Sick, Ordination, and Marriage.) But the Christian tradition also celebrates *informal* sacramental moments in everyday life. Consider the apostle Paul speaking to the Athenians in Acts 17: "God…is not far from each one of us. For in God we live and move and have our being." It's as if all of us are swimming in God's presence. In such a world, the holy is never far off. In such a world, "church isn't the only place where the holy happens. Sacramental moments can occur at any moment, any place, and to anybody. Watching something get born. Making love…Somebody coming to see you when you're sick. A meal with people you love…If we weren't blind as bats, we might see that life itself is sacramental."[2]

This book understands sacrament in this broader, less formal way. It sees the eating, procuring and growing of food as sacramental, ushering an awareness of "the holy" into everyday life. It sees in the need to be nourished daily the larger spiritual reality of our dependence on mysteries that we do not fully understand.

My Family and Farming

Other relationships, besides those with my immediate family and their tomatoes draw me back to Minnesota where most of my extended family lives. I feel rooted in this landscape, nurtured by lasting ties to family, friends, and the land itself. I feel at "home," which is not surprising considering my roots. My paternal grandparents, Henry Schut and Hazel Dalman, called the rolling hills, lakes and dairy country of central Minnesota home. Grandpa was born, reared and lived for sixty years in his family's farmhouse, on land farmed by his family for over seventy-five years. Henry Van Roekel and Wilma Van Ommen, my maternal grandparents, were born in the corn, hog and soybean country of southeastern Iowa. Grandpa was born in the house where he lived for the first seventy years of his life. The land he farmed was in his family for over one hundred years, one of Iowa's "century farms."

All of my grandparents grew up speaking Dutch and attending the Reformed Church. Sunday was always a Sabbath, reserved for rest and worship no matter the work left undone in the fields or the barn. There was a certain rhythm and regularity imposed on them by the farm, and a certain rhythm and regularity to their faith tradition, in some ways imposed on them by the culture in which they lived.

Each of the two families raised six children. Of these twelve, not one became a farmer. Not one of my aunts, uncles, or twenty-seven first cousins were able to purchase the family farms; none of us wanted to, considering the economics of farming today. Both sets of grandparents eventually sold their land to neighbor farmers needing more acreage. I carry a deep sadness that the land no longer belongs to the family.

The sadness is personal. I have lost a connection with a landscape that still in my bones feels very much like home. Though I probably could still become a farmer, learning to farm from my family on their land is no longer a possibility. The sadness is also ecological: modern crop farming and animal production is much more destructive of topsoil, water and wildlife than the methods my grandparents learned. The sadness is also cultural: modern crop farming and animal production is much more destructive of rural community than the scale and type of farming my grandparents employed.

Both my personal and my family's experiences—fewer and fewer farmers, larger and larger farms, a more distant relationship with the land that sustains us—mirror changes occurring around the world, and especially in the United States. These personal experiences therefore connect to many larger concerns related to our society's distance (even alienation) from our food, farmers and land: those concerns include ecosystem health, rural economic viability and the spirituality expressed in personal and cultural relationships to food.

Looking Further

This book explores a broad range of food-related themes. Many of these are reflected in my own family's stories. First, like my tomato pilgrimage, a number of the themes can help reveal the sacramentality of food. Second, like my extended family's farming history, several of those themes connect to the decline of the family farm, the reasons for that decline and the impacts it has on rural communities, the environment, migrant workers and farm animals. The sacramentality of food is reflected in this book's emphasis on celebration, communion and gratitude.

Celebration

Food adds joy to life. Meaningful, hilarious, community-enriching, soul-satisfying times are so often associated with a shared table. Close friends, candlelight, homemade bread, a meal prepared together and a prayer of thanks. Or a big party, potluck, the plates not big enough for all the variety, the second helping of those particularly tasty dishes, the familiar voices and laughter. Or a favorite holiday meal, feeding body and soul. The stories and settings are endless, but at each occasion the gift of food mediates a larger reality—the sanctity, preciousness and joy of life.

Communion

"To live, we must daily break the body and shed the blood of creation." Daily we participate in the mystery of other beings becoming part of our very tissue. And daily we have the opportunity to experience food as a sacrament, where the appropriate metaphor for food is not *fuel* but rather *communion*: with those family and friends sharing the meal, with those hands whose skill helped grow and harvest the food, with other creatures and ultimately with our Creator.

Communion in the Christian tradition also connotes the liturgical celebration instituted in remembrance of Jesus' last meal with his disciples. Just after college I spent a year as a resident manager at Samaritan Inns, a ministry of Church of the Savior in Washington, DC. I lived with formerly homeless men for a year. We ate our meals at Christ House, a thirty-four-bed medical recovery home for homeless men. Christ House held weekly worship services in their dining room where Holy Communion was celebrated each week. Those of us able to stand and file to the altar did so; others wheeled themselves.

One Sunday especially the "line-up" hit me. There's Don, a man in his 50s, a walking miracle, recovering from alcoholism and homelessness. There's David, the highly talented, well-educated and compassionate co-founder of Samaritan Inns. There's Carlton, a man in his 40s, angry with me because of the position of authority I have as the resident manager of his home. There's the elderly woman whose financial generosity helped make Christ House possible. There's David, a medical doctor on the Christ House staff who struggles mightily with his own depression. Rich and poor, young and old, black, white and in-between, sick and well, each in their own way recognizing their need for reconciliation and relationship with God and others, celebrating God's presence. Sharing bread and grape juice. The Kingdom of God is here, I thought. And the Kingdom of God will be like this: Communion.

Gratitude

Eating can nurture gratitude. "When we eat," Sharon Parks writes, "we must very soon eat again. If we dare to contemplate fully the act of eating, we will be led to the unavoidable awareness of our continual desire to live, and also our utter dependence upon the generosity of the Earth and its peoples and the power and grace by which our lives are sustained."[3] Thus, in the presence of a meal, we bow our heads. In receiving the gift of "our daily bread" we are reminded of our ultimate dependence on God's provision for this life and of the miracle of sun, water, seed, soil, and air contributing to what becomes food.

My extended family's farming history also connects to this book's emphasis on healing divisions, agriculture's environmental impacts, the explosion of industrial agriculture, political activism, and hope.

Healing Divisions

Generally speaking, Western culture does not see the words food and faith as closely related. For most of us, food comes from the supermarket (often diced, sliced, packaged and frozen beyond resemblance to anything living), not from the farm or the Earth. We live in a time when it is possible for children gardening in the inner city to refuse to eat the fruits of their labor, not wanting to eat anything that "comes from dirt." In addition, for many of us faith is relegated to a Sunday morning ritual, compartmentalized from the rest of our lives, having little impact on everyday choices such as food.

Environmental educator David Orr writes, "Our alienation from the natural world is unprecedented. Healing this division is a large part of the difference between survival and extinction." This book seeks to help heal a number of "divisions," including: the division between the foods we eat and our knowledge of how those foods impact not only our own health but the health of the rest of the natural world; the division between faith and faith's call to care for all creation and the division between food and faith.

Environmental Impacts

On some level we are all aware that eating ties us directly to Earth. Anything that so connects us to the natural world has significant environmental impacts. As Wendell Berry says, "How we eat determines to a considerable extent how the world is used." The accuracy of his statement is corroborated in the 1999 book *The Consumer's Guide to Effective Environmental Choices.* This well-researched book highlights those choices that individual consumers can make to decrease detrimental impacts on the environment. Rather than getting bogged down with detailed questions: paper or plastic? cloth diapers or disposables?, the book focuses consumers' attention on those choices that really make a difference.

Their findings? Two of the top three "most harmful consumer activities" involve what we eat, and where and how it is grown. The most harmful [individual] consumer activity: cars and light trucks. The second most harmful: meat and poultry. The third most harmful: fruit, vegetables, and grains. How we eat really does significantly determine how Earth is used. Their suggested "priority actions" for American consumers are to eat less meat, and buy certified organic produce.[4]

Let's consider their first suggestion, eating less meat. In the United States it takes 2,400 gallons of water to produce one pound of beef; over 70 percent of the U.S. grain harvest is fed to livestock each year, the majority of it to cattle. There's more, but you get the picture (simply eating one less quarter-pounder a month saves 600 gallons of water).[5]

Industrial Agriculture

The word "agriculture" refers to the culture that develops from the cultivation of land. Over the last fifty years that culture has changed dramatically. Corporate management has significantly replaced family and community stewardship. What often became an art form attuned to the complexities of local climate, soil, seasons and family knowledge has been largely replaced by agriscience and agribusiness, attuned to Wall Street, competition, and the bottom line. In the process, monocultures, petroleum-based fertilizers and pesticides, "factory farms" and soil erosion have greatly reduced the use of crop rotation, organic fertilizers, and animal and soil husbandry.

These shifts in agricultural practices are intricately connected to the increased ownership of agricultural land by multinational agribusiness corporations. Corporations are either less willing or less able to care for the long-term health of land than small-scale family farmers, concerned about passing the land on to their children. Between 1910 and 1920, the United States had 32 million farmers living on farms, about a third of the population. By 1991, the number was only 4.6 million, less than 2% of the national population.[6] These statistics begin to suggest the extent of the change in the "culture of agriculture."

Wendell Berry suggests that such a culture produces "industrial eaters," who may think of food as an agricultural product, but who do not think of themselves as "participants in agriculture. They think of themselves as passive consumers."[7] Passive consumers no longer know those who grow their food, or even how or where it was grown. When, as in the example of the young inner-city gardeners, our understanding of the source of our food is limited to "it comes from the supermarket," we do not know its geographical derivation or remember its ultimate dependence upon the fertility of the soil. Thus, we cannot know how healthful such food is for us, for the land, or for those who grew it.

On the other hand, if we begin to think of ourselves as participants in agriculture, we might begin to ask questions. Where and how was the food grown? Are those who planted, tended and harvested our food treated as pawns in the global food economy? Or do they own their land and are therefore more likely to care for its long-term health? To realize that our food choices influence not only our own health, but also the health of the land and rural communities, is to move toward taking responsibility for our participation. In accepting such responsibility, we honor those community connections that bring us our daily bread. With this awareness comes the possibility of eating more sacramentally, fostering healing.

Political Activism

It ought to be clear by now that *Food and Faith* is not only about *individuals* making changes in daily food choices. The book also recognizes the importance of political activism leading to systemic change. Both individual and systemic change are essential; to debate which is the more effective seems pointless. For example, if enough individuals choose to boycott eating "factory-farmed" animals, the system would find a way to meet the demand for meat raised more humanely and with less environmental impact. A similar result could be achieved through the application of political pressure. For example, taxing the owners of such factory farms to cover the costs of adequate animal waste disposal would increase the cost of the meat. Individual consumers would then begin to shift their meat-buying habits in order to get a better price.

Various essays highlight the necessity of working at both the individual and systemic level. In Section 2, Marion Nestle emphasizes that individuals need to be educated about how to eat well, *and* that political pressure must be applied to combat the food industry's marketing of foods high in salt, sugar, and fat. In Section 9, Mittal and McGovern point out that addressing hunger is not only about growing enough food for individual consumption, but also requires the political will to ameliorate poverty.

Hope

Industrial agriculture's influence on the food we eat, on its nutritional value, on ecosystems around the world, on migrant workers, on the treatment of animals, on the viability of rural farm communities can become overwhelming. Looking clearly at those realities is a necessity if we are to help create systems that value the integrity of creation. But shifting our gaze to see and celebrate the hopeful stories of individuals and agricultural systems which recognize that the eating, procuring, and growing of food can be sacramental is just as important.

Throughout this book, and particularly in the final section titled "Stories of Hope: Promising Directions," you will find examples of individuals eating, cooking, growing, and shopping for food in ways that are healthy for people, value the importance of clean water and healthy soil, pay farmers a fair wage, treat farm animals well, keep farmland protected from urban sprawl and support local agriculture rather than distant mega-farms. In various essays and within the Study Guide you will find suggested, "doable," small action steps you can take in your personal life that reflect a sacramental view of food.

Coming Home to Eat

I began this essay relating my experiences of returning home to eat, and how I am more than physically fed at such times. If we are fortunate enough to have a good home, we return there not only to eat, but also to be nurtured in a variety of ways. One of the ways we know we are home is through the food prepared for us. In the biblical story of the prodigal son, a young man takes his father's inheritance, quickly exhausting it on "reckless" living. Destitute and desperate for food, the son decides to return home. He plans to simply ask his father to treat him like one of his hired men, who at least are well fed. But the father, upon seeing his son, runs to him, kisses and hugs him, clothes him, kills the "fatted calf" and throws a feast. The feast's significance becomes clear if we try to imagine the story without it: if, say, after kissing, hugging and clothing him the father had said, "Welcome home— help yourself to what's in the fridge." The feast is a sign that the son is loved, forgiven, welcomed and truly "home."

There are other meanings within the phrase "coming home to eat." Gary Paul Nabhan spent a year eating foods that grew no further than 250 miles from his home. He titled his book about that year *Coming Home to Eat.* Most broadly understood, coming home to eat recognizes Earth as the home God created for us and all creatures. To eat in such a way honors and cares for the breadth of God's creation.

This book raises significant social and ecological concerns. If we are to live and eat in ways that will begin to ameliorate those concerns, the most fundamental shift we must make is a spiritual one. The essence of that shift is to live as if the Earth "is the Lord's" (Psalm 24:1), not a treasure chest for human plunder. Put differently, we must act as if our home is a sacred place, and remember that our faith traditions not only affirm that God is transcendent but also immanent, very near. Biblical scholar and Orthodox theologian Philip Sherrard puts it this way in the introduction to his book *Human Image: World Image:*

We are treating our planet in an inhuman and god-forsaken manner
because we see things in an inhuman, god-forsaken way. And we see
things in this way because that is basically how we see ourselves...
[we] look upon ourselves as little more than two-legged animals
whose destiny and needs can best be fulfilled through the pursuit of...
self-interest. To correspond with this self-image, we have invented a
worldview in which nature is seen as an impersonal commodity, a
soulless source of food, raw materials...which we think we are entitled to exploit and abuse by any technique we can devise....[8]

Significantly, in the epilogue to *Coming Home to Eat*, Nabhan comes to a similar
conclusion: "If we no longer believe that the Earth is sacred, or that we are blessed
by the bounty around us, or that we have a caretaking responsibility given to us by
the Creator...then it does not really matter to most folks how much ecological and
cultural damage is done by the way we eat."[9]

Finally, if this book is an invitation to come home to eat, to remember food's
sacramentality, then everyone is invited—farmers, environmentalists, corporate
executives, grocery store clerks, migrant workers, economists, theologians, artists,
politicians, truck drivers, scientists and activists (not to mention the whole host of
God's other creatures who also need to be fed and nurtured in this same home).
We all eat and we all wish to leave our children and grandchildren a healthy
world: we at least share that in common. Through individual choice and political
action we must work together to create and support food systems (as well as larger
economic systems) that recognize and celebrate food as sacramental.

I hope this book helps you discern ways you might embody love and compassion
through your everyday food choices and see how those choices can help create
agricultural and economic systems that embody love.

Notes

1. Wendell Berry, *The Gift of Good Land* (San Francisco: North Point Press, 1983, 1981), pp. 272-281.

2. Frederick Buechner, *Wishful Thinking: A Theological ABC* (New York: Harper and Row, 1973), p. 82.

3. Sharon Daloz Parks, "The Meaning of Eating and the Home As Ritual Space," from Elizabeth Gray, ed. *Sacred Dimensions of Women's Experience* (New York: Roundtable Press, 1988), pp. 184-192.

4. Michael Brower and Leon Warren, *The Consumer's Guide to Effective Environmental Choices* (New York: Three Rivers Press, Crown Publishers, 1999), pp. 50, 85.

5. Alan Durning and John Ryan, *Stuff: The Secret Lives of Everyday Things*, (Seattle, WA: Northwest Environment Watch, 1997), pp. 54-55.

6. Wendell Berry, "Conserving Communities," *Orion Magazine*, Summer, 1995.

7. Wendell Berry, "The Pleasures of Eating," in *What Are People For?* (San Francisco: North Point Press, 1990), p. 145.

8. Philip Sherrard, *Human Image: World Image* (Ipswich, UK: Golgonooza Press, 1992), pp. 2-3.

9. Gary Paul Nabhan, *Coming Home to Eat* (New York: W.W. Norton and Company, 2002), p. 304.

A Celebration of Food

Given honest flour, pure water, and a good fire, there is
really only one more thing needed to make the best
bread in the world, fit for the greatest gourmet
ever born: and that is honest love.

—M.F.K. Fisher

Oh taste and see that the Lord is good.

—Psalm 34:8

Long before institutionalized religions
came along—and temples, and
churches—there was an unquestioned
recognition that what goes on in the
kitchen is holy…Do we not hallow
places by our very commitment to
them? When we turn our home
into a place that nourishes and
heals and contents, we are meeting directly all the hungers that
a consumer society exacerbates
but never satisfies.

—Carol Flinders

Introduction

"I am thinking now of some of the best meals of my life," begins M.F.K. Fisher's story "Poor Food." In "A Thing Shared" Fisher has the same theme, reliving the first meal she and her sister shared with their father, away from mother's watchful eyes. In these two stories, as well as the subsequent essays by Ackerman and Nabhan, the goodness of food is intimately intertwined with the goodness of the relationships represented around the table. Nabhan's meal with his Lebanese cousins celebrates not only his relationships with his family, but also the relationships between his family, their food, and the Earth. Nabhan's piece foreshadows Wendell Berry's point (see "The Pleasures of Eating," p. 142) that the fullest possible celebration of food comes through knowing the sources (both human and non-human) from which one's food comes. A book bearing the title *Food and Faith* would be incomplete without stories celebrating the place of food within the fullness of life. Enjoy and recall some of your best meals!

A Thing Shared

by M. F. K. Fisher

For over sixty years, M.F. K. Fisher wrote about food, cooking and eating as human and cultural metaphors. She published fifteen books and many essays which first appeared in the *New Yorker* magazine.

One of our most widely read gourmet food writers, she recalls here an early childhood experience: a dinner shared with her father and younger sister which, 25 years later, is still fresh in each of their memories as one of their favorite meals. "Poor Food" describes the best sauce, the best stew, and the best bread she ever ate. Both articles remember meals made rich, wholesome, even holy, through the love with which they were prepared and made celebratory through the people with whom they were shared. Savor them.

∞

Now you can drive from Los Angeles to my Great-Aunt Maggie's ranch on the other side of the mountains in a couple of hours or so, but the first time I went there it took most of a day.

Now the roads are worthy of even the All-Year-Round Club's boasts, but twenty-five years ago, in the September before people thought peace had come again, you could hardly call them roads at all. Down near the city they were oiled, all right, but as you went farther into the hills toward the wild desert around Palmdale, they turned into rough dirt. Finally they were two wheelmarks skittering every which way through the Joshua trees.

It was very exciting: the first time my little round brown sister Anne and I had ever been away from home. Father drove us up from home with Mother in the Ford, so that she could help some cousins can fruit.

We carried beer for the parents (it exploded in the heat), and water for the car and Anne and me. We had four blowouts, but that was lucky, Father said as he patched the tires philosophically in the hot sun; he'd expected twice as many on such a long, hard trip.

The ranch was wonderful, with wartime crews of old men and loud-voiced boys picking the peaches and early pears all day, and singing and rowing at night in the bunkhouses. We couldn't go near them or near the pen in the middle of a green alfalfa field where a new prize bull, black as thunder, pawed at the pale sand.

We spent most of our time in a stream under the cottonwoods, or with Old Mary the cook, watching her make butter in a great churn between her mountainous knees. She slapped it into pats, and put them down in the stream where it ran hurriedly through the darkness of the butter-house.

She put stone jars of cream there, too, and wire baskets of eggs and lettuces, and when she drew them up, like netted fish, she would shake the cold water onto us and laugh almost as much as we did.

Then Father had to go back to work. It was decided that Mother would stay at the ranch and help put up more fruit, and Anne and I would go home with him. That was as exciting as leaving it had been, to be alone with Father for the first time.

He says now that he was scared daft at the thought of it, even though our grandmother was at home as always to watch over us. He says he actually shook as he drove away from the ranch, with us like two suddenly strange small monsters on the hot seat beside him.

Probably he made small talk. I don't remember. And he didn't drink any beer, sensing that it would be improper before two unchaperoned young ladies.

We were out of the desert and into deep winding canyons before the sun went down. The road was a little smoother, following streambeds under the live-oaks that grow in all the gentle creases of the dry tawny hills of that part of California. We came to a shack where there was water for sale, and a table under the dark, wide trees.

Father told me to take Anne down the dry streambed a little way. That made me feel delightfully grown-up. When we came back we held our hands under the water faucet and dried them on our panties, which Mother would never have let us do.

Then we sat on a rough bench at the table, the three of us in the deep green twilight, and had one of the nicest suppers I have ever eaten.

The strange thing about it is that all three of us have told other people that same thing, without ever talking of it among ourselves until lately. Father says that all his nervousness went away, and he saw us for the first time as two little brown humans who were fun. Anne and I both felt a subtle excitement at being alone for the first time with the only man in the world we loved.

(We loved Mother too, completely, but we were finding out, as Father was too, that it is good for parents and for children to be alone now and then with one another...the man alone or the woman, to sound new notes in the mysterious music of parenthood and childhood.)

That night I not only saw my Father for the first time as a person. I saw the golden hills and the live-oaks as clearly as I have ever seen them since; and I saw the dimples in my little sister's fat hands in a way that still moves me because of that first time; and I saw food as something beautiful to be shared with people instead of as a thrice-daily necessity.

I forget what we ate, except for the end of the meal. It was a big round peach pie, still warm from Old Mary's oven and the ride over the desert. It was deep, with lots of juice, and bursting with ripe peaches picked that noon. Royal Albertas, Father said they were. The crust was the most perfect I have ever tasted, except perhaps once upstairs at Simpson's in London, on a hot plum tart.

And there was a quart Mason jar, the old-fashioned bluish kind like Mexican glass, full of cream. It was still cold, probably because we all knew the stream it had lain in, Old Mary's stream.

Father cut the pie in three pieces and put them on white soup plates in front of us, and then spooned out the thick cream. We ate with spoons too, blissful after the forks we were learning to use with Mother.

And we ate the whole pie, and all the cream...we can't remember if we gave any to the shadowy old man who sold water...and then drove on sleepily toward Los Angeles, and none of us said anything about it for many years, but it was one of the best meals we ever ate.

Perhaps that is because it was the first conscious one, for me at least; but the fact that we remember it with such queer clarity must mean that it had other reasons for being important. I suppose that happens at least once to every human. I hope so.

Now the hills are cut through with super-highways, and I can't say whether we sat that night in Mint Canyon or Bouquet, and the three of us are in some ways even more than twenty-five years older than we were then. And still the warm round peach pie and the cool yellow cream we ate together that August night live in our hearts' palates, succulent, secret, delicious.

Poor Food

by M.F.K. Fisher

I am thinking now of some of the best meals in my life, and almost without exception they have been so because of the superlative honesty of "poor food," rather than sophistication. I admire and often even *like* what is now called the classical cuisine—the intricate sauces of great chefs, and the complexities of their entremets and their pastries. But for strength, both of the body and of the spirit, I turn without hesitation to the simplest cooks.

I remember the best sauce I ever ate.

It was not at Foyot's, in the old days in Paris. It was in a cabin with tar-paper walls on a rain-swept hillside in southern California. The air was heavy with the scent of wet sage from outside and the fumes of a cheap kerosene stove within. Three or four children piped for more, more, from the big bowl of steaming gravy in the center of the heavy old round table crowded between the family's cots. We ate it from soup plates, the kind you used to get free with labels from cereal packages. It was made from a couple of young cottontails, and a few pulls of fresh herbs from the underbrush, and springwater and some Red Ink from the bottom of Uncle Johnnie's birthday jug—and a great deal of love. It was all we had, with cold flapjacks left from breakfast to scoop it up. It was *good*, and I knew that I was indeed fortunate, to have driven up the hill that night in the rain and to have friends who would share with me.

I remember the best stew I ever ate, too.

It was not a bouillabaisse at Isnard's in Marseille. It was made, further east on the Mediterranean at Cassis, by a very old small woman for a great lusty batch of relatives and other people she loved. Little grandnephews dove for equally young octopuses and delicate sea eggs, and older sons sent their rowboats silently up the dark *calanques* for rockfish lurking among the sunken German U-boats from the First War, and grizzling cousins brought in from the deep sea a fine catch of rays and other curious scaly monsters. Little girls and their mothers and great-aunts went up into the bone-dry hills for aromatic leaves and blossoms, and on the way home picked up a few bottles of herby wine from the tiny vineyards where they worked in the right seasons.

The very old small woman cooked and pounded and skinned and ruminated, and about noon, two days later, we met in her one-room house and spent some twenty more hours, as I remember, eating and eating...and talking and singing and then eating again, from seemingly bottomless pots of the most delicious stew in my whole life. It, again, had been made with love...

And out of a beautiful odorous collection of good breads in my life I still taste, in my memory, the *best*.

There have been others that smelled better, or looked better, or cut better, but this one, made by a desolately lonesome Spanish-Greek Jewess for me when I was about five, was the best. Perhaps it was the shape. It was baked in pans just like the big ones we used every Saturday, but tiny, perhaps one by three inches. And it rose just the way ours did, but tinily. (Many years later, when I read *Memoirs of a Midget* and suffered for the difficulties of such a small person's meals, I wished I could have taken to her, from time to time and wrapped in a doll's linen napkin, a fresh loaf from my friend's oven.)

Yes, that was and still is the best bread. It came from the kitchen of a very simple woman, who knew instinctively that she could solace her loneliness through the ritual of honest cooking. It taught me, although I did not understand it then, a prime lesson in survival. I must eat well. And in these days of spurious and distorted values, the best way to eat is simply, without affectation or adulteration. Given honest flour, pure water, and a good fire, there is really only one more thing needed to make the best bread in the world, fit for the greatest gourmet ever born: and that is honest love.

The Social Sense

by Diane Ackerman

Diane Ackerman is a poet and author whose works include *On Extended Wings* and *A Natural History of the Senses*. Born in Waukegan, Illinois, she received an M.A., M.F.A. and Ph.D. from Cornell University. She has taught at several universities and writes for the *New Yorker*.

Her essay evokes a great diversity of familiar images associated with the gift of food, mediated through taste, which she calls the "intimate sense." No matter the context—from power lunches to wedding feasts, from the sacrament of communion to birthday cake—food is "close at hand to sanctify and bind it." Enjoy the memories she conjures and the reminders of how central food is to hospitality, religion and pleasure.

∞

The other senses may be enjoyed in all their beauty when one is alone, but taste is largely social. Humans rarely choose to dine in solitude, and food has a powerful social component. The Bantu feel that exchanging food makes a contract between two people who then have a "clanship of porridge." We usually eat with our families, so it's easy to see how "breaking bread" together would symbolically link an outsider to a family group. Throughout the world, the stratagems of business take place over meals; weddings end with a feast; friends reunite at celebratory dinners; children herald their birthdays with ice cream and cake; religious ceremonies offer food in fear, homage, and sacrifice; wayfarers are welcomed with a meal. As Brillat-

Savarin says, "every...sociability...can be found assembled around the same table: love, friendship, business, speculation, power, importunity, patronage, ambition, intrigue." If an event is meant to matter emotionally, symbolically, or mystically, food will be close at hand to sanctify and bind it. Every culture uses food as a sign of approval or commemoration, and some foods are even credited with supernatural powers, others eaten symbolically, still others eaten ritualistically, with ill fortune befalling dullards or skeptics who forget the recipe or get the order of events wrong. Jews attending a Seder eat a horseradish dish to symbolize the tears shed by their ancestors when they were slaves in Egypt. Malays celebrate important events with rice, the inspirational center of their lives. Catholics and Anglicans take a communion of wine and wafer. The ancient Egyptians thought onions symbolized the many-layered universe, and swore oaths on an onion as we might on a Bible. Most cultures embellish eating with fancy plates and glasses, accompany it with parties, music, dinner theater, open-air barbecues, or other forms of revelry. Taste is an intimate sense. We can't taste things at a distance. And how we taste things, as well as the exact makeup of our saliva, may be as individual as our fingerprints.

Food gods have ruled the hearts and lives of many peoples. Hopi Indians, who revere corn, eat blue corn for strength, but all Americans might be worshiping corn if they knew how much of their daily lives depended on it. Margaret Visser, in *Much Depends on Dinner*, gives us a fine history of corn and its uses: livestock and poultry eat corn; the liquid in canned foods contains corn; corn is used in most paper products, plastics, and adhesives; candy, ice cream, and other goodies contain corn syrup; dehydrated and instant foods contain cornstarch; many familiar objects are made from corn products, brooms and corncob pipes to name only two. For the Hopis, eating corn is itself a form of reverence. I'm holding in my hand a beautifully carved Hopi corn kachina doll made from cottonwood; it represents one of the many spiritual essences of their world. Its cob-shaped body is painted ocher, yellow, black, and white, with dozens of squares drawn in a cross-section-of-a-kernel design, and abstract green leaves spearing up from below. The face has a long, black, rootlike nose, rectangular black eyes, a black ruff made of rabbit fur, white string corn-silk-like ears, brown bird-feather bangs, and two green, yellow, and ocher striped horns topped by rawhide tassels. A fine, soulful kachina, the ancient god Maïs stares back at me, tastefully imagined.

Throughout history, and in many cultures, taste has always had a double meaning. The word comes from the Middle English *tasten*, to examine by touch, test, or sample, and continues back to the Latin *taxare*, to touch sharply. So a taste was always a trial or test. People who have taste are those who have appraised life in an intensely personal way and found some of it sublime, the rest of it lacking. Something in bad taste tends to be obscene or vulgar. And we defer to professional critics of wine, food, art, and so forth, whom we trust to taste things for us because we think their taste more refined or educated than ours. A companion is "one who eats bread with another," and people sharing food as a gesture of peace or hospitality like to sit around and chew the fat.

The first thing we taste is milk from our mother's breast,* accom[panied]
and affection, stroking, a sense of security, warmth, and well-being,
feelings of pleasure. Later on she will feed us solid food from her ha[nd]
chew food first and press it into our mouths, partially digested. Such [asso]
ciations do not fade easily, if at all. We say "food" as if it were a simple thing, an
absolute like rock or rain to take for granted. But it is a big source of pleasure in
most lives, a complex realm of satisfaction both physiological and emotional, much
of which involves memories of childhood. Food must taste good, must reward us, or
we would not stoke the furnace in each of our cells. We must eat to live, as we must
breathe. But breathing is involuntary, finding food is not; it takes energy and planning, so it must tantalize us out of our natural torpor. It must decoy us out of bed in
the morning and prompt us to put on constricting clothes, go to work, and perform
tasks we may not enjoy for eight hours a day, five days a week, just to "earn our
daily bread," or be "worth our salt," if you like, where the word *salary* comes from.
And, because we are omnivores, many tastes must appeal to us, so that we'll try new
foods. As children grow, they meet regularly throughout the day—at mealtimes—to
hear grown-up talk, ask questions, learn about customs, language, and the world. If
language didn't arise at mealtimes, it certainly evolved and became more fluent
there, as it did during group hunts.

We tend to see our distant past through a reverse telescope that compresses it: a
short time as hunter-gatherers, a long time as "civilized" people. But civilization is
a recent stage of human life, and, for all we know, it may not be any great achievement. It may not even be the final stage. We have been alive on this planet as rec-
ognizable humans for about two million years, and for all but the last two or three
thousand we've been hunter-gatherers. We may sing in choirs and park our rages
behind a desk, but we patrol the world with many of a hunter-gatherer's drives,
motives, and skills. These aren't knowable truths. Should an alien civilization ever
contact us, the greatest gift they could give us would be a set of home movies: films
of our species at each stage in our evolution. Consciousness, the great poem of matter, seems so unlikely, so impossible, and yet here we are with our loneliness and our
giant dreams. Speaking into the perforations of a telephone receiver as if through
the screen of a confessional, we do sometimes share our emotions with a friend, but
usually this is too disembodied, too much like yelling into the wind. We prefer to
talk *in person*, as if we could temporarily slide into their feelings. Our friend first
offers us food, drink. It is a symbolic act, a gesture that says: *This food will nourish
your body as I will nourish your soul.* In hard times, or in the wild, it also says *I will
endanger my own life by parting with some of what I must consume to survive.* Those
desperate times may be ancient history, but the part of us forged in such trials
accepts the token drink and piece of cheese and is grateful.

*This special milk, called colostrum, is rich in antibodies, the record of the mother's epidemiologic
experience.

Coming Home to Eat

by Gary Paul Nabhan

Gary Nabhan's interests and insights are as diverse as the wild seeds he gathers. Not only does he write beautifully about what he knows, he also goes out into the fields of native peoples collecting and conserving indigenous seeds, returning them to communities from which they have been lost. Winner of the John Burroughs Medal for nature writing for his first book, *Gathering the Desert*, Nabhan is a MacArthur Fellow, co-founder of Native Seeds/SEARCH, science advisor at the Arizona-Sonora Desert Museum and board member of the Seed Savers Exchange. He has published six books and over 100 technical articles on ethnobotany, nutrition, and plant conservation.

Like Fisher and Ackerman, Nabhan celebrates and testifies to the place of good food within community and of community itself nurtured by good food. In this unforgettable story Nabhan, a Lebanese American, begins to define what "good food" means to him. He does so through describing two meals enjoyed on his first pilgrimage to his homeland. One "reflected a desire for a life unsoiled by local...or even nationalistic constraints, where one could pick and choose from the planetary supermarket without any contact with local fishers or farmers, let alone any responsibility to them." The other "exuded the aroma of our aunts' and cousins' hands, the musk of goats and sheep grazed on the slopes above us, the salt and the bitter herbal bite of the alkaline earth itself." On returning to his Sonoran Desert home, he resolved to eat more like his far away cousins by eating from "the foodstuffs found in my own backyard."

∞

There are moments in this life that I recall not as visual snapshots but as tastes and fragrances. They make sense to me, to who I am, in ways that I suppose are profoundly rooted. At the same time they are blessedly involuntary; for I cannot control when they spring up within me and take me over. They are truly re-membered, that is, those moments seen as deeply etched into the matter of my body now as anything can be.

One such set of visceral recollections came from my first visit to eat and drink and walk on my grandparents' home ground in Lebanon. Like almost everyone else I know, I had eaten food of sorts and drunk various beverages all my life, and yet I am like that proverbial fish who had no clear concept of water. At last, in Lebanon, it became poignantly, perhaps painfully, evident to me that the kinds of food

I eat and who I've shared them with say more or less everything tangible about how I've lived. They mark how ethereally remote or how bodily close I've been to the land, to the sea, and to the labors of the harvest at various points in my life.

If food is the sumptuous sea of energy we dive into and swim through every day, I have lived but one brief moment leaping like a flying fish, and catching a glimmering glimpse of that sea roiling all around us. And then just as quickly, I splashed back beneath its surface, to be evermore immersed in what effortlessly buoys us up.

That brief moment of leaping came by way of juxtaposition in Lebanon. It sprung me loose from ever again being complacent about not knowing where true nourishment comes from.

Over the quarter century prior to that leap, I had dreamed of making a pilgrimage to taste Lebanon. I had grown up eating Lebanese American among my father's clan, as my mother and aunts adapted the recipes of their foremothers to fit the availability of *materia prima* in our newfound home. I craved to compare the kibble, koosa, tabbouleh, labneh and hummus bi tahini of my youth to that of the motherland, and to reconnect with relatives while doing so.

Fortunately my younger brother, Douglas, had the generosity and wherewithal to arrange a reunion with our distant cousins in the Bekáa Valley. Douglas had worked as a lawyer in Riyadh, Saudi Arabia, and on a brief business trip to Beirut the year before, had hooked up with the Nabhan clan for a glorious but emotionally exhausting twenty-four hours. He came back home sighing like a guy who had fallen in love for the first time in his life. He had been smitten by the shower of genuine affection poured onto him by our long-lost cousins, by their lovely children, and by the tangible sense of reconnection with our own heritage.

"You just can't believe it...I don't know what to do...I cried all the way back across the ocean." Douglas immediately proposed that he take me and my older brother, Norman, back with him to Beirut and the Bekáa Valley, even though the three of us had never traveled together as adults. Seeing how deeply Doug had been moved, Norm and I dropped everything else in order to join him. Douglas knew far more Arabic than we did, but he had also persuaded his Lebanon-born friend Sam Habboush to accompany us, just in case words failed him during his next venture into the surf of emotion.

"You might want to think about fasting for a few days before we arrive," Sam warned us. "If your cousins are anything like mine," he moaned, "they'll ask you if you're hungry every twenty minutes."

Doug concurred. "Get ready for an all-night feast. I swear our cousins won't let you leave the room until you've had every traditional dish they can fit on the table."

When we arrived at the Beirut airport, we were immediately met by a distant cousin in government services who had somehow positioned himself as the first official just outside the arrival gate. Our family from the Bekáa Valley had insisted that he guarantee our safe passage through customs. He led us straight to our other cousins and uncles, who not only escorted us but constantly held, hugged, and kissed us from the very moment we set foot on Lebanese soil. They tried to feed us immediately, but, seeing how tired we were, they graciously granted us a day to recover from jet lag. They would then drive us over the mountains to the Bekáa Valley, where they said the rest of our kin were already preparing for our arrival.

Lebanon was "in recovery," trying to break its twenty-two-year addiction to internecine strife that had been doped up by external political, economic, and religious forces. Beirut was not a pretty sight. It was a little like seeing someone who had just had plastic surgery after a car accident, but was still bandaged, bruised, and battered. "You're looking better," you offer optimistically, painfully aware that your reaction might be considered a bit premature.

Our cousins nonchalantly drove us past bombed-out buildings where, three stories up, families were trying to shape a refuge for themselves, despite the tons of twisted steel, crumbling plaster, and blasted concrete walls hanging above them. Shell-pocked buildings dotted the neighborhoods surrounding the airport, although more than a few edifices were being intentionally demolished to make way for new ones to go up in their stead. The city was struggling to regain its stature as an international trade center, even though its reputation as an intellectual and cultural forum remained badly crippled.

At the end of our day of rest in Beirut we were invited to dinner by a Lebanese Maronite businessman whom my brother knew. He urged us to join his entourage at the exclusive Club Du Lubnan before we headed for the hinterland, so that we could sample the finest the "New Beirut" had to offer. Although we were anxious to get out of the city to devote ourselves to our relatives, we accepted the invitation anyway. It would allow us a few more hours to restore our emotional energy before full immersion in family passions, politics, and personalities.

A taxi wound down narrow streets to the edge of the city not far from the ancient ports of Juniye and Byblos, and dropped us off at the glass-and-marble entranceway of an elite casino. Suddenly a wave of disorientation crashed around me, and when I resurfaced from it, I felt something had gone awry. I had a vague, unsettling feeling that I had been in that space before, not in the Club Du Lubnan per se but in some other hall of gambling with the same essential character.

We were escorted through double doors into an immense but disturbingly quiet lobby, decorated in marble, and mirrors. I glanced around feverishly, embarrassed to be having a déjà-vu moment in the presence of my brothers. Was this place reminiscent of a governor's palace I had once visited in central Mexico? A now-abandoned mansion of the Rockefeller family in western Massachusetts, or a recently erected resort hotel in Las Vegas? I could not put my finger on it.

Meanwhile, we were asked to present photo IDs and credit cards, put through financial and security checks by computer, and then given lifetime membership cards to the club. (Now *that* was something that gave me a false sense of "eternal belonging," as much as anything I'd ever received!) Next we were ushered into an exclusive dining room overlooking blackjack tables where Saudi oilmen, English

are so laughably clueless about the origins of their food that they are just as likely to mention Safeway as the Garden of Eden as the place where the first apple came from. Eve, honey, please forgive us for our sins, the freeze-dried ones, the ones we have spiced with MSG, and all the others we heave into our shopping carts.

While the younger generation's relative lack of historicity has always been an easy target, there are in fact a few things new under the sun. The markets are being flooded with nutraceuticals, transgenic foods, irradiated grains, and other such marginally edible gobbledygook. A handful of companies control the bulk of the global food economy, perhaps fewer now than ever before. Most of them are unwilling to tell us whether our food crops have been sprayed with toxins in the old-fashioned way, or ingeniously modified genetically to produce the same toxins, with no easy way to discern whether the results of such slippery engineering feats have been put in our mouths.

Still, we have become a nation of food worriers more than food savorers. We fatalistically concede that we hardly know anything about who grew our food and how, but we are fixated on whether today's fare is more nutritious or less so, more tasty or more toxic, higher in fiber, folic acid, fat, and antioxidants or less so. As conscientious consumers, we are told that we should be preoccupied with issues regarding the chemical composition, the days since initial packaging, and the densities of insect parts and fecal coliform found in the grains ground down to make our daily bread. Nonetheless we don't much fathom from whom or from whence they came.

Flying in the face of such ironies, I resolved myself to entertain a modest proposal on my return from Lebanon to my Sonoran Desert home. It was not so much to adopt or imitate my cousins' diets in Kfar Sibad, but to emulate their efforts by filling my larder as much as possible from the foodstuffs found in my own backyard, within my own horizons. My mouth, my heart, my belly, and my brain began ruminating over the same simple few questions:

Just what exactly is it that we want to have cross our lips, to roll off our tongues, down our throats, to fill our nostrils with hardly described fragrances, to slide to a brief halt within our bellies, to mix with our own gastric juices to be transformed and conjured into something new by the myriad microbes in our guts, to migrate across our stomach linings, to surge into our bloodstreams, and to be carried along with insulin for one last ride, and then to be lodged within our very own bodies? What do we want to be made of? What do we claim as our tastes? And what on earth do we ultimately want to taste like?

Your Health,
the Western Diet and Politics

Virtually every food and beverage product is represented by a trade association or public relations firm whose job it is to promote a positive image of that item...It is in the interest of food companies to have people believe that there is no such thing as a "good" food (except when it is theirs); that there is no such thing as a "bad" food (especially not theirs); that all foods (especially theirs) can be incorporated into healthful diets—which means that no advice to restrict intake of their particular product is appropriate.

—Marion Nestle

Here, in one of the wealthiest countries in the world, we now face an epidemic of malnutrition. By malnutrition we don't only mean the plight of those Americans who aren't getting enough calories; we also mean that of the millions who are filling their bodies with foods that don't healthfully nourish them. One-fourth of all Americans now eat a meal from a fast-food joint at least once a day, and if we choose a double whopper with cheese, we're downing in one meal 130 percent of the saturated fat we're supposed to eat in an entire day.

—Frances Moore Lappe and Anna Lappe

Introduction

Many of us first begin exploring the ramifications of our food choices out of concern for our own health—and rightly so. "Evidence for the importance of diet in health is overwhelming," writes nutritionist Marion Nestle. Thirty-five percent of American adults, and 14 percent of children aged 6-11, are overweight. As many people die from the combination of poor diet, sedentary lifestyle and excessive alcohol consumption as die from cigarette smoking.

The following essays share remarkable consistency in defining the hallmarks of a healthy diet: rich in fruits and vegetables, limited in animal foods and fats, largely plant-based. The recommendation is so common it begins to feel like a drumbeat. If there is such agreement, why do many feel confused about nutrition advice? Marion Nestle points out that the food industry contributes to and benefits from this confusion. She compares the "tactics of the food companies" to those employed by tobacco companies and argues that food companies ought to "attract the same kind of attention as purveyors of drugs or tobacco...because of the health consequences of dietary choices."

John Robbins' essay discusses the links between meat and dairy based diets and heart disease. Dr. Nestle's entire book (*Food Politics*) reveals the political power of the corporate food industry. She recognizes that if Americans are to change the way they eat, they must not only change individual food choices but also pool their political power to change societal systems. Dr. Nestle reinforces the emphasis of the opening essay ("Food As Sacramental"): individual change and political activism are both necessary in any movement.

Happily (as we will discover throughout this book), those foods most healthy for our own bodies also contribute to a healthy environment and a more equitable society. In a faith context that is good news, allowing us through our daily food choices to both treat our bodies as sacred and love our neighbors as ourselves.

Food Politics

by Marion Nestle

Marion Nestle is Professor and Chair of the Department of Nutrition and Food Studies at New York University. Author of *Nutrition in Clinical Practice*, she has served as a nutrition policy advisor to the Department of Health and Human Services. She frequently writes and lectures about a broad range of topics related to food and nutrition policy.

What is a healthy diet? Nestle answers, "The longest-lived populations in the world...traditionally eat diets that are largely plant-based," and "the advice to eat more fruits and vegetables and to avoid overweight as a means to promote health has remained constant for half a century." In this introduction, Nestle reminds us just how much diet does matter, and reveals why we often experience confusion about the components of a healthy diet. "It is in the interest of food companies," she writes, "to have people believe that there is no such thing as a 'good' food (except when it is theirs); that there is no such thing as a 'bad' food (especially not theirs); that all foods (especially theirs) can be incorporated into healthful diets; and that...no advice to restrict intake of their particular product is appropriate."

∞

What Is a "Healthy" Diet?

To promote health as effectively as possible, diets must achieve balance. They must provide enough energy (calories) and vitamins, minerals, and other essential nutrients to prevent deficiencies and support normal metabolism. At the same time, they must not include excessive amounts of these and other nutritional factors that might promote development of chronic diseases. Fortunately, the optimal range of intake of most dietary components is quite broad. It is obvious that people throughout the world eat many different foods and follow many different dietary patterns, many of which promote excellent health and longevity. As with other behavioral factors that affect health, diet interacts with individual genetic variation as well as with cultural, economic, and geographical factors that affect infant survival and adult longevity. On a population basis, the balance between getting enough of the right kinds of nutrients and avoiding too much of the wrong kinds is best achieved by diets that include large proportions of energy from plant foods —fruits, vegetables, and grains.

The longest-lived populations in the world, such as some in Asia and the Mediterranean, traditionally eat diets that are largely plant-based. Such diets tend to be relatively low in calories but high in vitamins, minerals, fiber, and other components of plants (phytochemicals) that—acting together—protect against disease. Dietary patterns that best promote health derive most energy from plant foods, considerably less from foods of animal origin (meat, dairy, eggs), and even less from foods high in animal fats and sugars...

Does Diet Matter?

In addition to consuming largely plant-based diets, people in long-lived populations are physically active and burn up any excess calories they obtain from food. An active lifestyle helps mitigate the harmful effects of overeating, but the evidence for the importance of diet in health also is overwhelming. Disease by chronic disease, scientists consistently have demonstrated the health benefits of diets rich in fruit and vegetables, limited in foods and fats of animal origin, and balanced in calories. Comprehensive reports in the late 1980s from the United States and

Europe documented the evidence available at that time, and subsequent research has only strengthened those conclusions.[1]

Health experts suggest conservatively that the combination of poor diet, sedentary lifestyle, and excessive alcohol consumption contributes to about 400,000 of the 2,000,000 or so annual deaths in the United States—about the same number and proportion affected by cigarette smoking. Women who follow dietary recommendations display half the rates of coronary heart disease observed among women who eat poor diets, and those who also are active and do not smoke cigarettes have less than one-fifth the risk. The diet-related medical costs for just six health conditions—coronary heart disease, cancer, stroke, diabetes, hypertension, and obesity—exceeded $70 billion in 1995. Some authorities believe that just a 1% reduction in intake of saturated fat across the population would prevent more than 30,000 cases of coronary heart disease annually and save more than a billion dollars in health care costs. Such estimates indicate that even small dietary changes can produce large benefits when their effects are multiplied over an entire population.[2]

Conditions that can be prevented by eating better diets have roots in childhood. Rates of obesity are now so high among American children that many exhibit metabolic abnormalities formerly seen only in adults. The high blood sugar due to "adult-onset" (insulin-resistant type 2) diabetes, the high blood cholesterol, and the high blood pressure now observed in younger and younger children constitute a national scandal. Such conditions increase the risk of coronary heart disease, cancer, stroke, and diabetes later in life. From the late 1970s to the early 1990s, the prevalence of overweight nearly doubled—from 8% to 14% among children aged 6-11 and from 6% to 12% among adolescents. The proportion of overweight adults rose from 25% to 35% in those years. Just between 1991 and 1998, the rate of adult *obesity* increased from 12% to nearly 18%. Obesity contributes to increased health care costs, thereby becoming an issue for everyone, overweight or not.[3]

The cause of overweight is an excess of calories consumed over calories burned off in activity. People gain weight because they eat too many calories or are too inactive for the calories they eat. Genetics affects this balance, of course, because heredity predisposes some people to gain weight more easily than others, but genetic changes in a population occur too slowly to account for the sharp increase in weight gain over such a short time period. The precise relationship between the diet side and the activity side of the weight "equation" is uncertain and still under investigation, in part because we lack accurate methods for assessing the activity levels of populations. People seem to be spending more time at sedentary activities such as watching television and staring at computer screens, and the number of hours spent watching television is one of the best predictors of overweight, but surveys do not report enough of a decrease in activity levels to account for the current rising rates of obesity.[4] This gap leaves overeating as the most probable cause of excessive weight gain…

Marketing Imperatives

To sell their products, companies appeal to the reasons why people choose to eat one food rather than another. These reasons are numerous, complex, and not always understood, mainly because we select diets within the context of the social, economic, and cultural environment in which we live. When food or money is scarce, people do not have the luxury of choice; for much of the world's population, the first consideration is getting enough food to meet biological needs for energy and nutrients. It is one of the great ironies of nutrition that the traditional plant-based diet consumed by the poor in many countries, some of which are among the world's finest cuisines, are ideally suited to meeting nutritional needs as long as caloric intake is adequate. Once people raised on such foods survive the hazards of infancy, their diets (and their active lifestyles) support an adulthood relatively free of chronic disease until late in life.[5]

Also ironic is that once people become better off, they are observed to enter a "nutrition transition" in which they abandon traditional plant-based diets and begin eating more meat, fat, and processed foods. The result is a sharp increase in obesity and related chronic diseases. In 2000 the number of overweight people in the world for the first time matched the number of undernourished people—1.1 billion each. Even in an industrialized country such as France, dietary changes can be seen to produce rapid increases in the prevalence of chronic disease. In the early 1960s, the French diet contained just 25% of calories from fat, but the proportion now approaches 40% as a result of increased intake of meat, dairy, and processed foods. Despite contentions that the French are protected from heart disease by their wine consumption (a phenomenon known as the French Paradox), they are getting fatter by the day and experiencing increased rates of diabetes and other health consequences of overeating and overweight. The nutrition transition reflects both taste preferences and economics. Food animals raised in feedlots eat grains, which makes meat more expensive to produce and converts it into a marker of prosperity. Once people have access to meat, they usually do not return to eating plant-based diets unless they are forced to do so by economic reversal or are convinced to do so for reasons of religion, culture, or health.[6]

Humans do not innately know how to select a nutritious diet; we survived in evolution because nutritious foods were readily available for us to hunt or gather. In an economy of overabundance, food companies can sell products to people who want to buy them. Whether consumer demands drive food sales or the industry creates such demands is a matter of debate, but much industry effort goes into trying to figure out what the public "wants" and how to meet such "needs." Nearly all research on this issue yields the same conclusion. When food is plentiful and people can afford to buy it, basic biological needs become less compelling and the principal determinant of food choice is personal preference. In turn, personal preferences may be influenced by religion and other cultural factors, as well as by considerations of convenience, price, and nutritional value. To sell food in an economy of abundant food choices, companies must worry about those other determinants much more than about the nutritional value of their products—unless the nutrient content helps to entice buyers.[7] Thus the food industry's marketing imperatives principally concern four factors: taste, cost, convenience, and (as we shall see) public confusion.

Taste: Make Foods Sweet, Fat, and Salty

Adults prefer foods that taste, look, and smell good, are familiar, and provide variety, but these preferences are influenced strongly by family and ethnic background, level of education, income, age, and gender. When asked, most of us say we choose foods because we like them, by which we mean the way we respond to their flavor, smell, sight, and texture. Most of us prefer sweet foods and those that are "energy-dense" (high in calories, fat, and sugar), and we like the taste of salt. The universality of such preferences suggests some physiologic basis for all of them, but the research is most convincing for sweetness. Ripe fruit is innately sweet and appealing, but many of us can and do learn to enjoy the complex and sometimes bitter taste of vegetables. Whether a taste for meat is innate or acquired can be debated, but many people like to eat steak, hamburgers, and fried chicken, along with desserts, soft drinks, and salty snacks. Such preferences drive the development of new food products as well as the menus in restaurants.

Cost: Add Value but Keep Prices Low

One result of overabundance is pressure to add value to foods through processing. The producers of raw foods receive only a fraction of the price that consumers pay at the supermarket. In 1998, for example, an average of 20% of retail cost—the "farm value" of the food—was returned to its producers. This percentage, which has been declining for years, is unequally distributed. Producers of eggs, beef, and chicken receive 50% to 60% of retail cost, whereas producers of vegetables receive as little as 5%. Once foods get to the supermarket, the proportion represented by the farm value declines further in proportion to the extent of processing. The farm value of frozen peas is 13%, of canned tomatoes 9%, of oatmeal 7%, and of corn syrup just 4%.[8]

...The remaining 80% of the food dollar goes for labor, packaging, advertising, and other such value-enhancing activities. Conversion of potatoes (cheap) to potato chips (expensive) to those fried in artificial fats or coated in soybean flour or herbal supplements (even more expensive) is an example of how value is added to basic food commodities. Added value explains why the cost of the corn in Kellogg's Corn Flakes is less than 10% of the retail price. With this kind of pricing distribution, food companies are more likely to focus on developing added-value products than to promote consumption of fresh fruits and vegetables, particularly because opportunities for adding value to such foods are limited. Marketers can add value to fruits and vegetables by selling them frozen, canned, or precut, but even the most successful of such products—prepackaged and branded "baby" carrots, salad mixes, and precut fruit—raise consumer concerns about freshness and price.

Despite the focus on adding value, overabundance keeps food costs low compared to those anywhere else in the world, and this is due only in part to our high average income. The average American pays less than 10% of income for food. People in low-income countries like Tanzania pay more than 70% of income for food, and those in middle-income countries like the Philippines up to 55%, but even people in high-income countries like Japan pay as much as 20%. Americans, however, strongly resist price increases. In the United States, lower prices stimulate sales, especially the sale of higher-cost items; price is a more important factor in the consumer's choice of steak than of ground beef. Cost is so important a factor in food choice that economists are able to calculate the effect of a change in price on nutrient intake. They estimate that a decline in the price of meat, for example, causes the average intake of calcium and iron to rise but also increases the consumption of calories, fat, saturated fat, and cholesterol.[9]

A more important reason for low food prices is that the government subsidizes food production in ways that are rarely evident. The most visible subsidies are price supports for sugar and milk, but taxpayers also support production quotas, market quotas, import restrictions, deficiency payments, lower tax rates, low-cost land leases, land management, water rights, and marketing and promotion programs for major food commodities. The total cost of agricultural subsidies rose rapidly at the end of the twentieth century from about $18 billion in 1996 to $28 billion in 2000…The large agricultural corporations that most benefit from federal subsidies spare no effort to persuade Congress and the administration to continue and increase this largesse.[10]

Convenience: Make Eating Fast

Convenience is a principal factor driving the development of value-added products. The demographic causes of demands for convenience are well understood. In the last quarter of the twentieth century, the proportion of women with children who entered the work force greatly expanded, and many people began to work longer hours to make ends meet. In 1900, women accounted for 21% of the labor force, and married women for less than 6%, but by 1999, women—married or not—accounted for more than 60%. The structure of American families changed once there was no longer a housewife who stayed home and cooked. Working women were unable or unwilling to spend as much time grocery shopping, cooking, and cleaning up after meals.[11]

Societal changes easily explain why nearly half of all meals are consumed outside the home, a quarter of them as fast food, and the practice of snacking nearly doubled from the mid-1980s to the mid-1990s. They explain the food industry's development of prepackaged sandwiches, salads, entrees, and desserts, as well as such innovations as "power" bars, yogurt and pasta in tubes, prepackaged cereal in a bowl, salad bars, hot-food bars, take-out chicken, supermarket "home meal replacements," McDonald's shaker salads, chips prepackaged with dips, and foods designed to be eaten directly from the package. Whether these "hyper-convenient" products will outlast the competition remains to be seen, but survival is more likely to depend on taste and price than on nutrient content. Many of these products are high in calories, fat, sugar, or salt but are marketed as nutritious because they contain added vitamins.

Nutritionists and traditionalists may lament such developments, because convenience overrides not only considerations of health but also the social and cultural meanings of meals and mealtimes. Many food products relegate cooking to a low-priority chore and encourage trends toward one-dish meals, fewer side dishes, fewer ingredients, larger portions to create leftovers, almost nothing cooked "from scratch," and home-delivered meals ordered by phone, fax or Internet. Interpreting the meaning of these developments no doubt will occupy sociologists and anthropologists for decades. In the meantime, convenience adds value to foods and stimulates the food industry to create even more products that can be consumed quickly and with minimal preparation.

Confusion: Keep the Public Puzzled

Many people find it difficult to put nutrition advice into practice, not least because they view the advice as ephemeral—changing from one day to the next. This view is particularly unfortunate because…advice to eat more fruits and vegetables and to avoid overweight as a means to promote health has remained constant for half a century. Confusion about nutrition is quite understandable, however. People obtain information about diet and health from the media—newspapers, magazines, television, radio and more recently the Internet. These outlets get much of their information from research publications, experts, and the public relations representatives of food and beverage companies. Media outlets require news, and reporters are partial to breakthroughs, simple take-home lessons, and controversies. A story about the benefits of single nutrients can be entertaining, but "eat your veggies" is old news. It is more interesting to read about a study "proving" that calcium does or does not prevent bone loss than a report that patiently explains the other factors—nutrients, foods, drinks, exercise—that might influence calcium balance in the body. Although foods contain hundreds of nutrients and other components that influence health, and although people eat diets that contain dozens of different foods, reporters rarely discuss study results in their broader dietary context.[12] News outlets are not alone in focusing on single nutrients or foods; researchers also do so. It is easier to study the effects of vitamin E on heart disease risk than it is to try to explain how current dietary patterns are associated with declining rates of coronary heart disease. Research on the effects of single nutrients is more likely to be funded, and the results are more likely to garner headlines, especially if they conflict with previous studies. In the meantime, basic dietary advice remains the same—constant, but dull.

Newspaper sales and research grants may benefit from confusion over dietary advice, but the greatest beneficiary of public confusion is the food industry…Virtually every food and beverage product is represented by a trade association or public relations firm whose job it is to promote a positive image of that item among consumers, professionals, and the media. These groups—and their lobbyists—can take advantage of the results of single-nutrient research to claim that products containing the beneficial nutrient promote health and to demand the right to make that claim on package labels. If people are confused about nutrition, they will be more likely to accept such claims at face value. It is in the interest of food companies to have people believe that there is no such thing as a "good" food (except when it is theirs); that there is no such thing as a "bad" food (especially not theirs); that all foods (especially theirs) can be incorporated into healthful diets; and that balance, variety, and moderation are the keys to healthful diets—which means that no advice to restrict intake of their particular product is appropriate. The Pyramid, however, clearly indicates that some foods are better than others from the standpoint of health.

Healthy Heart, Healthy Life

by John Robbins

John Robbins is the author of numerous bestsellers, including *Diet for a New America*. He serves as a director for many nonprofit organizations concerned with the environment, health, world hunger and genetic engineering. A popular speaker, founder of EarthSave International, and chairman of Youth for Environmental Sanity (YES!) he lives with his family in California.

"If I told you that you could join either group A, in which one out of every two men and one out of every three women would die of heart disease, or group B, in which heart disease deaths would be practically unknown and people would be healthier in every other way as well, which group would you join? Group B, of course." Robbins goes on to point out that most of us stand solidly within group A. The primary difference between the two groups? Diet.

∞

Scientific Data or Industry Propaganda?

The meat and dairy industries, naturally, disagree with everything I'm saying. They tell us repeatedly that their products are the cornerstones of a balanced and complete diet. They say we need the foods they produce to have adequate protein, calcium, iron, B-12, riboflavin, and zinc. They say that without the consumption of animal products, human health would decline dramatically.

What I think any sane person would want to know is this: Opinions aside, what does the hard data indicate? Does it support the contention of vegetarians and vegans that they have lower rates and less risk of heart disease, and indeed for almost all of the "diseases of affluence" that plague our culture? Is there sound science behind the claims that vegetarians are leaner and more fit people who outlive the rest of the population by six to 10 years? Or is this simply the fuzzy rhetoric of radical extremists?

The National Cattlemen's Beef Association and the National Dairy Council tell us again and again that we jeopardize our health and well-being if we do not consume the products they provide. Impartial researchers and nonprofit public health organizations such as the World Health Organization, the American Institute for Cancer Research, the American Heart Association, the Physicians Committee for Responsible Medicine, the National Cancer Institute, and the Center for Science in the Public Interest, however, have a different perspective.

It can get contentious.... [See box.]

When we see industry statements juxtaposed nakedly against those from

Is That So?

"[It's a] myth [that] people who eat vegetarian diets are healthier than people who eat meat."

—*National Cattlemen's Beef Association*[13]

"Studies indicate that vegetarians often have lower morbidity and mortality rates...Not only is mortality from coronary artery disease lower in vegetarians than in nonvegetarians, but vegetarian diets have also been successful in arresting coronary artery disease. Scientific data suggest positive relationships between a vegetarian diet and reduced risk for ...obesity, coronary artery disease, hypertension, diabetes mellitus, and some types of cancers."

—*American Dietetic Association Position Paper on Vegetarian Diets*[14]

more objective sources, it is possible to see the contrast, get a sense of the differences, and appraise which is more likely to be true. But in everyday life, we are hardly ever given the opportunity to compare the messages we receive from industries promoting the sale of their food products with messages from more reliable sources.

The statements of the meat and dairy industries are important to evaluate because, even though they are no more true than any other form of advertising, they are broadcast so pervasively in our culture that they very likely have insinuated themselves into your mind. The meat and dairy industries in the United States spend literally billions of dollars annually, not only on advertising, but on thousands of other ways by which they influence what you think and how you spend your money. They provide free educational materials to schools. They issue a constant stream of public service announcements to radio and TV stations. They continually flood newspapers and magazines with press releases. They promote their products heavily to doctors, nurses, and dieticians. And they typically proceed with a veneer that implies they're doing all this for your own good.

The amount of money spent on food in our culture is phenomenal, and these dollars are, of course, highly coveted. There are whole industries with massive budgets whose entire goal is to sell their products. From their point of view, if their products are healthy, great, and if not, they'll find another marketing angle. They typically spend the most money promoting the very foods that are most harmful. They'll want you to be more concerned with what's cool or what other people are doing than what's healthy. And they'll tell you that their foods are healthy even when they're not.

This is not just misinformation. It is really affecting people's lives, and probably yours. There are industries profiting from keeping you ignorant, confused, and mis-informed, buying and consuming products that lead to unnecessary suffering and death for you and your loved ones.

Today, heart disease is the number one killer of Americans.[15] More people die from heart and blood vessel diseases each year in the United States than from all other causes of death combined.

What is the single greatest risk factor for heart disease? A high blood cholesterol level.[16] And what is the single most important factor in raising blood cholesterol levels? The consumption of saturated fat. The correlations between cholesterol levels, saturated fat intake, and heart disease are among the strongest and most consistent in the history of world medical research. This is why every authoritative health body in the world, from the American Heart Association to the World Health Organization to the National Heart, Lung and Blood Institute, is calling for reductions in saturated fat consumption...

Scientists at the Center for Science in the Public Interest have studied the American diet for years, and have sought to give people sound information on which they can base healthy food choices. Recognizing the saturated fat in ham-burgers, they have been outspoken about the health consequences of such food. "If you had to pick a single food that inflicts the most damage in the American diet," they said in their newsletter in 1999, "ground beef would be a prime contender. Whether it's tacos, meatloaf, lasagna, or the ubiquitous hamburger, Americans stuff themselves with ground beef without a second thought about its consequences. 'Billions and billions served' means 'billions and billions spent'—on doctor's visits and hospital bills."[17]

How has the U.S. meat industry responded? Some of its representatives have called the Center for Science in the Public Interest "food fascists," "culinary dictators," and similar names.[18] This gives me pause. Name-calling has never impressed me as a valid form of argument. I suppose it shows the frustration of an industry with increasingly reduced scientific grounds on which to defend its products. Still, I would think these people could grasp that there is an enormous difference between dictating your food choices, which is a form of coercion, and providing education as to what science has learned about diet and health, so you can make informed choices about matters that affect your health.

Others, a little more thoughtfully, have pointed out that there are some kinds of saturated fat that don't raise cholesterol levels. Red meat, for example, contains a type of saturated fat—stearic acid—that has little effect on cholesterol levels. But these comparatively rare types of saturated fat are almost always accompanied by the kinds of saturated fat that do raise cholesterol levels. Red meat is very high in another kind of saturated fat—palmitic acid—that is notorious for raising cholesterol levels.

With what we've learned about diet and heart disease, it is not easy to defend animal fat consumption today. Even the American Meat Institute and National Dairy Council acknowledge that the primary suppliers of saturated fat in the American diet are animal products—beef, cheese, butter, chicken, milk, pork, eggs, and ice cream. They like to point out, however, that their products are not the only culprits. There are a few other foods that are also high in saturated fat, such as palm and palm kernel oil, hydrogenated oils, margarine, and chocolate.

They are correct. But the producers of chocolate aren't trying to convince you and me and the rest of the public that the foods they sell should be the mainstays of our diets. You won't see famous actors and celebrities in expensive ad campaigns telling you that palm kernel oil is "real food for real people." James Garner, speaking for the American beef industry, said that about beef. That was just before the actor, who was so fond of beef, was hospitalized for a quintuple bypass heart operation.

What We Know

Percentage of adult daily value for saturated fat in one Double Whopper with cheese: 130 percent

Percentage of eight-year-old child's daily value for saturated fat in one Double Whopper with cheese: More than 200 percent

Most of us grew up believing that animal protein is superior to plant protein, and that if we don't eat animal protein we are risking our health. This is ironic given that animal proteins, in particular, have been found to raise cholesterol levels.[23] Soy proteins, on the other hand, have consistently been found to lower cholesterol levels.[24]...

Blood cholesterol levels are of course not the only dietary factor affecting the risk of heart disease, but the advantages of having a lower level are enormous. William Castelli, M.D., Director of the Framingham Health Study, says that when people keep their cholesterol levels below 150, they are virtually assured of never suffering a heart attack. "We've never had a heart attack in Framingham in 35 years in anyone who had a cholesterol under 150."[25]

It can be stunning how quickly people with heart disease improve when they adopt a low-fat vegan diet. Patients enrolled in the McDougall Program at St. Helena Hospital in Santa Rosa, California, consistently show dramatic improvement after only two weeks on a very low-fat vegan diet...

The meat, dairy and egg industries have had a difficult time in recent years, as study after study has confirmed the link between their products and heart disease. In the effort to exonerate their products, they have often tried to make much of what is, in fact, very little.

In 1999, a study appeared in the *Archives of Internal Medicine* that has since been widely touted by the U.S. meat industry. This study, they say, "proves" that red meat should be part of a healthy diet. The reason for the industry's enthusiasm is that participants in the study who ate lean red meat lowered their cholesterol levels by 1 percent.[26]

People who eat low-fat, near-vegan, plant-based diets, on the other hand, regularly lower their cholesterol levels by 10 to 35 percent.[27]

What We Know

Drop in heart disease risk for every 1 percent decrease in blood cholesterol: 3-4 percent[19]

Blood cholesterol levels of vegetarians compared to nonvegetarians: 14 percent lower[20]

Risk of death from heart disease for vegetarians compared to nonvegetarians: Half[21]

Blood cholesterol levels of vegans (vegetarians who eat no meat, eggs, or dairy products) compared to nonvegetarians: 35 percent lower[22]

Another important risk factor in determining your risk of heart disease is the ratio of your total cholesterol to your HDL (high-density lipoprotein) level. The higher the ratio, the greater your danger of heart disease. The ideal ratio of total cholesterol to HDL is 3.0 to 1 or lower.[28]

The average American male's ratio is 5.1 to 1.[29] The average vegetarian's ratio, on the other hand, is 2.9 to 1.[30]

When it comes to heart disease, the evidence against animal products has today become so convincing and so thorough that even many in the livestock industry can see the handwriting on the wall. Dr. Peter R. Cheeke is a professor of animal science at Oregon State University and serves on the editorial boards of the *Journal of Animal Science* and *Animal Feed Science and Technology*. In his widely used animal science textbook, he says:

Many studies, involving hundreds of thousands of people, have shown...a positive relationship between coronary heart disease and serum (blood) cholesterol. The higher the serum cholesterol, the higher the risk for coronary heart disease. Populations in which the average serum cholesterol level is (low)...are those on the lower end of the per capita meat consumption scale, while those (with high cholesterol levels) are populations with high intakes of animal products...It's more useful to the livestock industries and animal scientists to come to grips with the demonstrated relationships among saturated fat and cholesterol intakes and coronary heart disease, than to claim that there is no relationship or that there's some sort of conspiracy against animal products by the medical community.[31]

Breaking Free

We know today that the same diets that help to prevent most heart attacks also help to prevent most cases of high blood pressure. And we know that these same diets also do wonders for those who, unfortunately, have already developed these problems. This is marvelous news, for it places in our hands the means to prevent massive amounts of unnecessary suffering.

Not everyone, however, is pleased that this knowledge has been attained. There are those who, perhaps a little biased by their own self-interest, say and do some remarkable things...

The irony is that many of us still think we must eat animal products in order to have balanced diets and be healthy. We still think heart attacks and high blood pressure are regrettable but more or less inevitable byproducts that come with living well and growing old. We think that the best we can do for heart attacks

Is That So?

"We must be eternally vigilant to guard against those who would undermine confidence in the health benefits of eating meat. If meat-eaters have high blood pressure, it's from the stress of having to defend the perfectly reasonable desire to chow down on a thick sirloin against the misguided and intrusive efforts of the food police."

—Sam Abrahamson, CEO Springfield Meats [32]

is to take cholesterol-lowering drugs, and that the best we can do for high blood pressure is take medication to bring it under control. These illnesses have become so much a part of the American scene as to virtually be institutions. We don't realize to what extent our destinies lie in our own hands, and on our own plates. We don't realize how powerfully and inexorably our food choices lead us toward or away from these afflictions.

Is That So?

"Blood pressure fell within hours of starting the (very low-fat vegan diet) McDougall Program. Twenty percent of the people were on blood pressure medications the day they began the program. In almost every case the medications were stopped that day. Yet the blood pressure dropped (significantly) by the second day. This data is from over 1,000 participants at the McDougall Program at St. Helena Hospital in the Napa Valley of California."

—*John McDougall, M.D.*

Many of us feel confused. There is so much information about diet and health all around us. How do we sort it out? Our task is not made easier when those who sell the foods that contribute to heart disease, high blood pressure, and many other diseases are doing everything they can, and spending billions of dollars in the effort, to influence how we think and what we eat.

Confused and disempowered, we too often end up not making the food choices that could dramatically improve the health of our cardiovascular systems, greatly reduce our risk of heart disease and high blood pressure, and vastly improve the quality of our lives. We complain, we feel bad, we get sick, but we don't do the one thing that could in fact go far to restore our inner vitality and the unimpeded circulation of our bloodstreams.

It's a shame that we allow people and industries to keep us bewildered and alienated from our personal power. It's a shame that we allow them to keep us ignorant of the enormous health advantages that would be ours with a shift toward a more healthy plant-based diet.

Fortunately, more and more of us are every day realizing we can choose a way of life, and a way of eating, that free us to our highest health potential and lead us to a far more fulfilling experience of our bodies and our lives. We can experience the joy of healthy cardiovascular systems and healthy hearts, and naturally healthy blood pressure levels. We don't need any longer to clog our arteries with saturated fat and cholesterol, but can feed our bodies with wholesome natural food so we can truly live to the heights of our potential. We can break out of the habits that tell us to conform and stay put, and say No to the lies of industries that profit from our pain.

We can do what gives us power, energy, and aliveness. We can say Yes to our vitality and passion. Leaving behind the standard American meat-based diet in favor of a healthy plant-based diet can be like breaking free from chains, to become, perhaps for the first time, truly free...

"Healthy Heart, Healthy Life", excerpted from *The Food Revolution* © 2001 by John Robbins, by permission of Conari Press, an imprint of Red Wheel/Weiser. Robbins' book may be ordered from Red Wheel/Weiser and Conari Press: 1-800-423-7087.

The Politics of Food Choice

by Marion Nestle

Dr. Nestle concludes her book, *Food Politics*, with very practical ideas on how to help create a food system and industry that values good nutrition and consumer education rather than corporate profit. She accurately points out the strategic necessity of political action to "counter food industry lobbying and marketing practices." Dr. Nestle also discusses the "marketing environment" which so powerfully influences our food choices.

∞

We have seen how the food industry uses lobbying, lawsuits, financial contributions, public relations, advertising, partnerships and alliances, philanthropy, threats, and biased information to convince Congress, federal agencies, nutrition and health professionals, and the public that the science relating diet to health is so confusing that they need not worry about diets: When it comes to diets, anything goes.[33]

Representatives of food companies and their trade associations repeatedly make the following claims:

- The keys to healthful diets are balance, variety, and moderation (especially when their products are included).
- All foods can be part of healthful diets (especially theirs).
- There is no such thing as a good or a bad food (except when their products are considered good).
- Dietary advice changes so often that we need not follow it (unless it favors their products).
- Research on diet and health is so uncertain that it is meaningless (except when it supports the health benefits of their products).
- Only a small percentage of the population would benefit from following population-based dietary advice (if that advice suggests restrictions on intake of their products).
- Diets are a matter of personal responsibility and freedom of choice (especially the freedom to choose their products).
- Advocacy for more healthful food choices is irrational (if it suggests eating less of their products).
- Government intervention in dietary choice is unnecessary, undesirable, and incompatible with democratic institutions (unless it protects and promotes their products).

Dr. Rhona Applebaum of the National Food Processors Association, for example, succinctly expresses such views when she says that diets should conform to
"the three principles of sound nutritional advice: balance, variety, and moderation"
and that societal measures to support more healthful food choices are unnecessary.
Changing the environment of food choice is possible, she maintains, only

> if the federal government, in the role of "Big Brother," mandates what foods
> can or cannot be produced—which is not the role of government in a free
> market economy. Controlling, limiting, and outright banning of products
> deemed "unfit" does not work, and history attests to the failure of such
> extremist measures...Food consumption is not supply driven, it is demand
> driven, and consumers are in the driver's seat...you cannot force people to
> comply with the *Dietary Guidelines* and it is wrong to try. It is an unwork-
> able, totalitarian approach that brings with it all the evils associated with
> such a philosophy.[34]

With such statements, food industry officials appeal to emotion (in this case,
fears of totalitarianism) to argue against something that no nutritionist, private or
governmental, advocates. Nutritionists are simply trying to educate the public that
some foods are better for health than others. The food industry fiercely opposes this
idea and uses its substantial resources, political skills, and emotional appeals to dis-
courage attempts to introduce "eat less" messages into public discussion of dietary
issues and, instead, to encourage people to eat more.

These tactics on the part of food companies are, in one sense, a routine part of
doing business; they are no different from those used by other large commercial
interests, such as drug companies, or—as we shall see—tobacco companies. But
sellers of food products do not attract the same kind of attention as purveyors of
drugs or tobacco. They should, not only because of the health consequences of
dietary choices, but also because of the ethical issues raised by industry marketing
practices. Food marketing raises ethical dilemmas, but so does attempting to regulate or change people's food choices, deciding how government should protect
health within the context of a free market economy, determining what kinds of
policy changes might support more healthful food choices, and identifying the role
of individual responsibility in making such choices...

The Ethics of Food Choice

Ethical issues arise whenever actions that benefit one group harm another. Food
choices have economic, political, social, and environmental consequences that
place improvements to the health of individuals or populations in conflict with
other considerations. Table 36 summarizes some of these conflicts. Underlying the
notion of food ethics is the assumption that following *Dietary Guidelines* improves
health and well-being. If ethics is viewed as a matter of good conduct versus bad,
then choosing a healthful diet—and advising people to do so—would seem to be

Table 36. Ethical dilemmas that arise in applying the 2000 *Dietary Guidelines* for Americans to food choices.

Dietary Guidelines	Ethical and Policy Dilemmas
Aim for fitness	
Aim for a healthy weight.	Eat less, *and cause economic harm to food producers.*
	Revise government agricultural support, advertising, tax, and other policies to promote "eat less," *and cause economic harm to some corporations and individuals.*
	In developing countries, establish policies to increase food intake, *and increase the risk of obesity.*
Be physically active each day.	Institute taxes and other policies to promote more active lifestyles, *and increase costs to consumers.*
Build a healthy base	
Let the *Pyramid* guide your food choices.	State "eat less" messages explicitly, *and provoke political opposition,* or say that there are no good or bad foods, *and confuse the public.*
	Insist that dietary advice be issued by independent agencies, *and incur political consequences,* or accept euphemistic dietary guidelines from agencies with conflicting missions, *and confuse the public.*
Eat a variety of grains daily, especially whole grains.	Recommend unprocessed grain products low in added fat, sugar, and salt, *and risk opposition and higher costs,* or advise "no good foods, no bad foods," *and add to public confusion.*
Eat a variety of fruits and vegetables daily.	Insist that fruits and vegetables be grown under conditions that conserve resources, limit pesticides and herbicides, and support workers adequately, *and pay more for food.*

Dietary Guidelines	**Ethical and Policy Dilemmas**
Keep foods safe to eat.	Require food companies to produce safe food and test for pathogens, *and risk political opposition and higher costs,* or focus safety efforts on consumer education, use of irradiation, or other post-market methods, *and ignore basic causes of safety problems.*

Choose sensibly

Choose a diet that is low in cholesterol and moderate in total fat.	Eat less meat, dairy, and eggs, *and cause economic harm to food and feed producers as well as inducing higher food costs.*
Choose beverages and foods to moderate intake of sugars.	Eat less of high-sugar foods, *and cause economic harm to sugar producers, product producers, and workers in those industries.*
	Remove price supports from sugar production, *and risk the companies' closing and moving elsewhere.*
	Regulate marketing of soft drinks and other high-sugar foods to children, especially in school, *and cause economic harm to soft-drink companies and to schools.*
Choose and prepare foods with less salt.	Eat less of high-salt foods, *and cause economic harm to their producers and to workers in those industries.*
	Advise salt restriction as a means of preventing hypertension, *and inconvenience people who do not need such advice.*
If you drink alcoholic beverages, do so in moderation.	Drink less alcohol to reduce social and health problems, *and eliminate a means of reducing heart-disease risk in certain population segments.*

virtuous actions. As we have seen, food industry representatives question this assumption when they say that *Dietary Guidelines* apply only to a small percentage of the population or claim that they do more harm than good by causing unnecessary deprivation and anxiety. I have heard ethicists call such problems "mass communication risks," meaning, in this case, that education about nutrition out of its dietary context makes people misinterpret advice, whether the advice comes from government, academics, or industry.[35]

Beyond concerns about whether it is appropriate for anyone to tell anyone else what to eat in the name of health, the principal ethical issues related to dietary practices involve the implications of advice to "eat less" for food producers and the food service industry. Some years ago, the

The range of economic sectors that would be affected if people changed their diets, avoided obesity, and prevented chronic diseases surely rivals the range of industries that would be affected if people stopped smoking cigarettes.

nutrition educators Joan Gussow and Kate Clancy began to ask whether it is ethical for food companies to market large numbers of resource intensive, high-calorie, low-nutrient food products to people who neither need nor can afford them and, in the case of children, do not understand the difference between advertising and education. They questioned the ethical implications of promoting a "seasonless, regionless" diet in which an average food travels thousands of miles before it is eaten—a practice that wastes natural resources; requires extensive use of pesticides, energy-intensive fertilizers, antibiotics, and hormones; and causes people in developing countries to produce food for export rather than for themselves.[36] In their view, the overriding ethical dilemma associated with *Dietary Guidelines* is the conflict between following the advice (and eating more plant foods but less meat, dairy, and processed foods) and the effects of doing so on food producers: "These economic realities are a problem worth worrying over. We all need to be concerned—if people start to eat less beef and sugar and Pringles—about the cattle growers, the cane raisers and the Pringle makers...but we must also recognize that consumers need help choosing foods, and there is no way we can help them select better diets without causing economic disruption to some sectors of the food industry."[37]

That "virtuous" dietary choices can result in economic harm to food producers is evident from U.S. Department of Agriculture (USDA) studies. USDA economists estimate that eating more fruit and vegetables and fewer foods of animal origin would upset the existing "volume, mix, production, and marketing of agricultural commodities" and would require large "adjustments" in international food trade, nonfood uses of basic commodities, and food prices.[38] Some agricultural sectors (fruits, vegetables) would benefit if people followed dietary guidelines, but others (beef, corn, sugar) would suffer. What might seem a virtue to some people might seem a vice to others—hence, ethical and policy dilemmas.

Ethical or not, a message to eat less meat, dairy, and processed foods is not going to be popular among the producers of such foods. It will have only limited popularity with producers of fruits and vegetables because their scale of production is limited and they cannot easily add value to their products. The message will not be popular with cattle ranchers, meat packers, dairy producers, or milk bottlers; oil seed growers, processors, or transporters; grain producers (most grain is used to feed cattle); makers of soft drinks, candy bars, and snack foods; owners of fast-food outlets and franchise restaurants; media corporations and advertising agencies; manufacturers and marketers of television sets and computers (where advertising takes place); and, eventually, drug and health care industries likely to lose business if people stay healthier longer. The range of economic sectors that would be affected if people changed their diets, avoided obesity, and prevented chronic diseases surely rivals the range of industries that would be affected if people stopped smoking cigarettes.

> **If we want to encourage people to eat better diets, we need to target societal means to counter food industry lobbying and marketing practices as well as the education of individuals.**

Perhaps for this reason, USDA officials believe that really encouraging people to follow dietary guidelines would be so expensive and disruptive to the agricultural economy as to create impossible political barriers. Rather than accepting the challenge and organizing a concerted national campaign to encourage more healthful eating patterns, they propose a more politically expedient solution: the industry should work to improve the food supply through nutrient fortification and the development of functional foods with added nutritional value.[39] Such proposals raise ethical dilemmas of their own. These foods are not necessarily "healthier," and they encourage people to eat more, not less.

Taking Action: Improving Public and Corporate Policies

Given the ethical and political implications just discussed, we must now ask two questions: What should health professionals and concerned citizens do to improve the social and political environment in which people make food choices? And how can we make sure that the actions we take are both responsible and effective? Once again, the parallel with tobacco is instructive. In the 30 years or so since publication of the surgeon general's first report on smoking and health, cigarettes have become socially unacceptable—on health grounds—among many groups and in many locations. Many of the lessons learned from the "tobacco wars" apply just as well to food, especially the lesson that the industry will relentlessly counter even the slightest suggestion to use less of its products. That actions typical of antismoking campaigns are only rarely applied to nutrition issues is a tribute to how well the food industry has sown confusion about the research linking diet to health, about advice based on that research, and about dietary choices based on that advice. The result is the widely held idea that "eat less" need not apply to categories of foods, to specific food products, or to food in general.

In this regard also, we have much to learn from the tobacco wars. Successful antismoking campaigns are based on four elements: a firm research base, a clear message, well-defined targets for intervention, and strategies that address the societal environment as well as the education of individual smokers. The research basis of antismoking messages is firmly established: Cigarettes cause lung cancer. The message is simple: don't smoke. The targets are well defined: antismoking efforts focus not only on individuals who smoke but also on the companies that produce cigarettes. The strategies include education but also encompass environmental measures, such as age thresholds for buying cigarettes, cigarette taxes, and bans on smoking in airplanes, restaurants, and workplaces.[40]

Could the four principal elements of antismoking campaign strategies—research, message, target, and tactics—be applied to dietary change? With regard to research, the evidence for the health benefits of hierarchical dietary patterns that emphasize fruits, vegetables, and grains is strong, consistent, and associated with prevention of as much illness as cessation of smoking. The message to follow *Pyramid*-like dietary patterns is more complicated than "don't smoke" but not impossible to understand. Just as "don't smoke" applies to everyone, so does the dietary message; everyone benefits from following a dietary pattern that contributes to prevention of so many diseases. Perhaps the most important lesson of all concerns tactics: antismoking campaigns succeeded when they began to focus on *environmental* issues rather than on the education of individuals. If we want to encourage people to eat better diets, we need to target societal means to counter food industry lobbying and marketing practices as well as the education of individuals.

Table 37 (see page 58) provides suggestions for actions that might improve the social environment of food choice in order to make it easier for people to eat better diets and be more active. Some of these suggestions involve government action—new policies as well as tweakings of existing policies. The government, of course, represents all constituencies and must balance a cacophony of diverse interests. In all too many instances, we have seen, the government serves business interests at the expense of public health.

Table 37: Modifications of public policies that would promote better food choices and more active lifestyles

Education
Mount a major, national campaign to promote "eat less, move more."
Teach teachers about nutrition and weight management.
In schools, ban commercials for foods of minimal nutritional value and teaching materials with corporate logos.
End the sale in schools of soft drinks, candy bars, and other foods of minimal nutritional value. Require school meals to be consistent with *Dietary Guidelines*.
Require daily opportunities for physical education and sports in schools.

Food labeling and advertising
Require fast-food restaurants to provide nutrition information on packages and wrappers.
Require containers for soft drinks and snacks to carry information about calorie, fat, or sugar content.
Restrict television advertising of foods of minimal nutritional value; provide equal time for messages promoting "eat less, move more."
Require print food advertisements to disclose calories.
Prohibit misleading health claims in advertising and on package labels.

Health care and training
Require health care training programs to teach nutrition and methods for counseling patients about diet, activity, and health.
Sponsor research on environmental determinants of food choice.

Transportation and urban development
Provide incentives for communities to develop parks and other venues for physical activity.
Modify zoning requirements to encourage creation of sidewalks, pedestrian malls and bicycle paths.

Taxes
Levy city, state, or federal taxes on soft drinks and other " junk" foods to fund "eat less, move more" campaigns.
Subsidize the costs of fruits and vegetables, perhaps by raising the costs of selected foods of minimal nutritional value.

From *Food Politics: How the Food Industry Influences Nutrition and Health*, by Marion Nestle. © 2002. Reprinted by permission of University of California Press.

Notes

1. Food and Nutrition Board. Diet and Health: Implications for Reducing Chronic Disease Risk. Washington, DC: National Academy Press, 1989. James WPT. Healthy Nutrition: Preventing Nutrition-Related Disease in Europe. Copenhagen: World Health Organization, 1988. World Cancer Research Fund. Food, Nutrition and the Prevention of Cancer: A Global Perspective. Washington, DC: American Institute for Cancer Research, 1997.

2. McGinnis JM, Foege WH. Actual causes of death in the United States. JAMA 1993; 270:2207-2212. Stampfer MJ, Hu FB, Manson JE, et al. Primary prevention of coronary heart disease in women through diet and lifestyle. N Engl J Med 2000; 343;16-22. Frazao E. High costs of poor eating patterns in the United States. In: Frazao E., ed. America's Eating Habits: Changes & Consequences. Washington, DC: USDA, 1999:5-32.

3. Troiano RP, Flegal KM, Kuczmarski RJ, et al. Overweight prevalence and trends for children and adolescents. Archives of Pediatric and Adolescent Medicine 1995;149:1085-1091. Mokdad AH, Serdula MK, Dietz WH, et al. The spread of the obesity epidemic in the United States, 1991-1998. JAMA 1999;282:1519-1522. Must A, Spadano J, Coakley EH, et al. The disease burden associated with overweight and obesity. JAMA 1999;282:1523-1529. Overweight and obesity are defined in relation to the Body Mass Index (BMI): body weight in kilograms divided by height in meters squared (kg/m^2). Overweight is defined as a BMI at or above the 85th percentile in a national survey conducted in 1976-1980, or a BMI of 25 or above. Obesity is defined as a BMI of 30 or above.

4. Physical activity trends—United States, 1990-1998. JAMA 2001;285:1835. Anderson RE, Crespo CJ, Bartlett SJ, et al. Relationship of physical activity and television watching with body weight and level of fatness among children. JAMA 1998;279:938-942.

5. Nestle M, Wing R, Birch L, et al. Behavioral and social influences on food choice. Nutrition Reviews 1998;56:s50-s74. Nestle M, Ed. Mediterranean diets: science and policy implications. Am J Clin Nutr 1995;61(supp):1313s-1427s.

6. Popkin BM. The nutrition transition and its health implications in lower-income countries. Public Health Nutrition 1998;I(I):5-21. Gardner G, Halwell B. Underfed and Overfed: The Global Epidemic of Malnutrition. Washington, DC: Worldwatch Institute, 2000.

7. Glanz K, Basil M, Maibach E, et al. Why Americans eat what they do: taste, nutrition cost, convenience, and weight. J Am Diet Assoc 1998;98:1118-1126.

8. Dunham D. Food Costs...From Farm to Retail in 1993. Washington, DC: USDA Economic Research Service, 1994.

9. Meade B, Rosen S. Income and diet differences greatly affect food spending around the globe. FoodReview 1996;19(3):39-44. Huang KS. Prices and incomes affect nutrients consumed. FoodReview 1998; 21(2):11-15.

10. Egan T. Failing farmers learn to profit from federal aid. New York Times December 24, 2000:A1,A20.

11. Zizza C, Siega-Riz AM, Popkin BM. Significant increase in young adults' snacking between 1977-1978 and 1994-1996 represents a cause for concern! Preventive Medicine 2001;32:303-310. Bowers DE Cooking trends echo changing roles of women. FoodReview 2000;23 (I):23-29.

12. Shim Y, Variyam JN, Blaylock J. Many Americans falsely optimistic about their diets. Food Review 2000;23(I):44-50. Hackman EM, Moe GL. Evaluation of newspaper reports of nutrition-related research J AM Diet Assoc 1999;99:1564-1566.

13. "Myths and Facts about Beef Production," National Cattlemen's Beef Association, displayed on the Web site of the National Cattlemen's Beef Association in 2001.

14. "Position of American Dietetic Association on Vegetarian Diets," *Journal of the American Dietetic Association* 97 (1997):1317-21.

15. American Heart Association, Heart Attack and Angina Statistics, 1999.

16. Roberts, William, "Atherosclerotic Risk Factors: Are There Ten or Is There Only One?" *American Journal of Cardiology* 64 (1989):552.

17. "Here's the Beef," *Nutrition Action*, September 1999.

18. Murphy, Dan, "Food Fascists on the Attack Again," October 27, 2000; www.meatingplace.com.

19. Law, M. R., Wald, N. J., Wu, T., et al., "Systematic Underestimation of Association between Serum Cholesterol Concentration and Ischaemic Heart Disease . . . ," *British Medical Journal* 308 (1994):363-6.

20. Resnicow, K., Barone, J., Engle, A., et al., "Diet and Serum Lipids in Vegan Vegetarians: A Model for Risk Reduction," *Journal of the American Dietetic Association* 91 (1991):447-53. See also West, R. O., et al., "Diet and Serum Cholesterol Levels: A Comparison between Vegetarians and Nonvegetarians . . . ," *American Journal of Clinical Nutrition* 21 (1968):853-62; Sacks, F. M., Omish, D., et al., "Plasma Lipoprotein Levels in Vegetarians: The Effect of Ingestion of Fats from Dairy Products," *Journal of the American Medical Association* 254 (1985):1337-41; Messina and Messina, *The Dietitian's Guide to Vegetarian Diets*.

21. Phillips, R., et al., "Coronary Heart Disease Mortality among Seventh-Day Adventists With Differing Dietary Habits," *American Journal of Clinical Nutrition* 31 (1978):S191-8; Burr, M., et al., "Vegetarianism, Dietary Fiber, and Mortality," *American Journal of Clinical Nutrition* 36 (1982) 873-7; Burr, M., et al., "Heart Disease in British Vegetarians," *American Journal of Clinical Nutrition* 48 (1988):830-2; Thorogood, M., et al., "Risk of Death from Cancer and Ischaemic Heart Disease in Meat and Non-meat Eaters," *British Medical Journal* 308 (1994):1666-71; Berkel, J., et al., "Mortality Pattern and Life Expectancy of Seventh-Day Adventists in the Netherlands," *International Journal of Epidemiology* 12 (1983):455-9; Chang-Claude, J., et al., "Mortality Pattern of German Vegetarians after 11 Years of Followup," *Epidemiology* 3 (1992):395-401.

22. Resnicow, et al., "Diet and Serum Lipids in Vegan Vegetarians." See also Messina and Messina, *The Dietitian's Guide to Vegetarian Diets*.

23. Anderson, J. W., et al., "Meta-Analysis of the Effects of Soy Protein Intake on Serum Lipids," *New England Journal of Medicine* 333 (1995):276-82. See also Carroll, K. K., "Dietary Protein in Relation to Plasma Cholesterol Levels and Atherosclerosis," *Nutrition Review* 36 (1978): 1-5.

24. Ibid.

25. Barnard, *The Power of Your Plate*, p. 15.

26. Davidson, M., et al., "Comparison of the Effects of Lean Red Meat vs. Lean White Meat on Serum Lipid Levels . . ., " *Archives of Internal Medicine* 159 (1999):13 31-8. See also Bamard, Neal, Letter to the Editor, *Archives of Internal Medicine*, February 14, 2000.

27. Omish, Dean, "Can Lifestyle Changes Reverse Coronary Heart Disease?" *Lancet* 336 (1990) 129-33; Omish, Dean, et al., "Intensive Lifestyle Changes for Reversal of Coronary Heart Disease," *Journal of the American Medical Association* 280 (1998):2001-7; Thorogood, M., et al., "Plasma Lipids and Lipoprotein Cholesterol Concentrations in People with Different Diets in Britain," *British Medical Journal* 295 (1987):351-3.

28. Barnard, Neal, *Food for Life* (New York: Harmony/Crown Publishers, 1993), p. 30.

29. Ibid.

30. Castelli, W., "Epidemiology of Coronary Heart Disease," *American Journal of Medicine* 76(2A) (1984):4-12.

31. Cheeke, Peter, *Contemporary Issues in Animal Agriculture*, 2nd ed. (Danville, IL: Interstate Publishers, 1999), p. 47.

32. Personal communication with author.

33. Parts of this chapter draw on material previously published as: Nestle M. Ethical dilemmas in choosing a healthful diet: Vote with your fork! Proceedings of the Nutrition Society (UK) 2000;59:619-629 (with permission) and Nestle M. Jacobson MF. Halting the Obesity Epidemic: A Public Health Policy Approach. Public Health Reports 2000;115:12-24 (courtesy of Michael Jacobson and Oxford University Press).

34. Applebaum RS. Commentary. Food Policy 1999;24:265-267.

35. Malm HM. Ethical considerations in dietary recommendations. American Society of Preventive Oncology, 14th annual meeting, Washington, DC, March 6, 2000.

36. Clancy KL. Ethical issues in food processing and marketing, or a nutritionist talks about "moral fiber." Agriculture, Change and Human Values, Proceedings of a Multidisciplinary Conference. Gainesville, FL: University of Florida, October 18-21, 1982. Gussow JD & Clancy K. Dietary guidelines for sustainability. J Nutrition Education 1986;18:1-5.

37. Gussow JD. Can industry afford a healthy America? CNI Weekly Report June 7, 1979:4-7.

38. O'Brien P. Dietary shifts and implications for US agriculture. Am J Clin Nutr 1995;61 (suppl):1390s-1396s. Young CE, Kantor LS. Moving Toward the Food Guide Pyramid: Implications for U.S. Agriculture. Washington, DC: USDA, 1999.

39. Kennedy E, Offutt S. Commentary: alternative nutrition outcomes using a fiscal food policy. British Medical J 2000;320:304-305.

40. Kluger R. Ashes to Ashes: America's Hundred-Year Cigarette War, the Public Health, and the Unabashed Triumph of Philip Morris. New York: Alfred A. Knopf, 1996. Advocacy Institute. Smoke & Mirrors: How the Tobacco Industry Buys & Lies Its Way to Power & Profits. Washington, DC: Advocacy Institute, 1998. Glantz SA Balbach ED. Tobacco War: Inside the California Battles. Berkeley: University of California Press, 2000.

Spirituality and Food

The outer harmony that we desire between our economy and the world depends finally upon an inward harmony between our own hearts and the originating spirit that is the life of all creatures, a spirit as near us as our flesh and yet forever beyond measures of this obsessively measuring age. We can grow good wheat and make good bread only if we understand that we do not live by bread alone.

—*Wendell Berry*

Eating is a sacrament. The grace we say clears our hearts and guides the children and welcomes the guest, all at the same time.

—*Gary Snyder*

Introduction

I suppose my own spirituality most connects with food when I walk through the grass in my backyard to my raised-bed garden and harvest tomatoes or spinach or broccoli for dinner, or when I sit down to a delicious meal at home with close friends. In such settings gratitude easily surfaces—for good soil, fresh food, good friends. All these are gifts. Protestant, Buddhist, and Catholic writers in this section reflect on their sense of how food connects them to their own spirituality and faith. Thomas Moore suggests that a deeper relationship with our food can lead to a "re-enchantment of everyday life." Carol Flinders believes that any ordinary work, such as cooking for someone, done with "one-pointed attention" is a form of prayer "which unifies our...attention and calms the mind."

In *Wishful Thinking: A Theological ABC*, Frederick Buechner writes, "Sacramental moments can occur at any moment, any place, and to anybody...If we weren't blind as bats, we might see that life itself is sacramental." Food can be sacramental: simply hold in your hand a piece of fruit. Is it not a window through which you can sense your connection to soil, farmers, sunlight, rain? In Buechner's words, is it not a window through which you see the "almost unbearable preciousness and mystery of life"? Gary Snyder reminds us of these themes in his evocative reflection on gratitude. Finally, in describing his grandfather's relationship to his chickens, Norman Wirzba depicts how eating chickens can itself be a sacramental act.

The Interiority of Food

by *Thomas Moore*

Thomas Moore is the best-selling author of *Care of the Soul, Soul Mates* and *Original Self*. His work helps people discover sacredness in everyday living.

Moore's words serve almost as an invocation, a gentle but powerful reminder that food nourishes both body *and* soul. He suggests that "re-membering" the soul of food—in shopping for it, in planting it, in preparing it—is one significant step toward the re-enchantment of everyday life.

∞

The Poetics of Food

The soul is not a mechanical problem that needs to be solved; it's a living being that has to be fed. I believe that if this simple, ancient idea were taken to heart, we would move close to the solution to many of our problems, but in this day of mechanistic thinking and problem solving, it isn't easy to appreciate such a simple notion. For some reason, we prefer to think of ourselves as a complicated apparatus in need of analysis more than a living being in need of good food.

The idea of feeding the soul is an old one, which can be found in mystical literature from around the world. Jesus said with utter simplicity: "I am the bread of life" (John 6:35). Ancient notions of soul food are summarized in the words of the modern poet Anne Sexton, in "The Jesus Papers":

> Mary, your great
> white apples make me glad...
> I close my eyes and suck you in like a fire.
> I grow. I grow. I'm fattening out.

The soul needs to be fattened, not explained, and certain things are nutritious, while others are without taste or benefit. Good food for the soul includes especially anything that promotes intimacy: a hike in nature, a late-night conversation with a friend, a family dinner, a job that satisfies deeply, a visit to a cemetery. Beauty, solitude, and deep pleasure also keep the soul well fed.

Religion teaches that sometimes spiritual food for the soul is closely connected to the body's food. The story in Genesis about Adam and Eve eating forbidden fruit is worth years of meditation. Somehow, eating the wrong thing brings a curse on life. The story has far-reaching and sublime theological implications, but it may also speak to the simple truth that we can be nourished or poisoned with whatever we take into ourselves—the books we read, the people we associate with, the religion we follow, or the food we eat.

Jesus begins his public life with his first miracle, transforming water into wine at a wedding, and then later he presents himself, his body and blood, as bread and wine. In one of his great miracles, he feeds five thousand people with five loaves of bread and two fish. In Greek religion the infant Dionysus was cut up, boiled, and eaten by the Titans, and in Judaism the Israelites were fed in the desert with miraculous manna. The ancient story of Gilgamesh tells of the hero's quest for the plant of immortality, and in Chinese Taoism we find a peach of immortality growing in a garden full of rare flowers and colorful birds.

In fasting and in feasting, in proscriptions and blessings, religions around the world stress the importance of food for the soul, not just for the body. When I was a child, we ate fish on Friday and fasted for hours before communion and gave up certain foods in Lent, and these simple food practices helped link religion with daily life in a simple but effective form of enchantment. When practices like these disappear, the fantasy associated with food, and therefore its soul and charm, diminishes. These days even religion seems to have forgotten the importance of lacing food with sacred imagination, and so we are left with food as a mere means of sustenance and health. We are getting fat in body, but not in soul. We are eating apples from the corner stand, but not Mary's apples.

Shunryu Suzuki Roshi ends his excellent little book of spiritual guidance, *Zen*

Mind, Beginner's Mind, with the sentence: "In Japan in the spring we eat cucumbers." Food is so ordinary that we overlook it as we make grand quests for spiritual understanding and enlightenment. Yet the religions of the world have understood its profound significance, its luscious imagery, and its weight in meaning. "Give us this day our daily bread"—is there a simpler yet more profound prayer in all of religious literature?

Many poets have recognized the secret of food's significance to the heart, and so we can turn to the poets to learn how to eat enchantingly. The American poet from Hartford, Wallace Stevens, tells us straight out: "The only emperor is the emperor of ice cream." In another poem he writes: "Meyer is a bum. What is it we share? Red cherry pie."

The fact that Meyer is a bum echoes the basic teaching of Shunryu Suzuki— "beginner's mind." To appreciate the importance of food, we may have to divest ourselves of our knowledge of chemicals and calories and, like a bum of the kitchen, discover food as if for the first time. We don't have to be self-conscious about our eating, yet we could give every kind of dining plenty of time and imagination. It's no accident that in our disenchanted times we have found hundreds of ways to short-circuit the production, preparation, and eating of food, and so it makes sense that to re-enchant our ordinary lives we could approach the supermarket, the kitchen, and the dining room differently, realizing that the extra time real food demands of us is not wasted but serves the soul.

Emily Dickinson, who once told her colleague Thomas Wentworth Higginson, "People must have puddings," makes a similar point about food's plainness and adds the rule of magic: the smallest ingredient is the most powerful, the slightest act the most potent.

> God gave a Loaf to every Bird—
> But just a Crumb—to Me—...
> I wonder how the Rich—may feel—
> An Indiaman—an Earl—
> I deem that I—with but a Crumb—
> Am Sovereign of them all—

Give us this day our daily crumb, our ice cream cone, our cherry pie. The slightest things—a walk, a word, a breeze, a passing view—please the soul immeasurably, and feed it. A dinner with a hint of imagination and effort, a tree bearing fruit outside the kitchen, a favorite market, an old recipe, can all feed the soul even as they nourish the body.

The health fantasy of food is not enough. That has its importance, of course, but if it is allowed to dominate, especially as we at present imagine it—a medical, scientific, chemical-genetic reduction of the human person to a materialistic object—the soul in food will vanish, and we will have lost one more important source of soul and enchantment in everyday experience.

Food Rituals

Religion and poetry teach us how to recapture the soul in food, but we don't have to "baptize" food by surrounding it with pomp and circumstance or elaborate symbolism. We could maintain food's simplicity while at the same time safeguarding all the fantasy, memory, and emotion that are associated with or contained in it. Such ordinary activities as shopping, canning, boxing, making a pantry, and filling a shelf are rites of food that give as much to the soul as they do to the body.

Shopping can be one of the most rewarding soul activities in daily life, but it can also be done obsessively or mindlessly. Good shopping makes a soulful life. But good shopping means taking time and care, knowing well the varieties of food and their seasons, and buying whenever possible from people who have some imagination about food. Consumerism could be defined as disenchanted shopping, while in soulful shopping we are profoundly aware of the wealth of culture that surrounds food—its seasons, national varieties, natural characteristics, and recipes.

A good food market that has excellent produce, in great variety, presented with imagination, and filled with sights and smells and gustatory possibilities can be one of the most enchanting places on earth. But not all food stores are real markets. A soul-inspiring market can make you passionate about buying and preparing food. "Market" is a "mercury" word, like "merchandise" and "commerce." "Store" also has a rich background, since it has the same root as "restaurant"—a place where we can be restored. If there is mercury in a market, and if it promises real restoration, then it is a treasure.

Even the disposal of food has soul in it. Garbage, compost, and trash, the underworld of food, is obviously full of fantasy. In every bucket of garbage we see the alchemical law of all life—the decomposing, the smells and sights of corruption, and, in our gardens, the great fertility in refuse. Every day we come in contact with garbage and "putrefaction," a process that has parallels in our personal and social lives, as when a marriage goes sour or a job becomes rotten.

Garbage is the shadow side of food, perhaps, but it is nevertheless enchanting in its own way. Any effort to avoid garbage by living in a sanitized environment contributes to our disenchantment. One of my household chores is to take the garbage to the recycling center in our town. Every time I pour food scraps into the great stinking bin that stands in the very middle of the melee, I think of Dante's inferno and Hieronymus Bosch's vivid portrayals of hell—a real benefit of my visit to the "dump."

Food can bring rich cultures from all over the world to our own table. It's exciting to come across an excellent spice for Indian food or a great salsa from the American Southwest. It's worth traveling great distances not only to see unusual sights but to eat local food. These notions are obvious to anyone even slightly sensitive to the richness of experience food offers, and yet in our modern world we are losing this source of enchantment too. Great, colorful, soul-drenching markets all over the world are gradually being replaced by cool, packaged, controlled supermarkets. At home, the American diet is filled with bland, overly processed, culture-poor, tasteless food that not only is inimical to our physical health but, worse, starves the soul of the enchantment calories it requires.

It wouldn't take much to change this unfortunate situation, and indeed there are signs here and there of movement back to soul food. In some cities, farmers come into town regularly to offer their fresh produce as well as their stories and advice. Some new supermarkets stock organic, locally grown food and positively refuse the overly processed food that bears the mark of the stainless-steel machine rather than the weathered hand. Some restaurants offer true seasonal menus and are always experimenting with ways to enrich the experience of food and dining.

Shops, restaurants, and our own dining room or kitchen tables can come to life quite easily with food that is ethnically evocative, individual, fresh, at least in part local, imaginatively prepared and presented, enjoyed, and lovingly disposed of. Food is an implement of magic, and only the most coldhearted rationalist could squeeze the juices of life out of it and make it bland. In a true sense, a cookbook is the best source of psychological advice and the kitchen the first choice of room for a therapy of the world.

Sacred Agriculture: Reflections of a Contemplative Farmer

By Miriam Therese MacGillis

Miriam Therese MacGillis, O.P. has traveled the world, leading groups and giving talks in order to explore and share her perspectives on the writings of Father Thomas Berry and cosmologist Brian Swimme. She is co-founder of Genesis Farm, an Earth Literacy Center in New Jersey which offers programs exploring the sacred universe as a new transforming context for our lives and culture.

In this selection, she speaks of her experiences living and working on Genesis Farm. She introduces the idea of "sacred agriculture" in which farmers "enter the sanctuary of the soil and engage the mysterious forces of creation in order to bless and nourish the inner and outer life of the community they serve." Within sacred agriculture, farmers would begin to take on a prophetic and priestly role where food is no longer primarily seen as fuel, but as an opportunity to be in communion with creation and God.

∞

In 1980 I came to live and work at Genesis Farm, a 140-acre farm bequeathed to my Dominican congregation in 1978. It was founded on a vision of creating a space where people of good will could come to ask the critical questions around our contemporary crises. It was to be a reflection center where we would also grapple with the challenges of our Western life-style, our alienation from the natural world, and the issues of land, agriculture, and food.

Genesis Farm is a "learning center for re-inhabiting the Earth," a descriptive phrase taken from the writings of Thomas Berry. The two primary dimensions of our work are in the areas of *learning* and *agriculture*.

The *learnings* lead us to alter radically our perceptions of the origin and nature of the universe as a bio-spiritual reality. We work to heal the separation of matter and spirit, as that single human perception that has so intrinsically affected the beliefs upon which the whole of Western culture is founded. Our programs and workshops are designed to help us experience ourselves as a dimension *of* the Earth and to expand our concept of *self* to include our *Earth self*, our *universe self* as one single reality. This is no small undertaking. Redefining ourselves in a bioregional context has become a primary source of personal transformation. This, too, is profoundly challenging. Each of our programs takes these learnings as its starting point.

The second major thrust of Genesis Farm is in the area of what we now call "sacred agriculture." In the words of Vincent McNabb, O.P.:

> If there is one truth more than any other, which life and thought
> have made us admit, against our prejudices, and even against our
> will, it is that there is little hope of saving civilization or religion
> except by the return of contemplatives to the land.[1]

Laying a contemplative foundation for our work in sacred agriculture rests on two central bodies of thought that we try to integrate.

The first is the exploration of the Earth as a self-nourishing organism. This concept displaces the prevalent cultural assumption about the role of farmers as the "growers" of food. When we begin to grapple with the differences in these perceptions, it becomes obvious how enormous is the shift of consciousness demanded to transform agriculture as practiced in the industrialized world. There are scientific, educational, and economic institutions that would virtually collapse if this understanding became evident and operable in our human communities.

If we understood the Earth as a *living being* whose activities are to *nourish, govern, learn, heal, regenerate, and transform itself*, then the mystery at the heart of human existence would open up and draw us into the sacramental aspect of our lives through the most ordinary and familiar ways.

The second major influence in our farming comes from the philosophy of Rudolf Steiner, a practice known as biodynamic agriculture. Steiner lived in Austria at the turn of the century, and while he did not have available the insight drawn from quantum physics, or from the Gaia theory, or the observations of our space explorers, his knowledge of the spiritual world pervading the world of matter resulted in an approach to farming and to the nourishing function of food that is extraordinary. Since 1987 the fields and gardens of Genesis Farm have been cultivated with this biodynamic approach. The food from this garden is literally a manifestation of Spirit.

It has become clear to me that the concept of food itself is key to the transformation of our ecological crisis. Unless our human species can open itself to the contemplation of food as a holy mystery through which *we eat ourselves into existence*, then the meaning of existence will continue to elude us. Our present cultural experience of food has degenerated into food as *fuel*, for supplying the energy for our insatiable search for that which will fill the hungers of our soul. When we understand that food is not a metaphor for spiritual nourishment, but is itself spiritual, then we eat food with a spiritual attitude and taste and are nourished by the Divine *directly*.

From early times Western culture has carried the burden of guilt for the existence of chaos in the universe. Only now are we realizing that the universe was divinely organized from the beginning with chaos as an integral dimension. Our earlier perceptions have cast a shadow over the attitude with which Western peoples have "discovered" and evolved "agriculture." Feeling doomed to earn our bread by the sweat of our brow explains part of the deep, hidden rage against the natural world described by Thomas Berry.[2] Our propensity toward favoritism has closed us off to the full diversity of nourishment offered by the Earth. It has constrained us by the narrow choices we elected in our methodology of monoculture. This clearly has shaped our present agricultural crisis.

The determination to redeem the Earth and transcend its natural limitations has played itself out in the industrialization and total mechanization of farming. The soils have been exhausted and drugged, their inner life forces depleted and poisoned, not because we are necessarily an evil species so much as that we are driven by our abstract *ideas* about a perfect world. We have been inculturated toward an inability to experience the universe as it actually is. We end up tearing apart the "garden planet" in our effort to redesign it.

If we were to accept the Earth on the terms and under the exquisite conditions in which it continues to evolve, the role of the farmer would be raised to a most honorable and sacred human profession. Relieved of the illusions that they are manufacturing food, or that they are worthy of success to the degree that they are also economists, cosmeticists, and managers, farmers might understand themselves as acting in something akin to a prophetic and priestly role. We need to see farmers as entering the sanctuary of the soil and engaging the mysterious forces of creation in order to bless and nourish the inner and outer life of the community they serve.

Villages, towns, and cities surrounded by farms practicing sacred agriculture would begin to regain the elemental prosperity of pure air, water, and diversity, and the possibility for health and vitality. The attention farmers would pay to the rhythms of the celestial world could reinspire the artists and poets. The music and texture of "place" would be grounded in the great seasonal cycles by which the human has been fashioned in our longing for communion with the Mystery at the heart of the world.

As our culture shrinks in its inner life and rages in violence between individuals and groups, and against the whole of nature, we might do well to reflect on the meaning of food. I do not believe that we are doomed to the inevitability of "engineering" food into a state of eternal shelf life, or that we must use our most deadly nuclear inventions to irradiate our food for its immortality. These compulsive tendencies can be changed.

We live in a universe with an inner spiritual reality. There is nothing that does not participate in this deep sacramental presence. The soils, the microbes, the animals are all holy, are all revelatory. Understanding the universe in this way has the capacity to transform our obsession with control and power.

It is my hope that the concept of sacred agriculture will find expression and authenticity on our land at Genesis Farm. By opening afresh the sacramental dimension of food, I hope to open the meaning of Eucharist and Gospel, so that we learn again to treat creation "knowingly, lovingly, skillfully, reverently"… as a sacrament. Let contemplatives return to the land.

The Work at Hand

By Carol Flinders

Carol Flinders is the co-author of *Laurel's Kitchen* and *The New Laurel's Kitchen*, and author of *Enduring Grace*. She holds a Ph.D. in Comparative Literature from the University of California at Berkeley, where she also teaches.

This lovely reflection comes from her introduction to *The New Laurel's Kitchen* cookbook. She expresses that which many of us experience: "Life really does militate against home-cooked wholesome meals—just as it does against friendships, marriage, parenting, and almost everything else that makes life worth living. It has to be like that, because the spirit of our time is to look only at the profit line." Whether or not you want to cook more wholesome meals at home, reflect on Flinders' words. She is really calling to us to pay attention and to seek relief from the oppression of time ("hurry-sickness" as she calls it). In doing so we may find that the attention we give to ordinary tasks becomes a form of prayer.

∞

Any way you cut it, preparing a balanced and truly appetizing meal with un-processed foods will take a chunk out of your day. If you're trying for healthful breakfasts and bag lunches too, the plot only thickens.

So there we are. Impasse. Collision. Gridlock, to use the dominant metaphor for our age. Life in the eighties really *does* militate against home-cooked wholesome meals—just as it does against friendships, marriage, parenting, and almost every-thing else that makes life worth living. It has to be like that, because the spirit of our time is to look only at the profit line.

It's good to clear the air on this point, and recognize that if you choose to live a different kind of life, it will take some doing. Think of yourself, then, as a pioneer. Celebrate the small, solid gains you *can* make, and don't dwell on the ones you can't make yet. And take heart from knowing that you are not alone.

No one can tell you how to fit those seemingly nonexistent hours into your own life, for the simple reason that it's your life. But I *can* tell you about some of the individuals I know who have managed to give priority to the kitchen, for whatever reasons and by whatever means, and about what has come of their choice.

Tragically, the turning point often comes when health—our own or that of someone we love—is threatened. Suddenly the games food advertisers play are no longer amusing. You find yourself angry now, seeing the damage they have done. Your priorities shift abruptly. And when you see that what you do in the kitchen might make the critical difference for someone you love, many of the subtler forms of resistance ("I'm being exploited," "This is tedious," or "But I cooked *last* night") lose their force. Life, we realize, is very short.

The change can be less dramatic and more positive. A baby comes. You nurse him or her, because there's no question today that it's the best possible start you could give your child. At first, all the sitting still and rocking might send you into paroxysms of restlessness. But then something in you gives way, relaxes, and your very reckoning of time alters. The present moment takes on an amazing luminos-ity. When the date you'd set to go back to work arrives, you may well let it pass. All that can wait; more is going on here than you'd anticipated. And as you begin to give your child solid foods, you balk at anything but the purest and most whole-some. After all, that's what you've been giving up to now! You buy your first nat-ural foods cookbook, and you're on your way. Short on money, maybe, and a little apprehensive, but quite certain, deep inside, that you're on the right track.

Whatever the actual turning point, something stops you and turns your atten-tion inward—puts you in touch with your deepest beliefs and desires, so that for a time, the contrary and conventional messages from outside can't penetrate. With this inward shift there come, inevitably, ideas on *how* to change, too.

> So I take the cucumber, and I cut off the two ends...I place the stem-end piece on the bottom and the bottom piece at the stem end, and I rub them together until I can see a milky substance. Then I set it aside, and gradually the bitter taste concentrated at one end goes? Hey, Laurel, do you believe this?

During a recent interview, Laurel was asked, "One of the main things that I got out of both your books is how valuable the work in the kitchen is. How do you find the time to do everything ideally?"

Laurel's response was simple but telling: "We all have important other things we want to work on. When you come into the kitchen, the thing to remember is that you're going to be there for a certain time. Drop everything else and concentrate on doing the very best you can."

It sounds simple, but what she's really talking about is a take-a-deep-breath-and-swallow-hard act of acceptance. An opening of yourself to the work before you, and an agreement with yourself not to be obsessed with looking for shortcuts—not to hurry, or to let awareness of other responsibilities get you tense or even resentful.

It comes with practice.

Of all the things we said in *Laurel's Kitchen*, I don't think any subject brought more appreciative response than the section on working with one-pointed attention—sanctifying ordinary work by the state of mind you bring to it. Any work you do for a selfless purpose, without thought of profit, is actually a form of prayer, which unifies our fragmented energy and attention and calms the mind. In the words of a monk of the seventeenth century, Brother Lawrence:

> The time of business does not with me differ from the time of prayer,
> and in the noise and clatter of my kitchen, while several persons are
> at the same time calling for different things, I possess God in as great
> tranquillity as if I were upon my knees at the blessed sacrament.

The approach may be catching on. Only last week I read of one homemaker's discovery that eggs are cooked to perfection after three Hail Mary's. "I use the boiling time," she adds, "to place myself in touch with earlier generations of cooks who measured their recipes with litanies, using time to get *beyond* time."

We are so oppressed by time these days—by "hurry sickness" and all its side effects. At moments of deep concentration, though, we are lifted clear *out* of time, and for a few minutes the stress of the day slips away. This may be why a very absorbing activity—chess, or fine needlework, or writing poetry—can leave us refreshed. Kitchen work, when it is undertaken in the spirit of Brother Lawrence, can heal and restore us in exactly the same way.

"I don't know, really, what changed," reflects my longtime friend Beth Ann. "I just know that one evening I walked in there grim as usual, determined to get it over with, and instead I found myself relaxing—accepting that I was there and willing to do it as well as I possibly could. And ever since then, it's been completely different.

"You know, partly I think it's the food itself. If you watch, so much beauty passes through your hands—of form, and color, and texture. And *energy* too." Abruptly her hands flew up into the air as if an electric current were passing between them. "Each grain of rice, each leaf of kale, charged with life and the power to nourish. It's heady, feeling yourself a kind of conduit for the life force!"

To be sure, everyday cooking ends up feeling more prosaic than this. Yet I suspect that what Beth Ann was groping to say has to do with an ancient, almost wordless truth. Long before institutionalized religions came along—and temples, and churches—there was an unquestioned recognition that what goes on in the kitchen is *holy*. Cooking involves an enormously rich coming-together of the fruits of the earth with the inventive genius of the human being. So many mysterious transformations are involved—small miracles like the churning of butter from cream, or the fermentation of bread dough. In times past there was no question but that higher powers were at work in such goings-on, and a feeling of reverence sprang up in response. I wonder sometimes whether the restorative effects of cooking and gardening arise out of similar—though quite unconscious—responses.

Gary Snyder has written compellingly about the importance of setting down deep roots wherever you live and forming a real relationship to the land itself. In his own way, he makes the same point M. F. K. Fisher does when he urges us to "find the holy places" where we live—the spring or grove or crest of a hill where you know that others have lingered before you and steeped themselves, like you, in its special stillness.

Perhaps, though, the real point is not so much to *find* the holy places as to *make* them. Do we not hallow places by our very commitment to them? When we turn our home into a place that nourishes and heals and contents, we are meeting directly all the hungers that a consumer society exacerbates but never satisfies. This is an enormously far-reaching achievement, because that home then becomes a genuine counterforce to the corporate powers-that-be, asserting the priority of a very different kind of power.

Grace
by Gary Snyder

In addition to *Practice of the Wild*, Gary Snyder is the author of *Turtle Island* (winner of the Pulitzer Prize), *Back Country*, *Left Out in the Rain*, *Myths and Texts* and many other collections of poetry and essays. His writing is influenced by Zen Buddhism, living in Japan, an appreciation for hard rural work and a commitment to the natural world.

∞

Everyone who ever lived took the lives of other animals, pulled plants, plucked fruit, and ate. Primary people have had their own ways of trying to understand the precept of nonharming. They knew that taking life required gratitude and care. There is no death that is not somebody's food, no life that is not somebody's death. Some would take this as a sign that the universe is fundamentally flawed. This leads to a disgust with self, with humanity, and with nature. Otherworldly philosophies end up doing more damage to the planet (and human psyches) than the pain and suffering that is in the existential conditions they seek to transcend.

The archaic religion is to kill god and eat him. Or her. The shimmering food-chain, the food-web, is the scary, beautiful condition of the biosphere. Subsistence people live without excuses. The blood is on your own hands as you divide the liver from the gallbladder. You have watched the color fade on the glimmer of the trout. A subsistence economy is a sacramental economy because it has faced up to one of the critical problems of life and death: the taking of life for food. Contemporary people do not need to hunt, many cannot even afford meat, and in the developed world the variety of foods available to us makes the avoidance of meat an easy choice. Forests in the tropics are cut to make pasture to raise beef for the American market. Our distance from the source of our food enables us to be superficially more comfortable, and distinctly more ignorant.

Eating is a sacrament. The grace we say clears our hearts and guides the children and welcomes the guest, all at the same time. We look at eggs, apples, and stew. They are evidence of plenitude, excess, a great reproductive exuberance. Millions of grains of grass seed that will become rice or flour, millions of codfish fry that will never, and *must* never, grow to maturity. Innumerable little seeds are sacrifices to the food-chain. A parsnip in the ground is a marvel of living chemistry, making sugars and flavors from earth, air, water. And if we do eat meat, it is the life, the bounce, the swish, of a great alert being with keen ears and lovely eyes, with foursquare feet and a huge beating heart that we eat, let us not deceive ourselves.

We too will be offerings—we are all edible. And if we are not devoured quickly, we are big enough (like the old down trees) to provide a long slow meal to the smaller critters. Whale carcasses that sink several miles deep in the ocean feed organisms in the dark for fifteen years. (It seems to take about two thousand to exhaust the nutrients in a high civilization.) At our house we say a Buddhist grace:

> We venerate the Three Treasures [teachers, the wild, and friends]
> And are thankful for this meal
> The work of many people
> And the sharing of other forms of life.

Anyone can use a grace from their own tradition (and really give it meaning) —or make up their own. Saying some sort of grace is never inappropriate, and speeches and announcements can be tacked onto it. It is a plain, ordinary, old-fashioned little thing to do that connects us with all our ancestors.

The Enjoyment of God and Creation
by Norman Wirzba

Norman Wirzba grew up in southern Alberta where he practiced farming and studied history. After studying for a Master's degree in theology at Yale, he completed the Master's and Doctorate degrees in Philosophy at Loyola University in Chicago. He writes in the areas of environmental philosophy and theology, and recent European philosophy. He is editor of *The Art of the Commonplace: The Agrarian Essays of Wendell Berry*. He lives with his family in Kentucky where he is Chair and Associate Professor of Philosophy at Georgetown College.

Wirzba asks us to consider how one of the gifts of creation—chickens!—might be properly enjoyed. He intimates that one important element of its proper enjoyment is through boycotting factory-produced poultry, raised in "misery and ill health." He then lovingly describes his own grandfather's care for his chickens. When grandfather ate chickens, Wirzba writes, "his was a sacramental eating."

∞

How does one properly enjoy a chicken? This is no paltry matter, for according to one Jewish tradition, we will need to give an account for the times we did not enjoy the gifts of creation when we had the chance. The enjoyment of creation—encompassing the gifts of family, friends, food, worms, chickens, buffalo, water, soil, air, and light—is not simply an activity we can postpone for our spare time, but rather goes to the heart of what we do now and who we are to become. The extent and character of our enjoyment, in other words, will be the test of our own righteousness, the measurement of our trust in the gracious goodness of God. This is why Sabbath observance, the festive time when we refrain from our own ambition so we can fully appreciate the gifts of God, became central to Jewish thought and life. If we observe the Sabbath properly we enter into God's own rest and delight in creative work well done. We anticipate and participate in the divine peace and joy. As the rabbis put it: "If Israel keeps one Sabbath as it should be kept, the Messiah will come..."

We will not come to the proper enjoyment of creation until we focus our atten-tion on the fundamentals of life, for it is here that the grace and blessing of God are most apparent. It seems odd to say this until we recognize how much of our time is spent occupying and responding to the demands of a purely human con-trived world: the world of the appointment calendar, instant messaging, etc. The course of our lives, viewed in its daily and most practical aspects, comes to be over-determined by and confined to the range of our ambition or fear. In this human world we live by our own effort and power, and so do not come face to face with our dependence on God's grace for our lives, our dependence on the complexity and blessing of creation for our lives.

To think and live fundamentally, however, is to willingly take ourselves out of the security and control of our personally designed worlds and immerse ourselves in the rich depth and beneficence of the lives we live with others. What this means is that we make ourselves vulnerable before and accountable to the lives of those we depend upon for our own life. It is to acknowledge that we live only because of the support and sacrifice of others (both seen and unseen), and so recognize that our lives are always and everywhere maintained by a grace we cannot comprehend or even intend.

When I think of a life lived fundamentally, a life open to the possibility of genuine enjoyment, I think of my grandfather Wilhelm Roepke. As a small-scale farmer he understood "in his bones" that his life was not his own. For his own livelihood he depended on an unending amount of support: good weather, soil fertility, healthy livestock, pest-free crops, generous (or at least cooperative) neigh-bors, the wisdom of forefathers and foremothers who taught him the skills of hus-bandry and care, a sufficient supply of water, his own health, and so on. None of these elements could be taken for granted, for the absence of even one had serious repercussions in his economy.

The acknowledgement of the graced character of his existence resulted in a life that stands out as unique among our current stressful and anxious ways. Put simply, my grandfather was able to enjoy the life he was given. This is not to say that his life was without sadness, grief, or tragedy. But it is to suggest that the context of his daily activities was a Sabbath context. Because he understood himself to be part of a vast and rich web of interdependencies, and because he saw these interdependen-cies as good, he was freed to enjoy the elements of his life as graciously given. In my grandfather's view the world simply could not be reduced to the human scale of personal ambition and fear because in that reduction too much of life was either overlooked, falsified, or destroyed. He understood, innately I think, that a purely human world, one limited to and driven by primarily human interests, breeds anxiety, destruction, and despair, whereas the world of creation experienced as the blessing of God produces joy, contentment, and peace. The most telling character-istic of my grandfather's enjoyment was the care with which he treated his depen-dents. Seeing and appreciating his dependence on others, he took seriously the dependence of others upon him.

For most of us the enjoyment of chicken is a thoughtless affair. We "enjoy" them as we consume, oblivious to the mostly gruesome conditions in which they were factory-produced. In certain respects our enjoyment is sacrilegious because it is premised on the misery and ill-health of chickens so produced. My grandfather's enjoyment of chickens, however, was of an entirely different order. As a child I still remember walking with my grandfather to various places in the yard where fresh grass could be cut, put in a pail, and then delivered to the chicken coop where hordes of chickens eagerly awaited his arrival (they knew he was coming and greeted his coming with obvious enthusiasm and delight). Did the chickens need this freshly cut grass, especially when performing this menial task interfered with more important work that needed to be done? Clearly not. What I remember, however, is my grandfather's pronouncement that it brought him such pleasure to see his chickens enjoying the fresh grass. These chickens, as with so much else in my grandfather's economy, were the object of affection and responsibility. In their well-being he saw his own. And so when grandfather sat down to a meal of chicken, his was a sacramental eating, a Sabbath eating that participated in God's own care for us and for the whole creation....

The modern food industry suggests that we have forfeited our trust in the grace of God and exchanged it for the control and profit that comes from industry. We have decided that we do not want to live within the limits of our created vulnerability and interdependence. The results of this choice have been serious. Control has replaced the contentment and joy that can come from attentive care. Our experience of the world has been seriously narrowed as we have come to think that the needs of creation are coterminous with human need (note the prevalence of "use-value" in economic accounting practices). And perhaps most seriously, we have prevented ourselves from seeing that in the care of creation we participate in God's own care and delight...

The whole creation is one lavish feast to which all of us are invited. There is...as my grandfather so calmly experienced, an interior beauty that shines within the creation. Nothing could please God more than for us to enjoy creation so lovingly made and maintained.

Reprinted with permission of the author. Excerpted from a forthcoming book tentatively titled *Becoming a Culture of Creation*, to be published by Oxford University Press in 2003.

Notes

1. Vincent McNabb, O.P., *Old Principles and the New World Order* (New York: Sheed and Ward, 1942).

2. Thomas Berry, *The Dream of the Earth* (San Francisco: Sierra Club, 1988), 215.

Christianity and Caring for the Land

Silence of the heart is necessary so you can hear God everywhere—in the closing of the door, in the person who needs
you, in the birds that sing, in the flowers, in the animals.

—*Mother Teresa*

If nature is the new poor, then the Christian mandate of
option for the poor and oppressed now includes the natural world. If we are to love our neighbor as ourselves,
then the range of neighbors now includes the whale,
the monarch butterfly, the local lake—the entire community of life. If the common good requires solidarity
with all who suffer, then our compassion extends to
suffering human beings and other species caught in
patterns of extinction.

—*Elizabeth Johnson*

Introduction

If, as Wendell Berry states, "how we eat determines to a considerable extent how the world is used" and if our faith traditions (in this case specifically Christianity) call us to care for Earth, then how we eat becomes an important way through which we can express care for creation. The following essays provide a theological underpinning to the Christian call to care for all life. Elizabeth Johnson develops Pope John Paul II's recognition that respect for life and the dignity of the human person extends to the rest of creation. Marcia Bunge continues this theme, exploring the biblical tradition for the basis of an ecological ethic. Such explorations are important because our theologies provide a lens through which we see the world and interpret reality. Our theologies place in the foreground certain concerns or relationships and place others in the background. As you read these essays, consider how your own perspectives, or society's perspectives, would be altered if these theologies were more influential within both the church and the larger culture.

God's Beloved Creation

by Elizabeth A. Johnson

Catholic theologian Elizabeth A. Johnson, C.S.J. is a Distinguished Professor of Theology at Fordham University, Bronx, N.Y. She is the author of *She Who Is* and *Friends of God and Prophets*.

"The more we gaze in wonder at Earth, the more we realize that human actions are ravaging and depleting the natural world." So Johnson summarizes her sense of modern humanity's paradox. She discusses three possible responses: contemplative, ascetic, and prophetic. Her thoughts help form what she sees as crucial: "a spirituality and ethics that will empower us to live in the web of life as sustainers rather than destroyers of the world."

∞

At the start of this third millennium, a new awareness of the magnificence and uniqueness of Earth as one intertwined community of life is growing among people everywhere. The image of our planet seen from space, a blue marble swirled around with white clouds, promotes realization of how fragile but tough life is. So too scientific study of the origins of the cosmos, the solar system and then the surprising uprising of life under conditions that are "just right" fosters insight into the wonder of life in this one little place. Gorgeous videos on public television about little-known species and the working of ecosystems, along with national wildlife conservation efforts, teaching units in schools, naturalistic zoos and an abundance of

photo books bring the beauty of the world before millions of eyes and boost a
sense of how interrelated all species of life truly are.

At the same time, however, the present moment is marked by a strange paradox: the more we gaze in wonder at Earth, the more we realize that human actions
are ravaging and depleting the natural world. Two major engines of destruction are
overconsumption and overpopulation. Every year, the 20 percent of Earth's people
in the rich nations use 75 percent of the world's resources and produce 80 percent
of the world's waste. An example: Chicago, with 3 million people, consumes as
much raw material in a year as Bangladesh, with 97 million people. Such overconsumption is driven by an economy that must constantly grow in order to be
viable, one whose greatest goal is a bottom line in the black. It does not factor
in the ecological cost.

Simultaneously, human numbers multiply exponentially. In 1950 the world
numbered two billion people. On Oct. 12, 1999, the announcement was made
that we now number six billion; current projections envision that by the year
2030 there will be ten billion persons on the planet. Earth's human population
will have multiplied five times during the average lifetime of someone born in
1950. To translate these statistics into a vivid image: another Mexico City is
added every 60 days; another Brazil is added every year.

The capacity of the planet to carry life is being exhausted by these human
habits. Not only is our species gobbling up resources faster than Earth's ability
to replenish itself, but our practices are causing damage to the very systems that
sustain life itself: holes in the ozone layer, polluted air and rain, clear-cut forests,
drained wetlands, denuded soils, fouled rivers and lakes, polluted patches of ocean.
Appallingly, this widespread destruction of habitats has as its flip side the death of
creatures that thrive in these ecosystems. By a conservative estimate, in the last
quarter of the 20th century, 20 percent of all living species have become extinct.
When these creatures, these magnificent plants and animals, large and small, go
extinct, they never come back again. We are killing birth itself, wiping out the
future of fellow creatures who took millions of years to evolve. We live in a time
of a great dying off caused by human hands.

On the one hand, we gaze in wonder at the world; on the other hand, we are
wasting the world. This is a sign of our times and should be filled with meaning for
people of faith. But the odd thing is that, with some notable exceptions, many
religious people and church business as a whole go on ignoring the plight of the
earth.

Respect for Life Extends to Earth

Much food for thought and action can be gleaned by rereading Pope John Paul
II's message for New Year's Day 1990 entitled "Peace With God the Creator, Peace
With All of Creation." Faced with widespread destruction of the environment, the
pope wrote, people everywhere are coming to understand that we cannot continue
to plunder the earth as we have in the past. Making this despoiling very concrete,

the message reels off a list of the ways humans have ravaged the earth. What is the root cause for this behavior? In a word, "lack of respect for life." Our disrespect is also due to placing economic profit for a few ahead of the common good of all peoples on the earth, to ignoring the interconnection of all processes and to ignoring the well-being of future generations (the earth is our common heritage).

In order to grow in due respect for nature, the pope continued, we need a morally coherent worldview. "For Christians, such a worldview is grounded in religious convictions drawn from revelation." These beliefs include the story of creation, sin and redemption; they also draw on incarnation, Eucharist and hope of future glory. God cre-

> **Sacramental theology has always taught that simple earthy things—bread, wine, water, oil, the embodied sexual relationship of marriage—can be bearers of divine grace.**

ated this beloved world "very good" (Gen. 1:31) and delivered it into the care of human beings. As they turn their back on God's plan through sinning, they create disorder to the point where all creation is "groaning in travail" (Rom. 8:22). The great act of redemption through the death and resurrection of Jesus Christ is intended not just for humanity but for the whole cosmos, for God reconciled "all things, whether on earth or in the heavens, making peace by the blood of his cross" (Col. 1:20). The view that the earth bears religious importance is also rooted in the rich biblical themes of incarnation (the Word becomes flesh, and so the divine joins with the matter of this world), Eucharist (sharing through bread and wine in the body and blood of Christ) and hope centered in Christ, "the first-born of all creation" (Col. 1:15) that in the future the cosmos will enjoy fullness of new life in the glory of God. In view of this faith, Christians must inevitably conclude that "the ecological crisis is a moral problem."

To address this, the pope proposes a series of righteous actions: be converted from a consumerist lifestyle, address poverty, avoid war and its devastating ecological effects, promote education in ecological responsibility starting with the family and appreciate the beauty of nature, which tells of the glory of God. All of these lead to peace within the human heart and between nations. Grounding these steps is a stunning principle: "Respect for life and for the dignity of the human person extends also to the rest of creation." This "extends also," I suggest, provides a doorway through which Catholics conversant with the church's stance of respect for life can be led to see the critical import of the ecological crisis. Pragmatically, humans will survive together with other creatures on this planet or not at all. Religiously, respect for life cannot be divided; not only human life but the whole living Earth is God's beloved creation, deserving of care.

Three Responses

Carrying forward this program of extending respect for life to all creation, a growing body of theological literature calls upon Christians to develop the virtue of "earth-keeping." The U.S. Catholic Conference in Washington, D.C., provides videos like "The Earth Is the Lord's," books like *And God Saw That It Was Good*, parish kits like "Let the Earth Bless the Lord: God's Creation and Our Responsibility" and grants to individuals, parishes, dioceses and regions to develop earthkeeping projects. Our response can take at least three forms: contemplative, ascetic and prophetic.

The *contemplative response* gazes on the world with eyes of love rather than with an arrogant, utilitarian stare. It learns to appreciate the astonishing beauty of nature, to take delight in its intricate and powerful workings and to stand in awe of the never-ending mystery of life and death played out in the predator-prey relationship. Nothing is too large (the farthest galaxies), nothing too small to escape our wonder. Recall the comment of the scientist Louis Agassiz: "I spent the summer traveling; I got half-way across my back yard." Within the context of faith, the contemplative gaze renders the world sacramental. Sacramental theology has always taught that simple earthy things—bread, wine, water, oil, the embodied sexual relationship of marriage—can be bearers of divine grace. We now realize that this is so because the earth, with all its creatures, is the primordial sacrament, the medium of God's gracious presence and blessing. It "is charged with the grandeur of God," in the prescient words of the Jesuit poet Gerard Manley Hopkins. More than just a stage for our human drama of sin and redemption, it is a marvelous creature in its own right, still evolving, loved by God for itself, of which we humans are a part. Therefore it bears intrinsic, not just instrumental, value. A great project lies ahead: drawing on the earth-loving resources of Scripture to design and frequently use liturgies, personal and communal prayers and meditations that would empower the whole church to see the natural world as God does, with a loving and appreciative eye.

The *ascetic response* practices discipline in using the things of Earth. The true purpose of asceticism has always been to make persons fully alive to the movement of grace in their lives. It does so by sacrificial acts of doing or abstaining that remove what blocks sensitivity to the presence of the Spirit. Traditional forms of asceticism have come upon hard days because of their alliance with a philosophical dualism that prized spirit at the expense of matter. In this framework, matter tends to entrap spirit within itself, and so spirit needs to control matter in order to ascend to a higher realm. Salvation is understood precisely as escape from this realm of bodiliness with its messiness and change in order to come to rest in the realm of light. For centuries a major path of spirituality was marked "Flee the world." To be holy one must reject the world, deny the body and its sexual needs, dismiss feelings (which "don't count") and seek union with God apart from the earth.

In light of Earth as God's beloved creation now being ravaged, however, there are whole new ways to engage in traditional ascetic practices such as fasting, retreats and almsgiving. We can fast from shopping, contribute money and time to ecological works, endure the inconvenience of running an ecologically sensitive household and conduct business with an eye to the green bottom line as well as the red or black. We do these things not to make ourselves suffer and not because we're anti-body, but so that we can become alert to how enslaved we are by the market-place and its effect on the planet. Our economy is structured to make us overcon-sume, with dire effects upon the earth. This is such a deep structural power that we are barely conscious of it—as if it were one of the principalities and powers ruling the world. An Earth-sensuous asceticism that is part of an Earth-affirming spiritual-ity is one response that sets us on the path of Earth-keeping virtue. It enables us to live more simply, with greater reverence for the earth and its creatures, out of religious conviction.

The *prophetic response* moves us to action on behalf of justice for Earth. If the earth is indeed creation, a sacrament of the glory of God with its own intrinsic value, then for Christians ongoing destruction of earth bears the marks of deep sinfulness. Realizing this, we experience a moral imperative to act in favor of care, protection and restoration. Indeed, one stringent criterion must now measure the morality of our actions: whether or not these contribute to a sustainable earth com-munity. A moral universe limited to the human community no longer serves the future of life.

Resisting the culture of death not only among humankind but also among "otherkind" requires a real conversion from the anthropocentric focus of the last five centuries. (My research seems to indicate that the loss of the natural world as a theological and moral issue dates to the Reformation, when everything boiled down to issues of how we are saved. Fights always make one lose perspective.) Here is where the fundamental principle of extension enunciated by John Paul II bears critical fruit: "Respect for life and for the dignity of the human person extends to the rest of creation." If nature is the new poor, then the Christian mandate of option for the poor and oppressed now includes the natural world. If we are to love our neighbor as ourselves, then the range of neighbors now includes the whale, the monarch butterfly, the local lake—the entire community of life. If the common good requires solidarity with all who suffer, then our compassion extends to suffer-ing human beings and other species caught in patterns of extinction. "Save the rain forest" becomes a concrete moral application of the commandment "Thou shalt not kill."

This in turn requires us to realize the deep connections between social injustice and ecological devastation. Ravaging of people and of the land go hand in hand. To be deeply true, prophetic action must not get caught in the trap of pitting social justice issues against issues of ecological health, but must include commitment to ecological wholeness within the struggle for a more just social order. We all share the status of creaturehood; we are all kin in the evolving community of life now under siege. A vision of justice as cosmic justice is the only adequate option. The practical aim is to establish and protect healthy ecosystems where all living crea-tures can flourish. The moral goal is to ensure vibrant life in community for all.

The U.N. Environment Programme's Interfaith Partnership publishes a resource book, *Earth and Faith*, and there is an excellent interfaith forum on religion and ecology at www.environment.harvard.edu/religion.

To Life

A flourishing humanity on a thriving earth in an evolving universe, all together filled with the glory of God: such is the theological vision needed in this critical age of Earth's distress. This moment of crisis calls for a spirituality and ethics that will empower us to live in the web of life as sustainers rather than destroyers of the world. Ignoring this need keeps religious persons locked in ultimately irrelevant concerns while the irreversible drama of life or death is being played out on the planet. But being converted to the earth sets our personal lives and church community off on a great adventure. Instead of living as thoughtless or greedy exploiters of the earth, we become sisters and brothers, friends and lovers, mothers and fathers, priests and prophets, co-creators and children of the earth that as God's beloved creation gives us life. Only then can we join in praying the Sanctus with integrity: "Holy, holy, holy, Lord God of power and might, heaven and earth are full of your glory. Hosanna!" No more monumental challenge faces those who are led by the Spirit of God, Lord and Giver of Life, at the start of the third millennium.

Biblical Views of Nature: Foundations for an Environmental Ethic

by Marcia Bunge

Dr. Marcia J. Bunge is Associate Professor of Theology and Humanities at Christ College, the Honors College of Valparaiso University in Valparaiso, Indiana. Her major areas of study are the history of Christian thought and contemporary issues in theology. She has had a strong commitment to environmental responsibility throughout her life. In addition to writing about the church and environmental responsibility, she has helped strengthen campus recycling programs and worked on several local environmental projects. She is the author of *Against Pure Reason: Writings on History, Language, and Religion* and *The Child in Christian Thought*.

In this reading, Bunge responds to the serious accusation that the Bible has often been accused of contributing to the environmental

crises in modern times. Rather than ignoring these accusations,
she presents the work of some modern biblical scholars (including
herself) who try to uncover alternative biblical interpretations
that "call human beings to preserve and protect the earth and its
creatures."

∞

A common perception is that the Bible shows little concern for our relationship
to nature and has perhaps even encouraged its exploitation. This perception is
often supported by reference to the biblical commands to "subdue" the earth and
"have dominion" over all living things (Genesis 1:28), which are interpreted to
mean that human beings can treat the non-human world in whatever way they
please. This interpretation of Genesis 1:28 and the perception that the Bible has
little else to say about our relation to the earth have led many people to reject the
Bible as a resource for developing a sound environmental ethic.

The view that the Bible has fostered the exploitation of nature is expressed
in an influential and often-cited article by Lynn White entitled, "The Historical
Roots of our Ecological Crisis."[1] Although several scholars have exposed weaknesses of White's position,[2] elements of his argument still prevail in discussions
about the Bible and the environment. Alluding to verses in Genesis 1-2, White
claims they emphasize that God planned creation "explicitly for [human] benefit
and rule: no item in the physical creation had any purpose save to serve [human]
purposes."[3] For White, Christianity accepted this biblical view of creation, fostering the attitude that human beings transcend nature and may exploit it. He argues
that this attitude has shaped the development of modern Western science and
technology, which have posed threats to our environment. He concludes that
Christianity therefore "bears a huge burden of guilt" for our ecological crisis.

Such interpretations of the Bible and our growing environmental problems have
prompted scholars to analyze carefully the biblical view of nature. In contrast to
common assumptions, they are discovering that the Bible contains insights that
can help form the basis of a sound environmental ethic. Although interpretations
of particular passages may vary, they indicate that the Bible affirms the goodness
and intrinsic value of all living things; it points out commonalties between human
beings and other living things; and it contains the mandate that we treat the natural world with care and respect. Such insights provide powerful grounds for environmental responsibility. This brief essay introduces some of the important biblical
passages that have implications for environmental ethics.

Genesis 1-11 contains several fundamental ideas about the natural world and
our place in it.[4] For example, the opening verses of Genesis clearly state that God
is the source of all life and that creation is good. Furthermore, the formation of
Adam from "the dust of the ground" (Genesis 2:7) highlights the connection
between human beings and the earth because *adam*, the word for "human being,"
is a play on *adamah*, the word for "ground" or "earth." The story of Noah and the

flood illustrates God's concern for all creatures because it states that God made the covenant not just with human beings but with "every living thing" and that God desires all creatures to "be fruitful and multiply." The ideas that God is the source of all life, that creation is good, that human beings are connected to the earth, and that God is concerned for all creatures strongly suggest that we are to value and respect the earth and its many forms of life.

Several recent interpretations have shown that Genesis 1:28 and 2:15 call human beings to preserve and protect the earth and its creatures. James Limburg, for example, interprets Genesis 1:28 in this way on the basis of a careful study of the Hebrew word, *radah*, which is usually translated as "to have dominion" or "to rule."[5] By examining the use of this word in other passages in the [Hebrew Bible], he finds it is most often used in political contexts to speak about the rule of a king or a nation. Limburg discovers that when the characteristics of the rule are discussed, the biblical texts emphasize a humane and compassionate rule that displays responsibility for others and that results in peace and prosperity. He therefore concludes that Genesis 1:28 does not advocate tyrannical exploitation of nature but rather responsible care of it.

Many of the Psalms, such as Psalm 8, 104, and 148, reaffirm the goodness of creation and provide additional insights into our relation to nature. For example, according to Terence Fretheim,[6] many of the Psalms indicate that God is active in nature and intimately involved in every aspect of the natural order. Furthermore, the Psalms suggest that all creatures, not merely human beings, witness to the glory of God. The language of Psalm 148 even seems to suggest that "it is only as all creatures of God join together in the chorus of praise that the elements of the natural order or human beings witness to God as they ought."[7] This insight implicitly calls human beings "to relate to the natural order in such a way that nature's praise might show forth with greater clarity."[8]

Insights relevant to an understanding of our relation to the natural world are also found in Wisdom literature [for example, in Proverbs, Ecclesiastes, and Wisdom of Solomon].[9] It emphasizes the importance of nature as a medium of God's revelation, for it presupposes that God's wisdom can be revealed through observation of the natural world. At the same time it points out the tremendous diversity and ultimate mystery of God's creation. Other wisdom texts, such as God's first speech from the whirlwind (Job 38-39), indicate that God takes great delight in non-human creatures and did not create them for human benefit alone. Such passages all imply that human beings need to respect nature, to recognize the intrinsic value of its many creatures, to learn from it, and to preserve its incredible diversity.

Passages from letters of the New Testament, such as Romans 8:18-25, Colossians 1:15-23, 1 Corinthians 15:20-28, and Ephesians 1:10, indicate that Christ's redemptive power affects the whole creation. The passage from Romans reveals that Paul had a universal vision of the "liberation of all the creatures of nature, along with human beings" through Christ's death.[10] Colossians 1:15-23 also claims that all things will be reconciled through Christ. Even if readers disagree about the nature of this universal reconciliation, the passages express God's concern for the whole creation and suggest that we, in turn, should respect God's handiwork.

All of the biblical passages that command us to love our neighbor also have strong implications for environmental responsibility, even if one does not extend the notion of "neighbor" to include non-human creatures, as some theologians have done. As we better understand the dimensions of our environmental problems, it is clear that they are often connected to social injustices. We cannot adequately show love to our neighbors, therefore, without taking into account the environmental problems that affect them.

The passages outlined above and many others[11] provide very strong grounds for respecting nature and its creatures and for living in ways that preserve and protect them. Although certainly not all elements of the Bible depict our relation to the natural world in this way,[12] the Bible clearly contains ample grounds for environmental responsibility. It provides valuable insights for building the foundations of an environmental ethic that, if lived out, can help solve today's environmental problems.

From *Care of the Earth: An Environmental Resource Manual for Church Leaders*, Tina Krause, editor. © 1994, pp. 19-21. Reprinted by permission from Lutheran School of Theology at Chicago.

Notes

1. Lynn White, "The Historical Roots of our Ecological Crisis," *Science* 155 (1967): 1203-7.

2. For an understanding of the debate surrounding this article see *Ecology and Religion in History*, David and Eileen Spring, ed. (New York: Harper, 1974), and James A. Nash, *Loving Nature: Ecological Integrity and Christian Responsibility*, (Nashville: Abingdon, 1991), pp. 68-92.

3. White, p. 1205.

4. For more detailed discussions of Genesis, see, for a few examples, James Limburg, "The Responsibility of Royalty: Genesis 1–11 and the Care of the Earth," *Word and World* 11 (1991): 124-30; William Dryness, "Stewardship of the Earth in the Old Testament," *Tending the Garden: Essays on the Gospel and the Earth*, Wesley Granberg-Michaelson, ed. (Grand Rapids: Eerdmans, 1987): 50-65; H. Paul Santmire, "The Genesis Narratives Revisited," *Interpretation* 45 (1991): 366-79.

5. Limburg, "The Responsibility of Royalty."

6. Terence Fretheim, "Nature's Praise of God in the Psalms," *ExAudit* 3 (1987): 16-30.

7. Ibid, p. 29.

8. Ibid.

9. See, for example, Bruce Malchow, "Nature from God's Perspective," *Dialog* 21 (Spring 1982): 130-133.

10. H. Paul Santmire, "The Liberation of Nature: Lynn White's Challenge Anew," *The Christian Century* 102 (May 22, 1985): 530-533.

11. See: Walter Brueggemann, *The Land* (Philadelphia: Fortress, 1977); Wendell Berry, *The Gift of Good Land* (San Francisco: North Point Press, 1981), pp. 267-281; Terence Fretheim, "The Plagues as Ecological Signs of Historical Disaster," *Journal of Biblical Literature* 110 (1991): 385-396 and "The Reclamation of Creation: Redemption and Law in Exodus," *Interpretation* (1991): 354-365; Richard Heier, "Ecology, Biblical Theology, and Methodology: Biblical Perspectives on the Environment," *Zygon* 19 (1984): 50.

12. See: Rosemary Radford Ruether, *Gaia and God: An Ecofeminist Theology of Earth Healing* (San Francisco: Harper, 1992).

The Family Farm

A new food system, one that uses dollars but is not ruled by them, is growing so fast that no one can keep track of it. There are at least 600 Community Supported Agriculture (CSA) farms across America, some count as many as a thousand....Farmers markets, consumer co-ops, and CSA farms practice a new economics, economics as if, as E.F. Schumacher once said, people mattered. As if the land mattered. As if we value farmers who work with love and beauty to bring forth from the earth health for us all.

—*Donella Meadows*

In the United States, where the vast majority of people were farmers at the time of the American Revolution, fewer people are now full-time farmers (less than 1 percent of the population) than are full-time prisoners.

—*Brian Halweil*

Introduction

This section uncovers some of the reasons behind the decline in the family farm and why some people are concerned about that loss. A common thread throughout much of the rest of this book is the industrialization of agriculture. Brian Halweil introduces the concept of "vertical integration"—how multi-national corporations like Cargill and Monsanto own the seed, the processors, the food companies, the supermarkets—allowing them to control our food supply, from the seed in the ground to the (prepared) food on the plate. The essays by Donella Meadows and Ben Jacques provide pictures of how some farmers are working together to restore the viability of smaller scale farming.

*W*here Have All the Farmers Gone?

by Brian Halweil

Brian Halweil is a staff researcher at the Worldwatch Institute. The globalization of industry and trade is bringing more and more uniformity to the management of the world's land and a spreading threat to the diversity of crops, ecosystems and cultures. As agribusiness takes over, farmers who have a stake in their land and who often are the most knowledgeable stewards of the land struggle to survive and many are driven out of business.

∞

An Endangered Species

Nowadays most of us in the industrialized countries don't farm, so we may no longer really understand that way of life. I was born in the apple orchard and dairy country of Dutchess County, New York, but since age five have spent most of my life in New York City—while most of the farms back in Dutchess County have given way to spreading subdivisions. It's also hard for those of us who get our food from supermarket shelves or drive-thru windows to know how dependent we are on the viability of rural communities.

Whether in the industrial world, where farm communities are growing older and emptier, or in developing nations where population growth is pushing the number of farmers continually higher and each generation is inheriting smaller family plots, it is becoming harder and harder to make a living as a farmer. A combination of falling incomes, rising debt, and worsening rural poverty is forcing more people to either abandon farming as their primary activity or to leave the countryside altogether—a bewildering juncture, considering that farmers produce perhaps the only good that the human race cannot do without.

Since 1950, the number of people employed in agriculture has plummeted in all industrial nations, in some regions by more than 80 percent. Look at the numbers, and you might think farmers are being singled out by some kind of virus:

- In Japan, more than half of all farmers are over 65 years old; in the United States, farmers over 65 outnumber those under 35 by three to one. (Upon retirement or death, many will pass the farm on to children who live in the city and have no interest in farming themselves.)
- In New Zealand, officials estimate that up to 6,000 dairy farms will disappear during the next 10 to 15 years—dropping the total number by nearly 40 percent.
- In Poland, 1.8 million farms could disappear as the country is absorbed into the European Union—dropping the total number by 90 percent.
- In Sweden, the number of farms going out of business in the next decade is expected to reach about 50 percent.
- In the Philippines, Oxfam estimates that over the next few years the number of farm households in the corn-producing region of Mindanao could fall by some 500,000—a 50 percent loss.
- In the United States, where the vast majority of people were farmers at the time of the American Revolution, fewer people are now full-time farmers (less than 1 percent of the population) than are full-time prisoners.
- In the U.S. states of Nebraska and Iowa, between a fifth and a third of farmers are expected to be out of business within two years.

Of course, the declining numbers of farmers in industrial nations does not imply a decline in the importance of the farming sector. The world still has to eat (and 80 million more mouths to feed each year than the year before), so smaller numbers of farmers mean larger farms and greater concentration of ownership. Despite a precipitous plunge in the number of people employed in farming in North America, Europe, and East Asia, half the world's people still make their living from the land. In sub-Saharan Africa and South Asia, more than 70 percent do. In these regions, agriculture accounts, on average, for half of total economic activity.

Some might argue that the decline of farmers is harmless, even a blessing, particularly for less developed nations that have not yet experienced the modernization that moves peasants out of backwater rural areas into the more advanced economies of the cities. For most of the past two centuries, the shift toward fewer farmers has generally been assumed to be a kind of progress. The substitution of high-powered diesel tractors for slow-moving women and men with hoes, or of large mechanized industrial farms for clusters of small "old fashioned" farms, is typically seen as the way to a more abundant and affordable food supply. Our urban-centered society has even come to view rural life, especially in the form of small family-owned businesses, as backwards or boring, fit only for people who wear overalls and go to bed early—far from the sophistication and dynamism of the city.

Urban life does offer a wide array of opportunities, attractions, and hopes—some of them falsely created by urban-oriented commercial media—that many farm families decide to pursue willingly. But city life often turns out to be a disappointment, as displaced farmers find themselves lodged in crowded slums, where unemployment and ill-health are the norm and where they are worse off than they were back home. Much evidence suggests that farmers aren't so much being lured to the city as they are being driven off their farms by a variety of structural changes in the way the global food chain operates. Bob Long, a rancher in McPherson County, Nebraska, stated in a recent *New York Times* article that passing the farm onto his son would be nothing less than "child abuse."

As long as cities are under the pressure of population growth (a situation expected to continue at least for the next three or four decades), there will always be pressure for a large share of humanity to subsist in the countryside. Even in highly urbanized North America and Europe, roughly 25 percent of the population—275 million people—still reside in rural areas. Meanwhile, for the 3 billion Africans, Asians, and Latin Americans who remain in the countryside—and who will be there for the foreseeable future—the marginalization of farmers has set up a vicious cycle of low educational achievement, rising infant mortality, and deepening mental distress.

Hired Hands on Their Own Land

In the 18th and 19th centuries, farmers weren't so trapped. Most weren't wealthy, but they generally enjoyed stable incomes and strong community ties. Diversified farms yielded a range of raw and processed goods that the farmer could typically sell in a local market. Production costs tended to be much lower than now, as many of the needed inputs were home-grown: the farmer planted seed that he or she had saved from the previous year, the farm's cows or pigs provided fertilizer, and the diversity of crops—usually a large range of grains, tubers, vegetables, herbs, flowers, and fruits for home use as well as for sale—effectively functioned as pest control.

Things have changed, especially in the past half-century, according to Iowa State agricultural economist Mike Duffy. "The end of World War II was a watershed period," he says. "The widespread introduction of chemical fertilizers and synthetic pesticides, produced as part of the war effort, set in motion dramatic changes in how we farm—and a dramatic decline in the number of farmers." In the postwar period, along with increasing mechanization, there was an increasing tendency to "out source" pieces of the work that the farmers had previously done themselves—from producing their own fertilizer to cleaning and packaging their harvest. That outsourcing, which may have seemed like a welcome convenience at the time, eventually boomeranged: at first it enabled the farmer to increase output, and thus profits, but when all the other farmers were doing it too, crop prices began to fall.

Before long, the processing and packaging businesses were adding more "value" to the purchased product than the farmer, and it was those businesses that became the dominant players in the food industry. Instead of farmers outsourcing to contractors, it became a matter of large food processors buying raw materials from farmers, on the processors' terms. Today, most of the money is in the work the farmer no longer does—or even controls. In the United States, the share of the consumer's food dollar that trickles back to the farmer has plunged from nearly 40 cents in 1910 to just above 7 cents in 1997, while the shares going to input (machinery, agrochemicals, and seeds) and marketing (processing, shipping, brokerage, advertising, and retailing) firms have continued to expand. The typical U.S. wheat farmer, for instance, gets just 6 cents of the dollar spent on a loaf of bread—so when you buy that loaf, you're paying about as much for the wrapper as for the wheat.

Ironically, then, as U.S. farms became more mechanized and more "productive," a self-destructive feedback loop was set in motion: over-supply and declining crop prices cut into farmers' profits, fueling a demand for more technology aimed at making up for shrinking margins by increasing volume still more. Output increased dramatically, but expenses (for tractors, combines, fertilizer, and seed) also ballooned —while the commodity prices stagnated or declined. Even as they were looking more and more modernized, the farmers were becoming less and less the masters of their own domain.

On the typical Iowa farm, the farmer's profit margin has dropped from 35 percent in 1950 to 9 percent today. In order to generate the same income, this farm would need to be roughly four times as large today as in 1950—or the farmer would need to get a night job. And that's precisely what we've seen in most industrialized nations: fewer farmers on bigger tracts of land producing a greater share of the total food supply. The farmer with declining margins buys out his neighbor and expands or risks being cannibalized himself.

There is an alternative to this huge scaling up, which is to buck the trend and bring some of the input-supplying and post-harvest processing—and the related profits—back onto the farm. But more self-sufficient farming would be highly unpopular with the industries that now make lucrative profits from inputs and processing. And since these industries have much more political clout than the farmers do, there is little support for rescuing farmers from their increasingly servile condition—and the idea has been largely forgotten. Farmers continue to get the message that the only way to succeed is to get big.

This shift of the food dollar away from farmers is compounded by intense concentration in every link of the food chain—from seeds and herbicides to farm finance and retailing.

The traditional explanation for this constant pressure to "get big or get out" has been that it improves the efficiency of the food system—bigger farms replace smaller farms, because the bigger farms operate at lower costs. In some respects, this is quite true. Scaling up may allow a farmer to spread a tractor's cost over greater acreage, for example. Greater size also means greater leverage in purchasing inputs or negotiating loan rates—increasingly important as satellite-guided combines and other equipment make farming more and more capital-intensive. But these economies of scale typically level off. Data for a wide range of crops produced in the

United States show that the lowest production costs are generally achieved on farms that are much smaller than the typical farm now is. But large farms can tolerate lower margins, so while they may not *produce* at lower cost, they can afford to *sell* their crops at lower cost, if forced to do so—as indeed they are by the food processors who buy from them. In short, to the extent that a giant farm has a financial benefit over a small one, it's a benefit that goes only to the processor— not to the farmer, the farm community, or the environment.

This shift of the food dollar away from farmers is compounded by intense concentration in every link of the food chain—from seeds and herbicides to farm finance and retailing. In Canada, for example, just three companies control over 70 percent of fertilizer sales, five banks provide the vast majority of agricultural credit, two companies control over 70 percent of beef packing, and five companies dominate food retailing. The merger of Philip Morris and Nabisco will create an empire that collects nearly 10 cents of every dollar a U.S. consumer spends on food, according to a company spokesperson. Such high concentration can be deadly for the bottom line, allowing agribusiness firms to extract higher prices for the products farmers buy from them, while offering lower prices for the crop they buy from the farmers.

An even more worrisome form of concentration, according to Bill Heffernan, a rural sociologist at the University of Missouri, is the emergence of several clusters of firms that—through mergers, takeovers, and alliances with other links in the food chain—now possess "a seamless and fully vertically integrated control of the food system from gene to supermarket shelf." Consider the recent partnership between Monsanto and Cargill, which controls seeds, fertilizers, pesticides, farm finance, grain collection, grain processing, livestock feed processing, livestock production, and slaughtering, as well as some well-known processed food brands. From the standpoint of a company like Cargill, such alliances yield tremendous control over costs and can therefore be extremely profitable.

But suppose you're the farmer. Want to buy seed to grow corn? If Cargill is the only buyer of corn in a hundred mile radius, and Cargill is only buying a particular Monsanto corn variety for its mills or elevators or feedlots, then if you don't plant Monsanto's seed you won't have a market for your corn. Need a loan to buy the seed? Go to Cargill-owned Bank of Ellsworth, but be sure to let them know which seed you'll be buying. Also mention that you'll be buying Cargill's Saskferco brand fertilizer. OK, but once the corn is grown, you don't like the idea of having to sell to Cargill at the prices it dictates? Well, maybe you'll feed the corn to your pigs, then, and sell them to the highest bidder. No problem—Cargill's Excel Corporation buys pigs, too. OK, you're moving to the city, and renouncing the farm life! No more home-made grits for breakfast, you're buying corn flakes. Well, good news: Cargill Foods supplies corn flour to the top cereal makers. You'll notice, though, that all the big brands of corn flakes seem to have pretty much the same hefty price per ounce. After all, they're all made by the agricultural oligopoly.

As these vertical food conglomerates consolidate, Heffernan warns, "there is little room left in the global food system for independent farmers"—the farmers being increasingly left with "take it or leave it" contracts from the remaining conglomerates. In the last two decades, for example, the share of American agricultural output produced under contract has more than tripled, from 10 percent to 35 percent—and this doesn't include the contracts that farmers must sign to plant genetically engineered seed. Such centralized control of the food system, in which farmers are in effect reduced to hired hands on their own land, reminds Heffernan of the Soviet-style state farms, but with the Big Brother role now being played by agribusiness executives. It is also reminiscent of the "company store" which once dominated small American mining or factory towns, except that if you move out of town now, the store is still with you. The company store has gone global.

With the conglomerates who own the food dollar also owning the political clout, it's no surprise that agricultural policies—including subsidies, tax breaks, and environmental legislation at both the national and international levels—do not generally favor the farms. For example, the conglomerates command growing influence over both private and public agricultural research priorities, which might explain why the U.S. Department of Agriculture (USDA), an agency ostensibly beholden to farmers, would help to develop the seed-sterilizing Terminator technology—a biotechnology that offers farmers only greater dependence on seed companies. In some cases the influence is indirect, as manifested in government funding decisions, while in others it is more blatant. When Novartis provided $25 million to fund a research partnership with the plant biology department of the University of California at Berkeley, one of the conditions was that Novartis has the first right of refusal for any patentable inventions. Under those circumstances, of course, the UC officials—mindful of where their funding comes from—have strong incentives to give more attention to technologies like the Terminator seed, which shifts profit away from the farmer, than to technologies that directly benefit the farmer or the public at large.

Even policies that are touted to be in the best interest of farmers, like liberalized trade in agricultural products, are increasingly shaped by non-farmers. Food traders, processors, and distributors, for example, were some of the principal architects of recent revisions to the General Agreement on Trade and Tariffs (GATT) —the World Trade Organization's predecessor—that paved the way for greater trade flows in agricultural commodities. Before these revisions, many countries had mechanisms for assuring that their farmers wouldn't be driven out of their own domestic markets by predatory global traders. The traders, however, were able to do away with those protections.

The ability of agribusiness to slide around the planet, buying at the lowest possible price and selling at the highest, has tended to tighten the squeeze already put in place by economic marginalization, throwing every farmer on the planet into direct competition with every other farmer. A recent UN Food and Agriculture Organization assessment of the experience of 16 developing nations in implementing the latest phase of the GATT concluded that "a common reported concern was with a general trend towards the concentration of farms," a process that tends to further marginalize small producers and exacerbate rural poverty and unemployment. The sad irony, according to Thomas Reardon, of Michigan State University, is that while small farmers in all reaches of the world are increasingly affected by cheap, heavily subsidized imports of foods from outside of their traditional rural markets, they are nonetheless often excluded from opportunities to participate in food exports themselves. To keep down transaction costs and to keep processing standardized, exporters and other downstream players prefer to buy from a few large producers, as opposed to many small producers.

As the global food system becomes increasingly dominated by a handful of vertically integrated, international corporations, the servitude of the farmer points to a broader society-wide servitude that OPEC-like food cartels could impose, through their control over food prices and food quality. Agricultural economists have already noted that the widening gap between retail food prices and farm prices in the 1990s was due almost exclusively to exploitation of market power, and not to extra services provided by processors and retailers. It's questionable whether we should pay as much for a bread wrapper as we do for the nutrients it contains. But beyond this, there's a more fundamental question. Farmers are professionals, with extensive knowledge of their local soils, weather, native plants, sources of fertilizer or mulch, native pollinators, ecology, and community. If we are to have a world where the land is no longer managed by such professionals, but is instead managed by distant corporate bureaucracies interested in extracting maximum output at minimum cost, what kind of food will we have, and at what price?

Agrarian Services

No question, large industrial farms can produce lots of food. Indeed, they're designed to maximize quantity. But when the farmer becomes little more than the lowest-cost producer of raw materials, more than his own welfare will suffer. Though the farm sector has lost power and profit, it is still the one link in the agri-food chain accounting for the largest share of agriculture's public goods—including half the world's jobs, many of its most vital communities, and many of its most diverse landscapes. And in providing many of these goods, small farms clearly have the advantage.

Local economic and social stability: Over half a century ago, William Goldschmidt, an anthropologist working at the USDA, tried to assess how farm structure and size affect the health of rural communities. In California's San Joaquin Valley, a region then considered to be at the cutting edge of agricultural industrialization, he identified two small towns that were alike in all basic economic and geographic dimensions, including value of agricultural production, except in farm size. Comparing the two, he found an inverse correlation between the sizes of the farms and the well-being of the communities they were a part of.

The small-farm community, Dinuba, supported about 20 percent more people, and at a considerably higher level of living—including lower poverty rates, lower levels of economic and social class distinctions, and a lower crime rate—than the large-farm community of Arvin. The majority of Dinuba's residents were independent entrepreneurs, whereas fewer than 20 percent of Arvin's residents were—most of the others being agricultural laborers. Dinuba had twice as many business establishments as Arvin, and did 61 percent more retail business. It had more schools, parks, newspapers, civic organizations, and churches, as well as better physical infrastructure—paved streets, sidewalks, garbage disposal, sewage disposal and other public services. Dinuba also had more institutions for democratic decision making, and a much broader participation by its citizens. Political scientists have long recognized that a broad base of independent entrepreneurs and property owners is one of the keys to a healthy democracy.

The distinctions between Dinuba and Arvin suggest that industrial agriculture may be limited in what it can do for a community. Fewer (and less meaningful) jobs, less local spending, and a hemorrhagic flow of profits to absentee landowners and distant suppliers means that industrial farms can actually be a net drain on the local economy. That hypothesis has been corroborated by Dick Levins, an agricultural economist at the University of Minnesota. Levins studied the economic receipts from Swift County, Iowa, a typical Midwestern corn and soybean community, and found that although total farm sales are near an all-time high, farm income there has been dismally low—and that many of those who were once the financial stalwarts of the community are now deeply in debt. "Most of the U.S. Corn Belt, like Swift County, is a colony, owned and operated by people who don't live there and for the benefit of those who don't live there," says Levin. In fact, most of the land in Swift County is rented, much of it from absentee landlords.

This new calculus of farming may be eliminating the traditional role of small farms in anchoring rural economies—the kind of tradition, for example, that we saw in the emphasis given to the support of small farms by Japan, South Korea, and Taiwan following World War II. That emphasis, which brought radical land reforms and targeted investment in rural areas, is widely cited as having been a major stimulus to the dramatic economic boom those countries enjoyed.

Not surprisingly, when the economic prospects of small farms decline, the social fabric of rural communities begins to tear. In the United States, farming families are more than twice as likely as others to live in poverty. They have less education and lower rates of medical protection, along with higher rates of infant mortality, alcoholism, child abuse, spousal abuse and mental stress. Across Europe, a similar pattern is evident. And in sub-Saharan Africa, sociologist Deborah Bryceson of the Netherlands-based African Studies Centre has studied the dislocation of small farmers and found that "as de-agrarian-

In the United States, official statistics say farmers are now five times as likely to commit suicide as to die from farm accidents, which have been traditionally the most frequent cause of unnatural death for them.

ization proceeds, signs of social disfunction associated with urban areas [including petty crime and breakdowns of family ties] are surfacing in villages."

People without meaningful work often become frustrated, but farmers may be a special case. "More so than other occupations, farming represents a way of life and defines who you are," says Mike Rosemann, a psychologist who runs a farmer counseling network in Iowa. "Losing the family farm, or the prospect or losing the family farm, can generate tremendous guilt and anxiety, as if one has failed to protect the heritage that his ancestors worked to hold onto." One measure of the despair has been a worldwide surge in the number of farmers committing suicide. In 1998, over 300 cotton farmers in Andhra Pradesh, India, took their lives by swallowing pesticides that they had gone into debt to purchase but that had nonetheless failed to save their crops. In Britain, farm workers are two and one-half times more likely to commit suicide than the rest of the population. In the United States, official statistics say farmers are now five times as likely to commit suicide as to die from farm accidents, which have been traditionally the most frequent cause of unnatural death for them. The true number may be even higher, as suicide hotlines report that they often receive calls from farmers who want to know which sorts of accidents (Falling into the blades of a combine? Getting shot while hunting?) are least likely to be investigated by insurance companies that don't pay claims for suicides.

Whether from despair or from anger, farmers seem increasingly ready to rise up, sometimes violently, against government, wealthy landholders, or agribusiness giants. In recent years we've witnessed the Zapatista revolution in Chiapas, the seizing of white-owned farms by landless blacks in Zimbabwe, and the attacks of European farmers on warehouses storing genetically engineered seed. In the book *Harvest of Rage*, journalist Joel Dyer links the 1995 Oklahoma City bombing that killed nearly 200 people—as well as the rise of radical right and antigovernment militias in the U.S. heartland—to a spreading despair and anger stemming from the ongoing farm crisis. Thomas Homer-Dixon, director of the Project on Environment, Population, and Security at the University of Toronto, regards farmer dislocation, and the resulting rural unemployment and poverty, as one of the major security threats for the coming decades. Such dislocation is responsible for roughly half of the growth of urban populations across the Third World, and such growth often occurs in volatile shantytowns that are already straining to meet the basic needs of their residents. "What was an extremely traumatic transition for Europe and North America from a rural society to an urban one is now proceeding at two to three times that speed in developing nations," says Homer-Dixon. And, these nations have considerably less industrialization to absorb the labor. Such an accelerated transition poses enormous adjustment challenges for India and China, where perhaps a billion and a half people still make their living from the land.

Ecological stability: In the Andean highlands, a single farm may include as many as 30 to 40 distinct varieties of potato (along with numerous other native plants), each having slightly different optimal soil, water, light, and temperature regimes, which the farmer—given enough time—can manage. (In comparison, in the

United States, just four closely related varieties account for about 99 percent of all the potatoes produced.) But, according to Carl Zimmerer, a University of Wisconsin sociologist, declining farm incomes in the Andes force more and more growers into migrant labor forces for part of the year, with serious effects on farm ecology. As time becomes constrained, the farmer manages the system more homogeneously —cutting back on the number of traditional varieties (a small home garden of favorite culinary varieties may be the last refuge of diversity), and scaling up production of a few commercial varieties. Much of the traditional crop diversity is lost.

Complex farm systems require a highly sophisticated and intimate knowledge of the land—something small-scale, full-time farmers are more able to provide. Two or three different crops that have different root depths, for example, can often be planted on the same piece of land, or crops requiring different drainage can be planted in close proximity on a tract that has variegated topography. But these kinds of cultivation can't be done with heavy tractors moving at high speed. Highly site-specific and management-intensive cultivation demands ingenuity and awareness of local ecology, and can't be achieved by heavy equipment and heavy applications of agrochemicals. That isn't to say that being small is always sufficient to ensure ecologically sound food production, because economic adversity can drive small farms, as well as big ones, to compromise sustainable food production by transmogrifying the craft of land stewardship into the crude labor of commodity production. But a large-scale, highly mechanized farm is simply not equipped to preserve landscape complexity. Instead, its normal modus is to use blunt management tools, like crops that have been genetically engineered to churn out insecticides, which obviate the need to scout the field to see if spraying is necessary at all.

In the U.S. Midwest, as farm size has increased, cropping systems have gotten more simplified. Since 1972, the number of counties with more than 55 percent of their acreage planted in corn and soybeans has nearly tripled, from 97 to 267. As farms scaled up, the great simplicity of managing the corn-soybean rotation—an 800 acre farm, for instance, may require no more than a couple of weeks planting in the spring and a few weeks harvesting in the fall—became its big selling point. The various arms of the agricultural economy in the region, from extension services to grain elevators to seed suppliers, began to solidify around this corn-soybean rotation, reinforcing the farmers' movement away from other crops. Fewer and fewer farmers kept livestock, as beef and hog production became "economical" only in other parts of the country where it was becoming more concentrated. Giving up livestock meant eliminating clover, pasture mixtures, and a key source of fertilizer in the Midwest, while creating tremendous manure concentrations in other places.

The world's agricultural biodiversity—the ultimate insurance policy against climate variations, pest outbreaks, and other unforeseen threats to food security—depends largely on the millions of small farmers who use this diversity in their local growing environments.

But the corn and soybean rotation—one monoculture followed by another—is extremely inefficient or "leaky" in its use of applied fertilizer, since low levels of biodiversity tend to leave a range of vacant niches in the field, including different root depths and different nutrient preferences. Moreover, the Midwest's shift to monoculture has subjected the country to a double hit of nitrogen pollution, since not only does the removal and concentration of livestock tend to dump inordinate amounts of feces in the places (such as Utah and North Carolina) where the live-stock operations are now located, but the monocultures that remain in the Mid-west have much poorer nitrogen retention than they would if their cropping were more complex. (The addition of just a winter rye crop to the corn-soy rotation has been shown to reduce nitrogen runoff by nearly 50 percent.) And maybe this dis-aster-in-the-making should really be regarded as a triple hit, because in addition to contaminating Midwestern water supplies, the runoff ends up in the Gulf of Mexico, where the nitrogen feeds massive algae blooms. When the algae die, they are decomposed by bacteria, whose respiration depletes the water's oxygen—suffo-cating fish, shellfish, and all other life that doesn't escape. This process periodically leaves 20,000 square kilometers of water off the coast of Louisiana biologically dead. Thus the act of simplifying the ecology of a field in Iowa can contribute to severe pollution in Utah, North Carolina, Louisiana, *and* Iowa.

The world's agricultural biodiversity—the ultimate insurance policy against climate variations, pest outbreaks, and other unforeseen threats to food security—depends largely on the millions of small farmers who use this diversity in their local growing environments. But the marginalization of farmers who have developed or inherited complex farming systems over generations means more than just the loss of specific crop varieties and the knowledge of how they best grow. "We forever lose the best available knowledge and experience of place, including what to do with marginal lands not suited for industrial production," says Steve Gleissman, an agroecologist at the University of California at Santa Cruz. The 12 million hogs produced by Smithfield Foods Inc., the largest hog producer and processor in the world and a pioneer in vertical integration, are nearly genetically identical and raised under identical conditions—regardless of whether they are in a Smithfield feedlot in Virginia or Mexico.

As farmers become increasingly integrated into the agribusiness food chain, they have fewer and fewer controls over the totality of the production process—shifting more and more to the role of "technology applicators," as opposed to managers making informed and independent decisions. Recent USDA surveys of contract poultry farmers in the United States found that in seeking outside advice on their operations, these farmers now turn first to bankers and then to the corporations that hold their contracts. If the contracting corporation is also the same company that is selling the farm its seed and fertilizer, as is often the case, there's a strong likelihood that company's procedures will be followed. That corporation, as a global enterprise with no compelling local ties, is also less likely to be concerned about the pollution and resource degradation created by those procedures, at least compared with a farmer who is rooted in that community. Grower contracts generally disavow any environmental liability.

And then there is the ecological fallout unique to large-scale, industrial agriculture. Colossal confined animal feeding operations (CAFOs)—those "other places" where livestock are concentrated when they are no longer present on Midwestern soy/corn farms—constitute perhaps the most egregious example of agriculture that has, like a garbage barge in a goldfish pond, overwhelmed the scale at which an ecosystem can cope. CAFOs are increasingly the norm in livestock production, because, like crop monocultures, they allow the production of huge populations of animals which can be slaughtered and marketed at rock-bottom costs. But the disconnection between the livestock and the land used to produce their feed means that such CAFOs generate gargantuan amounts of waste, which the surrounding soil cannot possibly absorb. (One farm in Utah will raise over five million hogs in a year, producing as much waste each day as the city of Los Angeles.) The waste is generally stored in large lagoons, which are prone to leak and even spill over during heavy storms. From North Carolina to South Korea, the overwhelming stench of these lagoons—a combination of hydrogen sulfide, ammonia, and methane gas that smells like rotten eggs—renders miles of surrounding land uninhabitable.

A different form of ecological disruption results from the conditions under which these animals are raised. Because massive numbers of closely confined livestock are highly susceptible to infection, and because a steady diet of antibiotics can modestly boost animal growth, overuse of antibiotics has become the norm in industrial animal production. In recent months, both the Centers for Disease Control and Prevention in the United States and the World Health Organization have identified such industrial feeding operations as principal causes of the growing antibiotic resistance in food-borne bacteria like *salmonella* and *campylobacter*. And as decisionmaking in the food chain grows ever more concentrated—confined behind fewer corporate doors—there may be other food safety issues that you won't even hear about, particularly in the burgeoning field of genetically modified organisms (GMOs). In reaction to growing public concern over GMOs, a coalition that ingenuously calls itself the "Alliance for Better Foods"—actually made up of large food retailers, food processors, biotech companies and corporate-financed farm organizations—has launched a $50 million public "educational" campaign, in addition to giving over $676,000 to U.S. lawmakers and political parties in 1999, to head off the mandatory labeling of such foods.

Perhaps most surprising, to people who have only casually followed the debate about small-farm values versus factory-farm "efficiency," is the fact that a wide body of evidence shows that small farms are actually more productive than large ones—by as much as 200 to 1,000 percent greater output per unit of area. How does this jive with the often-mentioned productivity advantages of large-scale mechanized operations? The answer is simply that those big-farm advantages are always calculated on the basis of how much *of one crop* the land will yield per acre. The greater productivity of a smaller, more complex farm, however, is calculated on the basis of how much food *overall* is produced per acre. The smaller farm can grow several crops utilizing different root depths, plant heights, or nutrients, on the same piece of land simultaneously. It is this "polyculture" that offers the small farm's productivity advantage.

To illustrate the difference between these two kinds of measurement, consider a large Midwestern corn farm. That farm may produce more corn per acre than a small farm in which the corn is grown as part of a polyculture that also includes beans, squash, potato, and "weeds" that serve as fodder. But in overall output, the poly-crop—under close supervision by a knowledgeable farmer—produces much more food overall, whether you measure in weight, volume, bushels, calories, or dollars.

The inverse relationship between farm size and output can be attributed to the more efficient use of land, water, and other agricultural resources that small operations afford, including the efficiencies of intercropping various plants in the same field, planting multiple times during the year, targeting irrigation, and integrating crops and livestock. So in terms of converting inputs into outputs, society would be better off with small-scale farmers. And as population continues to grow in many nations, and the agricultural resources per person continue to shrink, a small farm structure for agriculture may be central to meeting future food needs.

Rebuilding Foodsheds

Look at the range of pressures squeezing farmers, and it's not hard to understand the growing desperation. The situation has become explosive, and if stabilizing the erosion of farm culture and ecology is now critical not just to farmers but to everyone who eats, there's still a very challenging question as to what strategy can work. The agribusiness giants are deeply entrenched now, and scattered protests could have as little effect on them as a mosquito bite on a tractor. The prospects for farmers gaining political strength on their own seem dim, as their numbers—at least in the industrial countries—continue to shrink.

A much greater hope for change may lie in a joining of forces between farmers and the much larger numbers of other segments of society that now see the dangers, to their own particular interests, of continued restructuring of the countryside. There are a couple of prominent models for such coalitions, in the constituencies that have joined forces to fight the Mississippi River Barge Capacity and Hidrovía Barge Capacity projects (see description, p. 119) being pushed forward in the name of global soybean productivity.

The American group has brought together at least the following riverbedfellows:
- National environmental groups, including the Sierra Club and National Audubon Society, which are alarmed at the prospect of a public commons being damaged for the profit of a small commercial interest group;
- Farmers and farmer advocacy organizations, concerned about the inordinate power being wielded by the agribusiness oligopoly;
- Taxpayer groups outraged at the prospect of a corporate welfare payout that will drain more than $1 billion from public coffers;

- Hunters and fishermen worried about the loss of habitat;
- Biologists, ecologists, and birders concerned about the numerous threatened species of birds, fish, amphibians, and plants;
- Local-empowerment groups concerned about the impacts of economic globalization on communities;
- Agricultural economists concerned that the project will further entrench farmers in a dependence on the export of low-cost, bulk commodities, thereby missing valuable opportunities to keep money in the community through local milling, canning, baking, and processing.

A parallel coalition of environmental groups and farmer advocates has formed in the Southern hemisphere to resist the Hidrovía expansion. There too, the river campaign is part of a larger campaign to challenge the hegemony of industrial agriculture. For example, a coalition has formed around the Landless Workers Movement, a grassroots organization in Brazil that helps landless laborers to organize occupations of idle land belonging to wealthy landlords. This coalition includes 57 farm advocacy organizations based in 23 nations. It has also brought together environmental groups in Latin America concerned about the related ventures of logging and cattle ranching favored by large landlords; the mayors of rural towns who appreciate the boost that farmers can give to local economies; and organizations working on social welfare in Brazil's cities, who see land occupation as an alternative to shantytowns.

The Mississippi and Hidrovía projects, huge as they are, still constitute only two of the hundreds of agro-industrial developments being challenged around the world. But the coalitions that have formed around them represent the kind of focused response that seems most likely to slow the juggernaut, in part because the solutions these coalitions propose are not vague or quixotic expressions of idealism, but are site-specific and practical. In the case of the alliance forming around the Mississippi River project, the coalition's work has included questioning the assumptions of the Corps of Engineers analysis, lobbying for stronger antitrust examination of agribusiness monopolies, and calling for modification of existing U.S. farm subsidies, which go disproportionately to large farmers. Environmental groups are working to reestablish a balance between use of the Mississippi as a barge mover and as an intact watershed. Sympathetic agricultural extensionists are promoting alternatives to the standard corn-soybean rotation, including certified organic crop production, which can simultaneously bring down input costs and garner a premium for the final product, and reduce nitrogen pollution.

The United States and Brazil may have made costly mistakes in giving agribusiness such power to reshape the rivers and land to its own use. But the strategy of interlinked coalitions may be mobilizing in time to save much of the world's agricultural health before it is too late. Dave Brubaker, head of the Spira/GRACE Project on Industrial Animal Production at the Johns Hopkins University School of Public Health, sees these diverse coalitions as "the beginning of a revolution in the way we look at the food system, tying in food production with social welfare, human health, and the environment." Brubaker's project brings together public health officials focused on antibiotic overuse and water contamination resulting from hog waste; farmers and local communities who oppose the spread of new factory farms or want to close down existing ones; and a phalanx of natural allies with related campaigns, including animal rights activists, labor unions, religious groups, consumer rights activists, and environmental groups.

"As the circle of interested parties is drawn wider, the alliance ultimately shortens the distance between farmer and consumer," observes Mark Ritchie, president of the Institute for Agriculture and Trade Policy, a research and advocacy group often at the center of these partnerships. This closer proximity may prove critical to the ultimate sustainability of our food supply, since socially and ecologically sound buying habits are not just the passive *result* of changes in the way food is produced, but can actually be the most powerful *drivers* of these changes. The explosion of farmers markets, community-supported agriculture, and other direct buying arrangements between farmers and consumers points to the growing numbers of nonfarmers who have already shifted their role in the food chain from that of choosing from the tens of thousands of food brands offered by a few dozen companies to bypassing such brands altogether. And, since many of the additives and processing steps that take up the bulk of the food dollar are simply the inevitable consequence of the ever-increasing time commercial food now spends in global transit and storage, this shortening of distance between grower and consumer will not only benefit the culture and ecology of farm communities. It will also give us access to much fresher, more flavorful, and more nutritious food. Luckily, as any food marketer can tell you, these characteristics aren't a hard sell.

There's Farming And Then There's Farming

by Donella H. Meadows

Donella H. Meadows was a pioneering environmental scientist and writer, best known as the lead author of the international bestseller *The Limits to Growth* (1972), which reported on a study of long-term global trends in population, economics and the environment. She was also the lead author of the follow-up study, *Beyond the Limits* (1992). A leading voice in what has become known as the "sustainability movement," she taught environmental systems, ethics and journalism at Dartmouth College. She earned a Ph.D. in biophysics from Harvard University. Her weekly column called "The Global Citizen" was nominated for the Pulitzer Prize in 1991.

In this article, she tackles the question, "how do U.S. farmers survive?"

∞

A while ago Beth Sawin and Phil Rice, researchers at the Sustainability Institute, put together a graph that I can't get out of my mind. It shows Midwest corn yields doubling from about 60 bushels per acre in 1950 to 120 bushels on average today. Despite the doubled yield, gross earnings per acre have stayed essentially constant. The net return to the farmer, after the costs of growing the corn, has also stayed constant, right around zero. If it weren't for government farm payments, the average corn farmer would have been working for decades for free.

My first question on seeing that was: How does the system *do* that? How does it so infallibly keep farmers from making money? My next question was, why do farmers put up with it?

Later Beth and Phil showed me some figures that explain how they put up with it. Farm families in two Minnesota counties consistently get more than half their income from off the farm. In recent years 85 percent of their income has been off-farm. The farmers are living mainly on subsidies and outside jobs. They are literally farming at night by tractor light.

Why? Two whys. Why do we pay so little to the people who feed us? Why do they keep feeding us?

The proper economic answer to the first question is: there are too many farmers. With those higher yields they raise more food than the market wants, so price goes down and forces some of them out of business. Then yields go up more, price goes down further, more farmers go under. My economics professor taught me that this process is rational and admirable. It's the market weeding out inefficiency. It enables a tiny percent of us to feed everybody else, reducing food costs for all.

Now that I think for myself, I don't see the rationality, and I don't admire the process. *Why* should yields keep going up, when the market is not calling for more food? And what about soil erosion, water pollution, poisoned ecosystems, fossil fuel use, broken communities, shattered lives, dubious food quality? The market makes food look cheap only by not counting all the costs.

The answer to the second question, why farmers keep at it, has got to be, at bottom, because they love it. John Peterson of Angelic Organics in Caledonia, Illinois, explains why he farms: "The land has a feel under foot that can melt a person to it. There's the rhythm—the barn door opens and closes; the swallows return; the bromegrass swishes....I don't stay on this farm because bromegrass swishes. That's a fringe benefit. The closest I can describe my bond to it is a shudder I get ...when it's time to work in the fields....

"My legs take me to the work, put me on the tractor; I am all surrender. And the joy of pushing dirt around, the thrill of organizing little dots of green into straight lines on bare soil—these invoke in me a subtle delirium.

"Fuzzy rows of carrots streak to the west, flanking scalloped tufts of green and red lettuces. Palm-tree-shaped Brussels sprouts transform a service drive into The Grand Boulevard. Massive cabbage leaves gradually hug themselves into a big ball. Enormous heirloom tomatoes hang voluptuously on avenues of trellising. To gaze at the lush display of textures, forms, colors, to notice the daily changes, is a privilege of being a farmer."

Peterson is not farming a monocrop straight to the horizon by tractor at night. He grows organic vegetables for a Community Supported Agriculture (CSA) farm—a farm that serves nearby subscribers, who pick up once a week a bundle of whatever is ripe. Fresh food, straight from farm to kitchen. No chemicals. No subsidies. Payment direct from consumer to farmer, no middlemen, a decent living for the farmer.

That is a food system that works, though many of its benefits are not measured in dollars. Pat Mannix, a subscriber to the Genesee Valley Organic CSA in New York State, spent four hours helping out on "her" farm and found a new way of seeing: "I found myself preparing the vegetables in a loving, respectful manner. I planned with a passion so nothing would go to waste. When I ate what I had harvested, I clearly understood...that the Earth was alive and that it gave and sustained other life.... Food would never be the same for me again."

Wendell Berry said once in an interview: "Farming is a hard life. It's a hard life, therefore nobody ought to live it. What a remarkable conclusion! There are several steps that are left out. What causes the difficulty? Does freedom come out of it? Does family pride come with it, family coherence? Does some kind of idea of community come with it? Some kind of idea of stewardship, does that come with it? Do ideas of affection or love or loyalty or fidelity come with it?"

Freedom, stewardship, fidelity, family, community, all are casualties of a mechanism that selects only for cheapness and a narrowly measured efficiency that turns a living farm into a mechanized, chemicalized, one-product factory.

Here's the good news. A new food system, one that uses dollars but is not ruled by them, is growing so fast that no one can keep track of it. There are at least 600 CSA farms across America, some count as many as a thousand. Sales of organic produce have been growing by 20 percent per year.

Farmers markets, consumer co-ops, and CSA farms practice a new economics, economics as if, as E.F. Schumacher once said, people mattered. As if the land mattered. As if we valued farmers who work with love and beauty to bring forth from the earth health for us all.

(The quotes in this article come from a book on Community Supported Agriculture called *Sharing the Harvest* by Elizabeth Henderson with Robyn Van En, Chelsea Green Publishing Company, White River Junction VT, 1999.)

From the June 3, 1999 issue of *The Global Citizen*. Reprinted with permission of the Sustainability Institute. Donella Meadows (1941-2001) was director of the Sustainability Institute (www.sustainer.org) and an adjunct professor of environmental studies at Dartmouth College.

Family Farms

by Ben Jacques

A freelance writer and editor, Ben Jacques teaches journalism at Massachusetts College of Liberal Arts. He has written articles on education, health care, medical technology and sustainable agriculture for a number of magazines, newspapers and corporations.

"Honduras has plenty of fertile land, but most of it belongs to wealthy plantation owners or foreign corporations." In contrast, this hopeful story tells how a group of small farmers formed a co-op (highlighting the power of collective action) and fought for access to land, and how a local organization and Heifer Project International assisted them.

∞

We sit on makeshift stools in the shade of a large yuyuga tree beside the workhouse, a typical farm structure with bamboo and mud walls and a tin roof. A few steps away in the stables, calves wait for their feeding. On the slope below, several dozen goats graze on the hillside. Further down, toward the Ulua River that winds north through the rugged Honduran mountains, children take sheep to pasture.

The men who sit with me are fathers and grandfathers, campesino leaders of the CAPTAL collective farm in the town of Concepción del Norte. One has just arrived on horseback. Another has come up from the fields, placing his machete on the ground beside him. Nearby a grandson scoots up the trunk of a tree for a better view.

After *saludos* and *bienvenidos*—handshakes and welcomes—Hernán Rene Ríos, the collective's leader, begins to tell the story of the CAPTAL campesino families. Translating for me is my guide, Tim Wheeler, a Presbyterian Church missionary assigned to work with the Christian Commission for Development (CCD) and Heifer Project International (HPI). In a country marked by abject poverty Tim and his wife, Gloria, provide coordination and support to a wide range of projects that enable poor families to achieve self-reliance, health and dignity.

Thanking God for our visit, Don Hernán begins with the good news. Although the farmers lost their corn and bean crops to Hurricane Mitch in 1998, no animals were lost. In fact, 23 calves have been born this year. The cattle, a mix of hardy, cream-colored Brahmin and Brown Swiss, are giving good milk, as are the dairy goats, black-and-white alpines and floppy-eared nubians. Last month the animals gave 5,546 bottles of milk. This means that there is plenty for everyone in the collective and extra to sell or process into cheese.

"We have completely done away with malnutrition," Don Hernán says. And to make his point, he gestures to a boy and girl sitting on the barn stoop. "See how fat they are!" The children grin shyly. Which do they prefer, cow's milk or goat's? "Goat's milk," the boy responds. "Many families prefer goat's milk because it is so nutritious," Hernán states.

After the hurricane the collective had to rely on its animals. Those designated for meat were slaughtered and shared with all the families. And the cooperative continued to sell young animals to fund farm repairs, improvements, medicine and other necessities. They also decided to give two liters of milk a day to a widow in town whose house was washed away by El Mitch.

Although the farmers still face challenges—how to pay for seeds for the spring planting, how to obtain additional acreage to plant sugar cane, vegetables and forage crops, how to fund an irrigation system—they've come a long way in the past two decades. In 1980 they were desperate. They had neither land nor milk. The meager wages the men could earn as laborers on large farms did not pay for even the basic necessities. The children were malnourished and often sick.

That's when the families decided to organize and seek land where they could grow their own crops. Honduras has plenty of fertile land, but most of it belongs to wealthy plantation owners or foreign corporations like Standard Fruit or Chiquita Brand International, which produce bananas, coffee and other export crops. Hundreds of thousands of poor campesinos are forced to live and farm on the rugged sides of mountains. To make matters worse, traditional slash-and-burn techniques and the overharvesting of trees for firewood or lumber have led to widespread soil depletion and erosion.

In search of arable land, the campesinos sought to take advantage of Honduras's 1975 Agrarian Reform Law, which specified that landless farmers could claim unused land through a lengthy process of application and verification. Yet throughout the country campesinos making land claims were met with hostility, threats and violence. Some were arrested and jailed. A few were killed. "We were opposed by the ranchers in our own village," Don Hernán says. "They told us we could not do it, that we could not define our own destiny."

In 1980, staking out approximately 100 manzanas (one manzana equals 1.7 acres) of unused land on the slopes of the mountain, the Concepción del Norte families bolstered their claim by moving onto the land and refusing to leave. With the strength of numbers and the support of church people and agrarian reform advocates, their claim was eventually authorized.

Since then, however, land reform laws have repeatedly been weakened or nullified. In effect, the collective has been required to purchase the land it once claimed. Twenty-one years later, CAPTAL is in the final process of gaining a legal title to it.

In 1983, the farmers applied to a new ecumenical rural development agency, the Christian Commission for Development, for loans to plant corn and beans. Now providing community development services in over 400 villages and cities throughout Honduras, CCD provided the collective not only with money, but with training in organization and farming methods.

In 1984, CAPTAL applied for grants for cattle through CCD's partner agency, Heifer Project International. "We've started with ten cows and calves, and right away we started to get milk and distribute it to all our members," Don Hernán says.

In 1987, HPI delivered 13 goats to the collective. "At first, we distributed the goats to individual families," Don Hernán reports, "but within months eight goats died, so we decided at our meeting to care for our goats collectively." Now the goat herd numbers 60. The collective also has 26 sheep.

As in all HPI grants made to collectives and individual families, recipients contract to pass on the first female offspring to a neighbor. This practice is known around the world as "passing on the gift." A farm collective may pass on several animals as a startup project for another collective, or donate a single heifer, doe, ewe or sow to a neighboring family.

Because farmers can never raise enough cash from beans and corn to rise above subsistence, an animal is a monumental gift for a poor family. In addition to the dramatic increase in nutrition a dairy cow or goat provides, future offspring may be sold to raise money for medicine, building supplies, education or the purchase of additional land. The animals also provide invaluable fertilizer, used to enrich and rebuild depleted soil.

This explains why campesinos throughout Honduras often made heroic efforts to save their animals during Hurricane Mitch. During the flooding that devastated the area bordering Nicaragua, members of one cooperative secured their young children in trees while the men swam with their cattle to higher ground. Nevertheless, in a disaster that took almost 6,000 lives and left hundreds of thousands homeless, farmers also lost livestock. Thanks to a sharp increase in donations from churches and individuals in North America, both the CCD and HPI have been able to expand their work to meet both crisis and developing needs in Honduras. HPI has been able to replace all the livestock lost in the floods and open up programs in new areas. Wheeler, who has worked in Honduras for 24 years, has seen HPI grow steadily from a few small projects to partnerships with a wide array of nongovernmental organizations, extending its reach throughout the country.

For example, HPI has started a new dairy cattle project in the impoverished Banjo Agua area, where 95 percent of the residents have no access to milk. In all its projects, livestock grants are integrated into sustainable-agriculture programs, including controlled grazing, organic fertilization, terracing, agroforestry and reforestation. Involving cattle, goats, sheep, pigs, donkeys, mules, chickens, rabbits and even fish, these projects are helping poor farmers improve both their lives and land. By rebuilding the soil and structure of hillside acreage, they are making the land more resistant to natural disasters like El Mitch.

At the center of HPI and CCD work is the empowerment of people. Noemi de Espinoza, CCD's founder and executive director, is a veteran advocate for human and economic rights for Honduras's poorest citizens. In 1999, Espinoza was presented with the Honduran Human Rights Prize, awarded to CCD for its community development work throughout the country.

"The poor majority must be at the center of our focus," she said. "We have to change the way power is distributed and exercised, so that the poor and forgotten can participate in rebuilding their lives, and not just be spectators as the international assistance is used to rebuild an economy for the wealthy."

Few communities better exemplify this philosophy than the CAPTAL collective. "We give to the collective, and it gives back to us," says Don Hernán. All decisions affecting the group's welfare are made together— what new crops to plant, how many animals to sell, how to spend cash from sales, how to meet the emergency needs of individual families. Each day three families are assigned to maintain the farm, and one day a week all the members join in. This rotation of labor allows members to supplement their income with jobs away from the farm.

But there are new concerns. The high inflationary rate is driving up the cost of medicine, building supplies and salt, which must be added to animal feed. The cooperative is considering selling up to 50 percent of its milk while reducing the size of its herds to avoid overgrazing. Its members want to plant more forage crops and put in an irrigation system. They would like to set up a micro-credit program that would allow them to make small loans to members for individual needs. And if the 40 children from the collective now attending school wish to go beyond the sixth grade, they will need more money for education.

The success of the collective has allowed its members to break out of the cycle of poverty. It has also brought affirmation of their human and economic rights. The support of CCD and HPI "has helped us to be recognized as persons of value, of inherent self-worth," Don Hernán says. For these families the spirit of community is at the heart of what they do each day. It has brought them, finally, to a place of dignity.

Economics as if Creation Mattered

The ability of agribusiness to slide around the planet, buying at the lowest possible price and selling at the highest, has...[thrown] every farmer on the planet into direct competition with every other farmer.

—Brian Halweil

Industrialism, which is the name of our economy, and which is now virtually the only economy of the world, has been from its beginnings in a state of riot. It is based squarely upon the principal of violence toward everything on which it depends, and it has not mattered whether the form of industrialism was communist or capitalist or whatever; the violence toward nature, human communities, traditional agricultures, local economies has been constant.

—Wendell Berry

Introduction

Economics, externalities, and taxes, oh my! When such topics arise, many of us find our attention wandering, our eyes glazing over. This section's essays will hopefully begin to reveal why economics can not be left only to the economist and why gaining basic economic literacy is essential to creating an economic system that serves the broader well-being of human and non-human communities, not just the corporate bottom line.

The first essay introduces some of the limitations to our measure of "economic health," the Gross Domestic Product (GDP). Brian Halweil's selection tells the story of two rivers, and how their modification (trumpeted as a way to help small farmers and feed hungry people) actually lowers farmers' profits while contributing to the coffers of giants like Cargill, ADM, and Bunge. Alan Durning and John Ryan's "french fry exposé" reveals the hidden costs behind one of America's favorite foods. Wendell Berry's provocative article on local economies further critiques our current economic system. He proposes that currently the most readily available pathway toward a more localized, sustainable economy is to develop local food economies. The final two articles, by Jim Mulligan and Wendell Berry, provide practical advice on how to help create such an economy daily.

This section's readings point to the need for both individual change (e.g., movement along Mulligan's continuum) and political action paving the way for systemic change (e.g., society adopting an alternative measure of economic well-being).

Before going to the essays, a few more introductory words may be helpful, especially regarding "externalities" and "getting prices right."

Simply put, externalities are "spillover effects," those things which are seen as "external" to the monetary accounting system. A common example is the chemical factory whose effluent into a river kills the fish and ruins the fishers' livelihood. The costs of the externalities in this example are borne by the fish themselves and the fishers' loss of work. In Redefining Progress' examples (which you will read shortly), obesity and related health impacts could be seen as externalities, spillover effects, of American eating habits.

"Getting prices right" is one way to include the costs of externalities in the price of what we buy. In our factory example, the manufacturer could be taxed for polluting the river. Money raised from those taxes could then be used to both provide work for unemployed fishers and clean up the river. Because the manufacturer's taxes would decrease as their emissions decreased, the taxes would also serve as an incentive to not pollute.

Let's take one more example. Most scientists now agree that global warming is occurring. The United States, with 4 percent of the world's population, emits 25 percent of the world's greenhouse gasses. Emissions from our cars and trucks are the largest contributors to those gasses. The price we pay for a gallon of gasoline does not include the "externality" of global warming. Should we pay more for gasoline in order to get the price right?

The Gross Domestic Product, Well-Being, and Waistlines

by Redefining Progress

The Atlantic Monthly published an article in 1995 titled "If the GDP Is Up, Why Is America Down?" The GDP refers to the Gross Domestic Product. Economists measure it; pundits analyze it; and incumbent politicians pray it continues to grow. Most of us assume our personal and social well-being increases right along with GDP. Questioning that assumption is akin to questioning one of our culture's most religiously held beliefs. The following essay, however, suggests we adopt an alternative measure of economic well-being, the Genuine Progress Indicator (GPI). The GPI was developed by Redefining Progress, a think-tank concerned with the sustainability of the Earth's resources. After introducing the GPI, the article describes how things we do not value—like obesity and overeating—actually increase GDP. They suggest that adopting the GPI as a measure of economic health would more accurately value, measure and encourage those things we all value like volunteer work, clean air and water, and strong social connections.

Considering such perspectives can help us begin to see in a different way and ask different questions: "Just what does the GDP measure? Is its growth always worth celebrating?"

∞

Imagine receiving an annual holiday letter from distant friends, reporting the best year ever for their family, because they spent more money this year than ever before. It began during the unusually rainy winter sparked by El Niño, when the roof sprang leaks and their yard in the East Bay hills started to slide. The many layers of roofing had to be stripped to the rafters before the roof could be reconstructed, and engineers were required to keep the yard from eroding away. Shortly after, Jane broke her leg in a car accident: A hospital stay, surgery, physical therapy, and replacing the car took a bite out of their savings. Jane, of course, couldn't maintain her usual routine of caring for their two small children, shopping, cooking, and cleaning duties, so they hired people to help. Then they were robbed and replaced a computer, two TVs, a VCR, and a video camera; they also bought a home security system to keep these new purchases safe.

Essentially, Jane and John's equating money spent with well-being is like using the gross domestic product (GDP) as the barometer of a nation's economic health.

The GDP is simply a gross tally of money spent—goods and services purchased by households or government and business investments, regardless of whether they enhance our well-being or not. Designed as a planning tool to guide the massive production effort for World War II, the GDP was never intended to be a yardstick of economic progress; yet, gradually it has assumed totemic stature as the ultimate measure of economic success. When it rises, the media applaud and politicians rush to take credit. When it falls, there is hand-wringing and general alarm.

The GDP as a Flawed Measure of the Economy and of Progress

As a measure of economic health, the GDP is badly flawed. First, by counting only monetary transactions as economic activity, the GDP omits much of what people value and activities that serve basic needs. For example, it doesn't count free services, such as community volunteer work or caring for children or elderly parents in the home, that would show up in the GDP if they were paid for. It also ignores the value of leisure time spent in recreation, relaxation, or with family and friends. The GDP omits crucial contributions of the environment, such as pure air and water, moderate climate, and protection from the sun's harmful rays, even though these services, which the earth provides for free, become expensive if they need to be bought instead. It is appropriate that an economic indicator include such measures, because common sense and history tell us that the economy is a tool to address needs and enhance well being, not an end in itself.

More significantly, the GDP fails to distinguish between monetary transactions that genuinely add to well being and those that diminish it, try to maintain the status quo, or make up for degraded conditions. Much that contributes to economic growth is perceived by most people as losses rather than gains…. For example, the GDP treats crime, divorce, legal fees, and other signs of social breakdown as economic gains. Car wrecks, medical costs, locks and security systems, and insurance are also pluses to the GDP.

Further, the GDP ignores the environmental costs of economic activities. It takes no account of the depletion of natural resources used to produce goods and services. For example, the harvesting of ancient redwood trees adds the market value of the wood to the GDP. The GDP counts pollution as a double gain to the economy. The production of oil that creates pollution adds to the GDP; then the clean-up of toxic waste sites or the Exxon Valdez oil spill ups the GDP even more. In treating the depletion or degradation of our natural resources as income rather than depreciation of an asset, the GDP violates both basic accounting principles and common sense...

The Genuine Progress Indicator

To address the inadequacies of the GDP as a guide for public policy, the Genuine Progress Indicator was developed in 1994 by Redefining Progress [www.redefiningprogress.org]…The Genuine Progress Indicator (GPI) takes from the GDP the financial transactions that are relevant to well being. It then adjusts them for aspects of the economy that the GDP ignores. The GPI thus reveals the relationship between factors conventionally defined as purely economic and those traditionally defined as purely social and environmental.

Like the GDP, the GPI begins with the nation's personal consumption expenditures. But the GPI assesses the well being of households, rather than focusing exclusively on the number of dollars they spend… It is often assumed that the rising GDP lifts all boats, but this is not necessarily true. From 1973 to 1993, for example, while the GDP rose by 55%, real wages declined by 3.4%. In the 1980s alone, the poorest fifth of American families lost 0.5% of their income each year, while the top 5% of households increased their real income by 3.9% per year. Growth did not benefit everyone, and a true measure of well being should take this inequality into account….

The following nonmonetary benefits—ignored by the GDP—are included in the GPI:

1. the value of time spent on household work, parenting, and volunteer work.
2. the value of services of consumer durables (such as cars and refrigerators).
3. services of highways and streets.

The GPI then subtracts three categories of expenses that do not improve well-being:

1. defensive expenditures, defined as money spent to maintain the household's level of comfort, security, or satisfaction, in the face of declines in quality of life due to such factors as crime, auto accidents, or pollution. Examples include personal water filters, locks or security systems, hospital bills from auto accidents, or the cost of repainting houses damaged by air pollution.
2. social costs, such as the cost of divorce, household costs of crime, or loss of leisure time.
3. the depreciation of environmental assets and natural resources, including loss of farmland, wetlands, and old-growth forests; reduction of stocks of natural resources, such as fossil fuels or other mineral deposits; and damaging effects of wastes and pollution.

[Editor's note: With this introduction to the GDP and GPI, the authors turn their attention to our eating habits, revealing how things we do not value—like obesity—increase the GDP.]

The GDP Is Padded with Fat—Ours

Americans spend $30 to 50 billion a year on dieting, trying to get rid of the extra growth around their midsections (Berg 1997). When it comes to food, the all-too-common cycle of overeating or eating poorly, buying diet products and exercise machines, paying the medical bills for obesity and poor nutrition, and then eating more for consolation hardly adds up to progress. That growth is unwanted by the American people, but every dollar spent advertising food products, gaining weight, and then trying to shed those unwanted pounds contributes to the GDP.

Surplus Food

Unless we've grown our own food, each bite that we take is digested by the GDP. Including agriculture, restaurants, and the like, $700 billion flowed through the U.S. food industry last year (Rowe and Silverstein 1999). No one will contest the need for a strong food industry, but as with other financial transactions counted as progress by the GDP, not all food-related purchases really increase well-being.

The thriving food industry nourishes what Marion Nestle, the head of the Department of Nutrition at New York University, calls the 3,800-calorie-a-day problem. America's food producers produce enough food to supply 3,800 calories every day to every American (Perl 1999). However, the average woman only needs 2,000 calories a day, the average man 2,500, and children even less.

So what happens to all of this extra food we produce? Some is exported, but the food industry spends $10 billion each year in direct advertising and another $20 billion on coupons, games, and other gimmicks trying to convince Americans to absorb the surplus calories (Nestle 1998). Psychologists have found that when food is put in front of people, they will eat it—whether they are hungry or not. In the end, 40% of Americans admit that they eat more calories than they should (USDA 1997).

Excess Weight

And so we grow. As the GDP goes up, so does the percentage of overweight Americans. According to the Third National Health and Nutrition Examination Survey (NHANES III), over half (55%) of American adults are currently overweight or obese (severely overweight) (National Institutes of Health 1998). While the GDP nearly tripled from 1960 to 1994 (in inflation-adjusted dollars), the rates of obese Americans nearly doubled, increasing from 12.8% to 22.5% of adults (Flegal et al. 1998). Evidence suggests an accelerating upward trend since 1994. According to the journal of the American Medical Association, the prevalence of obesity increased by 6% between 1991 and 1998 (Mokdad et al. 1999).

No demographic group is immune. The data show that obesity increased in every state, in both sexes, and across all age groups, races, educational levels, and smoking statuses (Mokdad et al. 1999).

Similar trends of increasing numbers of overweight and obese Americans are also showing up in children. Two successive Surgeons General have pronounced childhood obesity an "epidemic." Indeed, over the last two decades, the number of overweight children has increased by more than 50%, and the number of obese (extremely overweight) children has nearly doubled to roughly 14% of children and 12% of adolescents. Less than a third of children ages 6 to 17 meet the minimum standards for cardiovascular fitness, flexibility, and strength (CDC 1997).

Evidence of our increasing size takes many forms. Seats in sports stadiums, concert venues, movie theaters, and airplanes are becoming more capacious, as the old standard of 18 inches no longer comfortably accommodates the expanding American girth. In 1992, more than twenty automotive and apparel companies sponsored a project to take new measurements of the American physique and develop new standards, updating those developed by the U.S. military in 1947 (Abend 1993). Trade magazines report an ongoing controversy in the apparel industry over the new standards for women's clothing sizes, developed partly because of the aging population and partly to address the confusion caused when designers make clothing two sizes larger than the label indicates. One instructor at the New York Fashion Institute explained the psychological ploy: "A lot of times in designer houses the cut is a bit fuller to make the woman feel she is wearing a smaller size" (Abend 1993). Inflate the sizes and sales rise, contributing to economic growth.

Pay the Doctor

Denial may sell clothes, but it cannot protect us from the health consequences and the economic costs associated with being overweight. Being overweight raises children's risks for serious illness. Type II diabetes alone, the type associated with weight problems, has quadrupled among kids since 1982, which boosts spending on pharmaceuticals and other health costs (National Institutes of Health 1995). Evidence also suggests that risks for high cholesterol, clogged arteries, and heart disease begin in childhood, with poor diets and sedentary lifestyles (Vessey 1998).

Overweight people run a higher risk of premature death, according to a recent American Cancer Society study, the largest ever done on obesity and mortality. "The evidence is now compelling and irrefutable," says the lead researcher, Dr. JoAnn Manson of the American Cancer Society. "Obesity is probably the second-leading preventable cause of death in the United States after cigarette smoking" (Associated Press 1999). Obesity leads to such serious diseases as type II diabetes, gallbladder disease, heart disease, breast and colon cancer, and higher risk of stroke. An estimated 300,000 Americans die each year from the combined effects of an unhealthy diet and inactivity (McGinnis 1993).

These health misfortunes of Americans plump up the GDP as well. Medical spending on diseases associated with obesity amounted to $51.6 billion in 1995, including medical costs for obesity-related heart disease, cancer, stroke, and hypertension. These costs represent 5.7% of national health expenditures within the United States (Wolf and Colditz 1998). Although this spending contributes to the GDP, it would be tough to argue that it makes us better off.

The indirect costs of obesity, such as lost productivity, are also substantial, and may have an even greater impact, both on the overall economy and on society, than direct medical spending. Obesity exacted another $47.6 billion in such costs in 1995 (Wolf and Colditz 1998), for a total cost of $99.2 billion.

But the costs and effects of a poor diet go beyond obesity. Diets high in calories, fat, cholesterol, and salt, and low in fiber and nutrition, contribute to heart disease, certain types of cancer, stroke, diabetes, hypertension, and osteoporosis, as well as to obesity. Taken together, these health conditions cost an estimated $250 billion each year in medical spending and lost productivity (Frazao 1996).

More than two-thirds of Americans are trying to lose or maintain their weight, according to a recent study of more than one million Americans by Mary K. Serdula at the Centers for Disease Control and Prevention. They spend $33 billion each year on weight-loss products and services (Serdula 1999). The medical costs associated with dieting are harder to count, but evidence suggests that dieting itself can undermine health: one recent study found that radical reductions in calorie intake reduce the effectiveness of protective cells in the immune system that fight viruses and tumors (USDA 1997).

If eating too many calories and leading a sedentary lifestyle lead to weight gain, it only makes sense that moderately limiting calorie intake and increasing physical activity would lead to weight loss. In fact, that is what both the U.S. Department of Agriculture's Dietary Guidelines and the National Heart, Lung, and Blood Institute's Clinical Guidelines recommend. Yet only one in five people in the U.S. who are actively trying to control their weight follow these recommendations (Serdula 1999).

Eating fewer calories and exercising for at least thirty minutes each day do not require spending any money. In fact, this dieting regime could even decrease spending on food. If more dieters followed the recommended guidelines, they would probably have more success at achieving their weight-loss goals and could reduce the $33 billion spent on dieting in the process. Not to mention the costs of roughly 110,000 liposuctions last year, at $2,000 or more apiece (Rowe and Silverstein 1999).

Buying Weight Loss

But so many Americans are habituated to buying solutions to problems that they prefer diet drinks disguised as pop or milkshakes and even surgery to altering their unhealthy eating habits and sedentary lifestyles. No pain. Just gain.

Retail trade magazines report record expansion in sales of weight control products, now a billion-dollar business. For example, sales in the "meal replacement" category—including products such as Slim Fast Food's Meal on the Go, USA Nutritional's MaxiFat Burning System, and CyperGenics' Super Weight Loss Shakes—hit $957 million in 1998, a 28.5% increase over 1997. Diet pill sales rose 4.9% to $153.8 million in the same period (Chain Drug Review 1999). Consumers spent another $3.5 million on home exercise equipment in 1995 (Business Wire 1996), and $5 billion in 1997 (Business Wire 1998). One trade magazine hailed this remarkable growth, calling the treadmill "the exercise machine of the nineties," unwittingly coining an apt symbol for our current sense of progress (Business Wire 1998).

While many Americans eat too many calories and spend money trying to lose the excess weight that results, 10% of Americans are going hungry or do not have enough food for an active and healthy life (USDA 1999). Nationally, 9.7% of households were rated "food insecure" in 1996-1998, according to a recent USDA study of census statistics (USDA 1999). But the GDP is blind to how food is distributed. It goes up just as much when some go hungry and some overeat as when everyone has a reasonable amount.

If increasing the size of our economy means spending lots of money on empty calories and then more money to get rid of the results, it is no wonder that eating disorders are increasing and appearing in younger and younger children. Researchers have found that almost half of American elementary students between the first and third grades want to be thinner (Mellin et al.). Further, cases of anorexia and bulimia have doubled in the past ten years, according to the National Institute of Mental Health, with the sharpest increases in teenage girls (Schuster 1999). "Bulimia may be the trademark affliction of the growth era," as Jonathan Rowe and Judith Silverstein (1999) assert. "It is a disease of literal obedience to the schizoid messages that barrage young girls: indulge yourselves wantonly but also be taut and svelte."

Scanning through magazines for teenage girls and women, one finds advertising for high-calorie energy drinks as well as svelte models touting the benefits of diet shakes. Both sales show up in the GDP. If we were attending to genuine progress, as does the GPI, overeating, then dieting, then treating eating disorders and surgically removing excess fat would be considered a net loss for our psyches, our perceptions of ourselves, and our well-being. The physical and mental health costs of our dysfunctional relationship with food should not be included in any true measure of progress.

Reprinted by permission of Redefining Progress, www.redefiningprogress.org.

References

Abend, Jules. 1993. "Our Fits over Fit, Apparel Sizing." *Bobbin* 35 (11) (July).

Associated Press. 1999. "Study Provides Best Evidence That Obesity Can Shorten Life." *Dallas Morning News*, 7 October.

Berg, Frances M. 1997. *Afraid to Eat; Children and Teens in Weight Crisis*. Hettinger, ND: Healthy Weight Network.

Business Wire. 1998. "Treadmill Popularity Helps Manufacturers' Sales of Fitness Equipment Pass 3-Billion Mark in '97." 26 May.

_____. 1996. "Sales of Fitness Equipment Increased in 1995 as Spending Continued on Serious Machines for Home Use." 3 June.

Centers for Disease Control. 1997. "Update: Prevalence of Overweight among Children, Adolescents, and Adults—U.S. 1988-1994." *Morbidity and Mortality Weekly Report* 46(9)(7 March):199-202.

Chain Drug Review. 1999. "Weight Loss Hits New Heights." 21(7):50.

Flegal, K. M., M. D. Carroll, R. J. Kuczmarski, and C. L. Johnson. 1998. "Overweight and Obesity in the United States: Prevalence and Trends, 1960-1994." *International Journal of Obesity* 22:39-47.

Frazao, Elizabeth. 1996. "The American Diet: A Costly Health Problem." *Food Review*, January.

Mcginnis, J. M., and W. H. Foege. 1993. "Actual Causes of Death in the United States." *Journal of the American Medical Association* 270:2207-2212.

Mellin et al. 1991. Cited in "Eating Disorders in the USA: Statistics in Context." [WWW Document]. Accessed 14 October 1999: http://www.edap.org/stats.html

Mokdad, Ali H., Mary K. Serdula, William H. Dietz, Barbara A. Bowman, James S. Marks, and Jeffrey P. Koplan. 1999. "The Spread of the Obesity Epidemic in the United States, 1991-1998." *Journal of the American Medical Association* 282(16):1519-1522.

National Institutes of Health. National Heart, Lung, and Blood Institute. 1998. *National Institutes of Health Guidelines*. [PDF Document]. Accessed 23 October 1999: http://www.nhlbi.nih.gov/guidelines/obesity/ob_guidelines.pdf

National Institutes of Health. National Institutes of Diabetes and Digestive and Kidney Diseases. 1995. *Diabetes in America*. 2nd Edition. Washington, DC: National Institutes of Health.

Nestle, Marion. 1998. "Toward More Healthful Dietary Patterns—A Matter of Policy; Commentary on Lowfat Milk." *Public Health Reports* 113(5):420.

Perl, Rebecca. 1999. "Americans Are Eating More and Exercising Less." Weekly Edition: *The Best of NPR News*, 2 October.

Rowe, Jonathan, and Judith Silverstein. 1999. "The GDP Myth: Why 'Growth' Isn't Always a Good Thing." *Washington Monthly*, March 17-21.

Schuster, Karoly. 1999. "The Dark Side of Nutrition." *Food Management* 34(6):34-39.

Serdula, Mary K., Ali H. Mokdad, David F. Williamson, Deborah A.Galuska, James M. Mendlein, and Gretory W. Heath. 1999. "Prevalence of Attempting Weight Loss and Strategies for Controlling Weight." *Journal of the American Medical Association* 282(14):1353-1358.

U.S. Department of Agriculture. 1997. *Human Nutrition, ARS Quarterly Report*, April-June.

_____. 1999. "Fact Sheet on State Food Insecurity Rankings: State Prevalence Rates of Food Insecurity, Average 1996-8." Release No. f414.99. [WWW Document]. Accessed 15 October 1999: http://www.usda.gov/news/releases/1999/10/f414

Vessey, Judith A., Paula K. Yim-Chiplis, and Nancy R. Mackenzie. 1998. "Effects of Television Viewing on Children's Development." *Pediatric Nursing* 23:483.

Wolf, A. M., and G. A. Colditz. 1998. "Current Estimates of the Economic Costs of Obesity in the United States." *Obesity Research* 6:97-106.

Introduction to Where Have All the Farmers Gone?

by Brian Halweil

Halweil tells of two major riverine construction projects: one on the Mississippi, the other on the Paraguay-Parana River. Both are touted as necessary to the economic survival of farmers. Halweil examines this claim, and uses the story to introduce some of the "externalities"—such as ecological degradation—of our global economic system.

∞

Since 1992, the U.S. Army Corps of Engineers has been developing plans to expand the network of locks and dams along the Mississippi River. The Mississippi is the primary conduit for shipping American soybeans into global commerce—about 35,000 tons a day. The Corps' plan would mean hauling in up to 1.2 million metric tons of concrete to lengthen ten of the locks from 180 meters to 360 meters each, as well as to bolster several major wing dams which narrow the river to keep the soybean barges moving and the sediment from settling. This construction would supplement the existing dredges which are already sucking 85 million cubic meters of sand and mud from the river's bank and bottom each year. Several different levels of "upgrade" for the river have been considered, but the most ambitious of them would purportedly reduce the cost of shipping soybeans by 4 to 8 cents per bushel. Some independent analysts think this is a pipe dream.

Around the same time the Mississippi plan was announced, the five governments of South America's La Plata Basin—Bolivia, Brazil, Paraguay, Argentina, and Uruguay—announced plans to dredge 13 million cubic meters of sand, mud, and rock from 233 sites along the Paraguay-Paraná River. That would be enough to fill a convoy of dump trucks 10,000 miles long. Here, the plan is to straighten natural river meanders in at least seven places, build dozens of locks, and construct a major port in the heart of the Pantanal—the world's largest wetland. The Paraguay-Paraná flows through the center of Brazil's burgeoning soybean heartland—second only to the United States in production and exports. According to statements from the Brazilian State of Mato Grasso, this "Hidrovía" (water highway) will give a further boost to the region's soybean export capacity.

Lobbyists for both these projects argue that expanding the barge capacity of these rivers is necessary in order to improve competitiveness, grab world market share, and rescue farmers (either U.S. or Brazilian, depending on whom the lobbyists are addressing) from their worst financial crisis since the Great Depression. Chris Brescia, president of the Midwest River Coalition 2000, an alliance of commodity shippers that forms the primary lobbying force for the Mississippi plan, says, "The sooner we provide the waterway infrastructure, the sooner our family farmers will benefit." Some of his fellow lobbyists have even argued that these projects are essential to feeding the world (since the barges can then more easily speed the soybeans to the world's hungry masses) and to saving the environment (since the hungry masses will not have to clear rain forest to scratch out their own subsistence).

Probably very few people have had an opportunity to hear both pitches and compare them. But anyone who has may find something amiss with the argument that U.S. farmers will become more competitive versus their Brazilian counterparts, at the same time that Brazilian farmers will, for the same reasons, become more competitive with their U.S. counterparts. A more likely outcome is that farmers of these two nations will be pitted against each other in a costly race to maximize production, resulting in short-cut practices that essentially strip-mine their soil and throw long-term investments in the land to the wind. Farmers in Iowa will have stronger incentives to plow up land along stream banks, triggering faster erosion of topsoil. Their brethren in Brazil will find themselves needing to cut deeper into the savanna, also accelerating erosion. That will increase the flow of soybeans, all right—both north and south. But it will also further depress prices, so that even as the farmers are shipping more, they're getting less income per ton shipped. And in any case, increasing volume can't help the farmers survive in the long run, because sooner or later they will be swallowed by larger, corporate farms that can make up for the smaller per-ton margins by producing even larger volumes.

So, how can the supporters of these river projects, who profess to be acting in the farmer's best interests, not notice the illogic of this form of competition? One explanation is that from the advocates' (as opposed to the farmers') standpoint, this competition isn't illogical at all—because the lobbyists aren't really representing farmers. They're working for the commodity processing, shipping, and trading firms who want the price of soybeans to fall, because these are the firms that buy the crops from the farmers. In fact, it is the same three agribusiness conglomerates—Archer Daniels Midland (ADM), Cargill, and Bunge—that are the top soybean processors and traders along both rivers.

Welcome to the global economy. The more brutally the U.S. and Brazilian farmers can batter each other's prices (and standards of living) down, the greater the margin of profit these three giants gain. Meanwhile, another handful of companies controls the markets for genetically modified seeds, fertilizers, and herbicides used by the farmers—charging oligopolistically high prices both north and south of the equator.

In assessing what this proposed digging-up and reconfiguring of two of the world's great river basins really means, keep in mind that these projects will not be the activities of private businesses operating inside their own private property. These are proposed public works, to be undertaken at huge public expense. The motive is neither the plight of the family farmer nor any moral obligation to feed the world, but the opportunity to exploit poorly informed public sentiments about farmers' plights or hungry masses as a means of usurping public policies to benefit private interests. What gets thoroughly Big Muddied, in this usurping process, is that in addition to subjecting farmers to a gladiator-like attrition, these projects will likely bring a cascade of damaging economic, social, and ecological impacts to the very river basins being so expensively remodeled.

What's likely to happen if the lock and dam system along the Mississippi is expanded as proposed? The most obvious effect will be increased barge traffic, which will accelerate a less obvious cascade of events that has been underway for some time, according to Mike Davis of the Minnesota Department of Natural Resources. Much of the Mississippi River ecosystem involves aquatic rooted plants, like bullrush, arrowhead, and wild celery. Increased barge traffic will kick up more sediment, obscuring sunlight and reducing the depth to which plants can survive. Already, since the 1970s, the number of aquatic plant species found in some of the river has been cut from 23 to about half that, with just a handful thriving under the cloudier conditions. "Areas of the river have reached an ecological turning point," warns Davis. "This decline in plant diversity has triggered a drop in the invertebrate communities that live on these plants, as well as a drop in the fish,

mollusk, and bird communities that depend on the diversity of insects and plants."
On May 18, 2000, the U.S. Fish and Wildlife Service released a study saying that
the Corps of Engineers' project would threaten the 300 species of migratory birds
and 127 species of fish in the Mississippi watershed, and could ultimately push
some into extinction. "The least tern, the pallid sturgeon, and other species that
evolved with the ebbs and flows, sandbars and depths, of the river are progressively
eliminated or forced away as the diversity of the river's natural habitats is removed
to maximize the barge habitat," says Davis.

The outlook for the Hidrovía project is similar. Mark Robbins, an ornithologist
at the Natural History Museum at the University of Kansas, calls it "a key step in
creating a Florida Everglades-like scenario of destruction in the Pantanal, and an
American Great Plains-like scenario in the Cerrado in southern Brazil." The
Paraguay-Paraná feeds the Pantanal wetlands, one of the most diverse habitats on
the planet, with its populations of woodstorks, snailkites, limpkins, jabirus, and
more than 650 other species of birds, as well as more than 400 species of fish and
hundreds of other less-studied plants, mussels, and marshland organisms. As the
river is dredged and the banks are built up to funnel the surrounding wetlands
water into the navigation path, bird nesting habitat and fish spawning grounds will
be eliminated, damaging the indigenous and other traditional societies that depend
on these resources. Increased barge traffic will suppress river species here just as it
will on the Mississippi. Meanwhile, herbicide-intensive soybean monocultures—
on farms so enormous that they dwarf even the biggest operations in the U.S. Midwest—are rapidly replacing diverse grasslands in the fragile Cerrado. The heavy
plowing and periodic absence of ground cover associated with such farming erodes
100 million tons of soil per year. Robbins notes that "compared to the Mississippi,
this southern river system and surrounding grassland is several orders of magnitude
more diverse and has suffered considerably less, so there is much more at stake."

Supporters of such massive disruption argue that it is justified because it is the
most "efficient" way to do business. The perceived efficiency of such farming might
be compared to the perceived efficiency of an energy system based on coal. Burning coal looks very efficient if you ignore its long-term impact on air quality and
climate stability. Similarly, large farms look more efficient than small farms if you
don't count some of their largest costs—the loss of the genetic diversity that under-
pins agriculture, the pollution caused by agrochemicals, and the dislocation of rural
cultures. The simultaneous demise of small, independent farmers and rise of multi-
national food giants is troubling not just for those who empathize with dislocated
farmers, but for anyone who eats.

"Where Have All the Farmers Gone?" from *World Watch* magazine Sep/Oct 2000, Worldwatch Institute,
© 2002, www.worldwatch.org.

French Fries

by John C. Ryan & Alan Thein Durning

This light-hearted look at one of America's favorite food items un-covers the real costs behind that little bag of fries. Try reading it through quickly, out loud, and see if you don't run out of breath, or at least feel exhausted, once you recognize what it really takes to deliver those tasty, deep-fried carbohydrates to your plate.

[Editor's Note: *Stuff* follows a day in the life of a fictitious middle class North American woman. Ryan and Durning reveal the secret lives of things she uses—coffee, clothing, newspapers, computer—during her day. We pick up the story at lunch where she has ordered french fries (*Stuff* also looks at the burger and cola she ordered with it).]

∞

I ordered french fries with my burger. Not the healthiest lunch, I admit—lots of grease and salt. But it's what I was raised on, and like I said, I was in a rush.

The fries arrived, 90 of them, in a paper box. The box was made of bleached pine pulp from an Arkansas mill. My fries weighed five ounces. They were made from a single 10-ounce potato, sliced into remarkably uniform four-inch-long strips.

Potato

The potato, a russet Burbank, was grown on one-half square foot of sandy soil in the upper Snake River valley of Idaho. Ninety percent of Idaho potatoes are russet Burbanks. They were selected in the early sixties by McDonald's and other fast-food chains because they make good fries. They stay stiff after cooking.

The growing season was 150 days; my potato was watered repeatedly. Seven and a half gallons of water were applied to the potato's half foot plot. If all of it had been applied at once, it would have submerged the soil to a depth of two feet. The water came from the Snake River, which drains a basin the size of Colorado. The Snake River valley and its downstream neighbor, the Columbia Basin, produce 80 percent of U.S. frozen french fries. Along the Snake's upper reaches, irrigators of potatoes and other crops take all the river's water. Directly below Milner Dam, west of Pocatello, the riverbed is bone-dry much of the year.

Eighty percent of the Snake's original streamside, or riparian, habitat is gone, most of it replaced by reservoirs and irrigation canals. Dams have stopped 99 per-cent of salmon from running up the Snake River, and sturgeon are gone from all but three stretches. Like salmon, sturgeon migrate between fresh water and the sea, but sturgeon live up to 100 years. They do not stop growing until they die and can

Salt of the Earth

Sodium chloride (table salt) is one of the Earth's most common minerals. Modern miners usually inject steam underground to dissolve salt deposits. Then they pump up the brine and evaporate it to get salt.

Only 3 percent of salt ends up on food. It is much more commonly used as a de-icer and as a source of chlorine for the chemical and plastic industries. The world's largest salt eaters by far are actually cars. Every winter, road crews and property owners use 145 pounds of salt for each American— melting ice and snow from roads, parking lots, and driveways. The salty runoff heads for sewers and local streams, where it can harm aquatic life.

weigh more than 1,000 pounds. There are undoubtedly sturgeon in the Snake River that remember the smell of the Pacific Ocean even though they have not been there for half a century.

My potato was treated with fertilizers and pesticides to ensure that its shape and quality were just like those of other potatoes. (My fries were so uniform that it was hard to believe they'd ever been potatoes.) These chemicals accounted for 38 percent of the farmer's expenses. Much of the fertilizer's nitrogen leached into groundwater; that, plus concentrated salts, made the water unfit even for irrigation.

Some of the fertilizers and pesticides washed into streams when rain fell. Among these were pesticides like Telone II (acutely toxic to mammals, and probably birds, through the skin or lungs) and Sevin XLR Plus (nontoxic to birds but highly toxic to fish). The Environmental Protection Agency's tests of waters in the Columbia Basin found agricultural contaminants in every tributary, including the Snake.

Processing

A diesel-powered harvester dug up my potato, which was trucked to a processing plant nearby. Half the potato's weight; mostly water, was lost in processing. The remainder was potato parts, which the processing plant sold as cattle feed.

Processing my potato created two-thirds of a gallon of wastewater. This water contained dissolved organic matter and one-third gram of nitrogen. The wastewater was sprayed on a field outside the plant. The field was unplanted at the time, and the water sank underground.

Freezing

Freezing the potato slices required electrical energy, which came from a hydroelectric dam on the Snake River. Frozen foods often require 10 times more energy to produce than their fresh counterparts. In 1960, 92 percent of the potatoes Americans ate were fresh; by 1990, Americans ate more frozen potatoes, mostly french fries, than fresh ones.

My fries were frozen using hydrofluoro-carbon coolants, which have replaced the chlorofluorocarbons (CFCs) that harm the ozone layer. Some coolants escaped from the plant. They rose 10 miles up, into the stratosphere, where they depleted no ozone, but they did trap heat, contributing to the greenhouse effect. A refrigerated 18-wheeler brought my fries to Seattle. They were fried in corn oil from Nebraska, sprinkled with salt mined in Louisiana, and served with ketchup made in Pittsburgh of Florida tomatoes. My ketchup came in four aluminum and plastic pouches from Ohio.

What To Do?

- Push your elected officials to support sustainable agriculture and to stop subsidizing irrigation. The subsidies hurt the environment, taxpayers, and those who don't receive the subsidies—such as growers of rain-fed potatoes.
- Instead of buying fried, overpackaged fast food, cook some organic produce for yourself. Eat it on a real plate.
- Buy local foods or, best of all, grow your own. Garden produce is fresher, uses almost no energy except the sun, and puts to use un(der)used land—your lawn.

Blue Baby Syndrome

Several infants in the Tri-Cities area of southeastern Washington have developed methemoglobinemia, or "blue baby syndrome," a rare but deadly malady afflicting infants. It is caused by nitrates in drinking water. Dark-skinned babies are at higher risk because changes in their skin color can be harder to detect. Many Hispanic families work in potato fields and processing plants in the Tri-Cities area, where the Snake River joins the Columbia. Nitrates in nearly half the area's residential water wells exceed standards in the Safe Drinking Water Act.

From *Stuff*, by John C. Ryan and Alan Thein Durning, © 1997, Northwest Environment Watch, Seattle. Used with permission.

The Idea of a Local Economy

by Wendell Berry

Wendell Berry's many books of poetry and prose include *The Unsettling of America*, *What Are People For?* and *Another Turn of the Crank*. His more recent books include *A Place on Earth*, *Life is a Miracle* and *Jayber Crow*.

The primary cause of environmental degradation is "economic over-simplification," according to Wendell Berry: the gifts of God's creation (otherwise known as natural resources) are reduced to a free or very cheap supply of raw materials. Stick with Berry—his economic analysis is heavy at times, but very provocative, and can reveal a new way of looking at the global economy. Berry proposes that the place to begin shifting toward a more localized, sustainable economy is to develop local food economies.

∞

Let us begin by assuming what appears to be true: that the so-called "environmental crisis" is now pretty well established as a fact of our age. The problems of pollution, species extinction, loss of wilderness, loss of farmland, loss of topsoil may still be ignored or scoffed at, but they are not denied. Concern for these problems has acquired a certain standing, a measure of discussability, in the media and in some scientific, academic, and religious institutions.

This is good, of course; obviously, we can't hope to solve these problems without an increase of public awareness and concern. But in an age burdened with "publicity," we have to be aware also that as issues rise into popularity they rise also into the danger of oversimplification. To speak of this danger is especially necessary in confronting the destructiveness of our relationship to nature, which is the result, in the first place, of gross oversimplification.

The "environmental crisis" has happened because the human household or economy is in conflict at almost every point with the household of nature. We have built our household on the assumption that the natural household is simple and can be simply used. We have assumed increasingly over the last five hundred years that nature is merely a supply of "raw materials," and that we may safely possess those materials merely by taking them. This taking, as our technical means have increased, has involved always less reverence or respect, less gratitude, less local knowledge, and less skill. Our methodologies of land use have strayed from our old sympathetic attempts to imitate natural processes, and have come more and more to resemble the methodology of mining, even as mining itself has become more technologically powerful and more brutal.

And so we will be wrong if we attempt to correct what we perceive as "environmental" problems without correcting the economic oversimplification that caused them. This oversimplification is now either a matter of corporate behavior or of behavior under the influence of corporate behavior. This is sufficiently clear to many of us. What is not sufficiently clear, perhaps to any of us, is the extent of our complicity, as individuals and especially as individual consumers, in the behavior of the corporations.

What has happened is that most people in our country, and apparently most people in the "developed" world, have given proxies to the corporations to produce and provide all of their food, clothing, and shelter. Moreover, they are rapidly giving proxies to corporations or governments to provide entertainment, education, child care, care of the sick and the elderly, and many other kinds of "service" that once were carried on informally and inexpensively by individuals or households or communities. Our major economic practice, in short, is to delegate the practice to others.

> **The trouble with this is that a proper concern for nature and our use of nature must be practiced not by our proxy-holders, but by ourselves.**

The danger now is that those who are concerned will believe that the solution to the "environmental crisis" can be merely political—that the problems, being large, can be solved by large solutions generated by a few people to whom we will give our proxies to police the economic proxies that we have already given. The danger, in other words, is that people will think they have made a sufficient change if they have altered their "values," or had a "change of heart," or experienced a "spiritual awakening," and that such a change in passive consumers will cause appropriate changes in the public experts, politicians, and corporate executives to whom they have granted their political and economic proxies.

The trouble with this is that a proper concern for nature and our use of nature must be practiced not by our proxy-holders, but by ourselves. A change of heart or of values without a practice is only another pointless luxury of a passively consumptive way of life. The "environmental crisis," in fact, can be solved only if people, individually and in their communities, recover responsibility for their thoughtlessly given proxies. If people begin the effort to take back into their own power a significant portion of their economic responsibility, then their inevitable first discovery is that the "environmental crisis" is no such thing; it is not a crisis of our environs or surroundings; it is a crisis of our lives as individuals, as family members, as community members, and as citizens. We have an "environmental crisis" because we have consented to an economy in which by eating, drinking, working, resting, traveling, and enjoying ourselves we are destroying the natural, the god-given world.

We live, as we must sooner or later recognize, in an era of sentimental economics and, consequently, of sentimental politics. Sentimental communism holds in effect that everybody and everything should suffer for the good of "the many" who, though miserable in the present, will be happy in the future for exactly the same reasons that they are miserable in the present.

Sentimental capitalism is not so different from sentimental communism as the corporate and political powers claim. Sentimental capitalism holds in effect that everything small, local, private, personal, natural, good, and beautiful must be sacrificed in the interest of the "free market" and the great corporations, which will bring unprecedented security and happiness to "the many"—in, of course, the future.

These forms of political economy may be described as sentimental because they depend absolutely upon a political faith for which there is no justification, and because they issue a cold check on the virtue of political and/or economic rulers. They seek, that is, to preserve the gullibility of the people by appealing to a fund of political virtue that does not exist. Communism and "free-market" capitalism both are modern versions of oligarchy. In their propaganda, both justify violent means by good ends, which always are put beyond reach by the violence of the means. The trick is to define the end vaguely—"the greatest good of the greatest number" or "the benefit of the many"—and keep it at a distance.

The fraudulence of these oligarchic forms of economy is in their principle of displacing whatever good they recognize (as well as their debts) from the present to the future. Their success depends upon persuading people, first, that whatever they have now is no good, and second, that the promised good is certain to be achieved in the future. This obviously contradicts the principle—common, I believe, to all the religious traditions—that if ever we are going to do good to one another, then the time to do it is now; we are to receive no reward for promising to do it in the future. And both communism and capitalism have found such principles to be a great embarrassment. If you are presently occupied in destroying every good thing in sight in order to do good in the future, it is inconvenient to have people saying things like "Love thy neighbor as thyself" or "Sentient beings are numberless, I vow to save them." Communists and capitalists alike, "liberal" and "conservative" capitalists alike, have needed to replace religion with some form of determinism, so that they can say to their victims, "I am doing this because I can't do otherwise. It is not my fault. It is inevitable." The wonder is how often organized religion has gone along with this lie.

The idea of an economy based upon several kinds of ruin may seem a contradiction in terms, but in fact such an economy is possible, as we see. It is possible however, on one implacable condition: the only future good that it assuredly leads to is that it will destroy itself. And how does it disguise this outcome from its subjects, its short-term beneficiaries, and its victims? It does so by false accounting. It substitutes for the real economy, by which we build and maintain (or do not maintain) our household, a symbolic economy of money, which in the long run, because of the self-interested manipulations of the "controlling interests," cannot symbolize or account for anything but itself. And so we have before us the spectacle of unprecedented "prosperity" and "economic growth" in a land of degraded farms, forests, ecosystems, and watersheds, polluted air, failing families, and perishing communities.

Wal-Mart, for example, as a large corporation "freely" competing against local, privately owned businesses has virtually all the freedom, and its small competitors virtually none.

This moral and economic absurdity exists for the sake of the allegedly "free" market, the single principle of which is this: commodities will be produced wherever they can be produced at the lowest cost, and consumed wherever they will bring the highest price. To make too cheap and sell too high has always been the program of industrial capitalism. The idea of the global "free market" is merely capitalism's so-far-successful attempt to enlarge the geographic scope of its greed, and moreover to give to its greed the status of a "right" within its presumptive territory. The global "free market" is free to the corporations precisely because it dissolves the boundaries of the old national colonialisms, and replaces them with a new colonialism without restraints or boundaries. It is pretty much as if all the rabbits have now been forbidden to have holes, thereby "freeing" the hounds.

The "right" of a corporation to exercise its economic power without restraint is construed, by the partisans of the "free market," as a form of freedom, a political liberty implied presumably by the right of individual citizens to own and use property.

But the "free market" idea introduces into government a sanction of an inequality that is not implicit in any idea of democratic liberty: namely that the "free market" is freest to those who have the most money, and is not free at all to those with little or no money. Wal-Mart, for example, as a large corporation "freely" competing against local, privately owned businesses has virtually all the freedom, and its small competitors virtually none.

To make too cheap and sell too high, there are two requirements. One is that you must have a lot of consumers with surplus money and unlimited wants. For the time being, there are plenty of these consumers in the "developed" countries. The problem, for the time being easily solved, is simply to keep them relatively affluent and dependent on purchased supplies.

The other requirement is that the market for labor and raw materials should remain depressed relative to the market for retail commodities. This means that the supply of workers should exceed demand, and that the land-using economy should be allowed or encouraged to overproduce.

To keep the cost of labor low, it is necessary first to entice or force country people everywhere in the world to move into the cities—in the manner prescribed by the United States' Committee for Economic Development after World War II —and second, to continue to introduce labor-replacing technology. In this way it is possible to maintain a "pool" of people who are in the threatening position of being mere consumers, landless and also poor, and who therefore are eager to go to work for low wages—precisely the condition of migrant farm workers in the United States.

To cause the land-using economies to overproduce is even simpler. The farmers and other workers in the world's land-using economies, by and large, are not organized. They are therefore unable to control production in order to secure just prices. Individual producers must go individually to the market and take for their produce simply whatever they are paid. They have no power to bargain or make demands. Increasingly, they must sell, not to neighbors or to neighboring towns and cities, but to large and remote corporations. There is no competition among the buyers (supposing there is more than one), who are organized, and are "free" to exploit the advantage of low prices. Low prices encourage overproduction as producers attempt to make up their losses "on volume," and overproduction inevitably makes for low prices. The land-using economies thus spiral downward as the money economy of the exploiters spirals upward. If economic attrition in the land-using population becomes so severe as to threaten production, then governments can subsidize production without production controls, which necessarily will encourage overproduction, which will lower prices—and so the subsidy to rural producers becomes, in effect, a subsidy to the purchasing corporations. In the land-using economies production is further cheapened by destroying, with low prices and low standards of quality, the cultural imperatives for good work and land stewardship.

This sort of exploitation, long familiar in the foreign and domestic economies and the colonialism of modern nations, has now become "the global economy," which is the property of a few supranational corporations. The economic theory used to justify the global economy in its "free market" version is again perfectly groundless and sentimental. The idea is that what is good for the corporations will sooner or later—though not of course immediately—be good for everybody.

That sentimentality is based in turn, upon a fantasy: the proposition that the great corporations, in "freely" competing with one another for raw materials, labor, and market share, will drive each other indefinitely, not only toward greater "efficiencies" of manufacture, but also toward higher bids for raw materials and labor and lower prices to consumers. As a result, all the world's people will be economically secure—in the future. It would be hard to object to such a proposition if only it were true.

But one knows, in the first place, that "efficiency" in manufacture always means reducing labor costs by replacing workers with cheaper workers or with machines.

In the second place, the "law of competition" does not imply that many competitors will compete indefinitely. The law of competition is a simple paradox: Competition destroys competition. The law of competition implies that many competitors, competing on the "free market" will ultimately and inevitably reduce the number of competitors to one. The law of competition, in short, is the law of war.

In the third place, the global economy is based upon cheap long-distance transportation, without which it is not possible to move goods from the point of cheapest origin to the point of highest sale. And cheap long-distance transportation is the basis of the idea that regions and nations should abandon any measure of economic self-sufficiency in order to specialize in production for export of the few commodities or the single commodity that can be most cheaply produced. Whatever may be said for the "efficiency" of such a system, its result (and I assume, its purpose) is to destroy local production capacities, local diversity, and local economic independence.

This idea of a global "free market" economy, despite its obvious moral flaws and its dangerous practical weaknesses, is now the ruling orthodoxy of the age. Its propaganda is subscribed to and distributed by most political leaders, editorial writers, and other "opinion makers." The powers that be, while continuing to budget huge sums for "national defense," have apparently abandoned any idea of national or local self-sufficiency, even in food. They also have given up the idea that a national or local government might justly place restraints upon economic activity in order to protect its land and its people.

The folly at the root of this foolish economy began with the idea that a corporation should be regarded, legally, as "a person." But the limitless destructiveness of this economy comes about precisely because a corporation is not a person.

The global economy is now institutionalized in the World Trade Organization, which was set up, without election anywhere, to rule international trade on behalf of the "free market"—which is to say on behalf of the supranational corporations—and to overrule, in secret sessions, any national or regional law that conflicts with the "free market." The corporate program of global free trade and the presence of the World Trade Organization have legitimized extreme forms of expert thought. We are told confidently that if Kentucky loses its milk-producing capacity to Wisconsin, that will be a "success story." Experts such as Stephen C. Blank, of the University of California, Davis, have proposed that "developed" countries, such as the United States and the United Kingdom, where food can no longer be produced cheaply enough, should give up agriculture altogether.

The folly at the root of this foolish economy began with the idea that a corporation should be regarded, legally, as "a person." But the limitless destructiveness of this economy comes about precisely because a corporation is not a person. A corporation, essentially, is a pile of money to which a number of persons have sold their moral allegiance. As such, unlike a person, a corporation does not age. It does not arrive, as most persons finally do, at a realization of the shortness and smallness of human lives; it does not come to see the future as the lifetime of the children and grandchildren of anybody in particular. It can experience no personal hope or remorse, no change of heart. It cannot humble itself. It goes about its business as if it were immortal, with the single purpose of becoming a bigger pile of money. The stockholders essentially are usurers, people who "let their money work for them," expecting high pay in return for causing others to work for low pay. The World Trade Organization enlarges the old idea of the corporation-as-person by giving the global corporate economy the status of a super government with the power to overrule nations. I don't mean to say, of course, that all corporate executives and stockholders are bad people. I am only saying that all of them are very seriously implicated in a bad economy.

Unsurprisingly, among people who wish to preserve things other than money—for instance, every region's native capacity to produce essential goods—there is a growing perception that the global "free market" economy is inherently an enemy to the natural world, to human health and freedom, to industrial workers, and to farmers and others in the land-use economies; and furthermore, that it is inherently an enemy to good work and good economic practice. I believe that this perception is correct and that it can be shown to be correct merely by listing the assumptions implicit in the idea that corporations should be "free" to buy low and sell high in the world at large. These assumptions, so far as I can make them out, are as follows:

1. Stable and preserving relationships among people, places, and things do not matter and are of no worth.
2. Cultures and religions have no legitimate practical or economic concerns.
3. There is no conflict between the "free market" and political freedom, and no connection between political democracy and economic democracy.
4. There can be no conflict between economic advantage and economic justice.
5. There is no conflict between greed and ecological or bodily health.
6. There is no conflict between self-interest and public service.
7. The loss or destruction of the capacity anywhere to produce necessary goods does not matter and involves no cost.
8. It is all right for a nation's or a region's subsistence to be foreign based, dependent on long-distance transport, and entirely controlled by corporations.
9. Therefore, wars over commodities—our recent Gulf War, for example—are legitimate and permanent economic functions.
10. This sort of sanctioned violence is justified also by the predominance of centralized systems of production supply, communications, and transportation, which are extremely vulnerable not only to acts of war between nations, but also to sabotage and terrorism.
11. It is all right for poor people in poor countries to work at poor wages to produce goods for export to affluent people in rich countries.
12. There is no danger and no cost in the proliferation of exotic pests, weeds, and diseases that accompany international trade and that increase with the volume of trade.
13. An economy is a machine, of which people are merely the interchangeable parts. One has no choice but to do the work (if any) that the economy prescribes, and to accept the prescribed wage.
14. Therefore, vocation is a dead issue. One does not do the work that one chooses to do because one is called to it by Heaven or by one's natural or god-given abilities, but does instead the work that is determined and imposed by the economy. Any work is all right as long as one gets paid for it.

These assumptions clearly prefigure a condition of total economy. A total economy is one in which everything—"life forms," for instance, or the "right to pollute"—is "private property" and has a price and is for sale. In a total economy significant and sometimes critical choices that once belonged to individuals or communities become the property of corporations. A total economy, operating internationally, necessarily shrinks the powers of state and national governments, not only because those governments have signed over significant powers to an international bureaucracy or because political leaders become the paid hacks of the corporations but also because political processes—and especially democratic processes—are too slow to react to unrestrained economic and technological development on a global scale. And when state and national governments begin to act in effect as agents of the global economy, selling their people for low wages and their people's products for low prices, then the rights and liberties of citizenship must necessarily shrink. A total economy is an unrestrained taking of profits from the disintegration of nations, communities, households, landscapes, and ecosystems. It licenses symbolic or artificial wealth to "grow" by means of the destruction of the real wealth of all the world.

Among the many costs of the total economy, the loss of the principle of vocation is probably the most symptomatic and, from a cultural standpoint, the most critical. It is by the replacement of vocation with economic determinism that the exterior workings of a total economy destroy the character and culture also from the inside.

In an essay on the origin of civilization in traditional cultures, Amanda K. Coomaraswamy wrote that "the principle of justice is the same throughout...[it is] that each member of the community should perform the task for which he is fitted by nature..." The two ideas, justice and vocation, are inseparable. That is why Coomaraswamy spoke of industrialism as "the mammon of injustice," incompatible with civilization. It is by way of the principle and practice of vocation that sanctity and reverence enter into the human economy. It was thus possible for traditional cultures to conceive that "to work is to pray."

Aware of industrialism's potential for destruction, as well as the considerable political danger of great concentrations of wealth and power in industrial corporations, American leaders developed, and for a while used, the means of limiting and restraining such concentrations, and of somewhat equitably distributing wealth and property. The means were: laws against trusts and monopolies, the principle of collective bargaining, the concept of one-hundred-percent parity between the land-using and the manufacturing economies, and the progressive income tax. And to protect domestic producers and production capacities it is possible for governments to impose tariffs on cheap imported goods. These means are justified by the government's obligation to protect the lives, livelihoods, and freedoms of its citizens. There is, then, no necessity or inevitability requiring our government to sacrifice the livelihoods of our small farmers, small business people, and workers, along with our domestic economic independence to the global "free market." But now all of these means are either weakened or in disuse. The global economy is intended as a means of subverting them.

In default of government protections against the total economy of the supranational corporations, people are where they have been many times before: in danger of losing their economic security and their freedom, both at once. But at the same time the means of defending themselves belongs to them in the form of a venerable principle: powers not exercised by government return to the people. If the government does not propose to protect the lives, livelihoods, and freedoms of its people, then the people must think about protecting themselves.

How are they to protect themselves? There seems, really, to be only one way, and that is to develop and put into practice the idea of a local economy—something that growing numbers of people are now doing. For several good reasons, they are beginning with the idea of a local food economy. People are trying to find ways to shorten the distance between producers and consumers, to make the connections between the two more direct, and to make this local economic activity a benefit to the local community. They are trying to learn to use the consumer economies of local towns and cities to preserve the livelihoods of local farm families and farm communities. They want to use the local economy to give consumers an influence over the kind and quality of their food, and to preserve and enhance the local landscapes. They want to give everybody in the local community a direct, long-term interest in the prosperity, health, and beauty of their homeland. This is the only way presently available to make the total economy less total. It was once, I believe, the only way to make a national or a colonial economy less total. But now the necessity is greater.

> So far as I can see, the idea of a local economy rests upon only two principles: neighborhood and subsistence. In a viable neighborhood, neighbors ask themselves what they can do or provide for one another, and they find answers that they and their place can afford.

I am assuming that there is a valid line of thought leading from the idea of the total economy to the idea of a local economy. I assume that the first thought may be a recognition of one's ignorance and vulnerability as a consumer in the total economy. As such a consumer, one does not know the history of the products that one uses. Where, exactly, did they come from? Who produced them? What toxins were used in their production? What were the human and ecological costs of producing them and then of disposing of them? One sees that such questions cannot be answered easily, and perhaps not at all. Though one is shopping amid an astonishing variety of products, one is denied certain significant choices. In such a state of economic ignorance it is not possible to choose products that were produced locally or with reasonable kindness toward people and toward nature. Nor is it possible for such consumers to influence production for the better. Consumers who feel a prompting toward land stewardship find that in this economy they can have no stewardly practice. To be a consumer in the total economy, one must agree to be totally ignorant, totally passive, and totally dependent on distant supplies and self-interested suppliers.

And then, perhaps, one begins to see from a local point of view. One begins to ask, What is here, what is in me, that can lead to something better? From a local point of view, one can see that a global "free market" economy is possible only if nations and localities accept or ignore the inherent instability of a production economy based on exports and a consumer economy based on imports. An export economy is beyond local influence, and so is an import economy. And cheap long-distance transport is possible only if granted cheap fuel, international peace, control of terrorism, prevention of sabotage, and the solvency of the international economy.

Perhaps one also begins to see the difference between a small local business that must share the fate of the local community and a large absentee corporation that is set up to escape the fate of the local community by ruining the local community.

So far as I can see, the idea of a local economy rests upon only two principles: neighborhood and subsistence. In a viable neighborhood, neighbors ask themselves what they can do or provide for one another, and they find answers that they and their place can afford. This, and nothing else, is the practice of neighborhood. This practice must be, in part, charitable, but it must also be economic, and the economic part must be equitable; there is a significant charity in just prices.

Of course, everything needed locally cannot be produced locally. But a viable neighborhood is a community; and a viable community is made up of neighbors who cherish and protect what they have in common. This is the principle of subsistence. A viable community, like a viable farm, protects its own production capacities. It does not import products that it can produce for itself. And it does not export local products until local needs have been met. The economic products of a viable community are understood either as belonging to the community's subsistence or as surplus, and only the surplus is considered to be marketable abroad. A community, if it is to be viable, cannot think of producing solely for export, and it cannot permit importers to use cheaper labor and goods from other places to destroy the local capacity to produce goods that are needed locally. In charity, moreover, it must refuse to import goods that are produced at the cost of human or ecological degradation elsewhere. This principle applies not just to localities, but to regions and nations as well.

The principles of neighborhood and subsistence will be disparaged by the globalists as "protectionism"—and that is exactly what it is. It is a protectionism that is just and sound, because it protects local producers and is the best assurance of adequate supplies to local consumers. And the idea that local needs should be met first and only surpluses exported does not imply any prejudice against charity toward people in other places or trade with them. The principle of neighborhood at home always implies the principle of charity abroad. And the principle of subsistence is in fact the best guarantee of giveable or marketable surpluses. This kind of protection is not "isolationism."

Albert Schweitzer, who knew well the economic situation in the colonies of Africa, wrote nearly sixty years ago: "Whenever the timber trade is good, perma-nent famine reigns in the Ogowe region because the villagers abandon their farms to fell as many trees as possible." We should notice especially that the goal of production was "as many...as possible." And Schweitzer makes my point exactly: "These people could achieve true wealth if they could develop their agriculture and trade to meet their own needs." Instead they produced timber for export to "the world economy," which made them dependent upon imported goods that they bought with money earned from their exports. They gave up their local means of subsistence, and imposed the false standard of a foreign demand ("as many trees as possible") upon their forests. They thus became helplessly dependent on an econ-omy over which they had no control.

Such was the fate of the native people under the African colonialism of Schweitzer's time. Such is, and can only be, the fate of everybody under the global colonialism of our time. Schweitzer's description of the colonial economy of the Ogowe region is in principle not different from the rural economy now in Ken-tucky or Iowa or Wyoming. A total economy for all practical purposes is a total government. The "free trade" which from the standpoint of the corporate economy brings "unprecedented economic growth," from the standpoint of the land and its local populations, and ultimately from the standpoint of the cities, is destruction and slavery. Without prosperous local economies, the people have no power and the land no voice.

This article originally appeared in *Orion* (Winter 2001). 187 Main Street, Great Barrington, MA 01230. www.oriononline.org.

The Great Hunter-Gatherer Continuum

by Jim Mulligan

Jim Mulligan, one of the founders of Earth Ministry, an ecumenical, Christian, environmental, nonprofit organization, also serves as its Executive Director. Ordained as a Presbyterian minister, Mulligan spent 23 years as a Pastoral Counselor with the Presbyterian Coun-seling Service in Seattle, Washington.

In the previous essay, Berry discusses the merits of a (more) local economy. One of the most immediate—as in everyday and do-able—ways to create local economies is to consider how we obtain our food. The "Hunter-Gatherer Continuum" thoughtfully explores the various food-purchasing choices available to many of us, and briefly discusses the social and ecological ramifications of those choices.

∞

We all eat. What we eat, where it comes from, how it was grown, how workers were treated, the process of obtaining it—all of these factors leave their impact upon us and the earth. In the earliest times of human history, hunting-and-gathering was the chief pathway for obtaining food. From what we are able to learn of these times, this pathway had the least detrimental impacts on land and people—depending on the availability of an adequate variety of game and plants. Gradually, as animal domestication and agriculture arose, people increasingly impacted the natural environment in procuring their food. In this country we are not that far removed from a time when a much greater percentage of our population were active farmers. Many of us need look back only to our parents or grandparents generation to find personal examples of "people living close to the land"—by which I mean they had a cognitive and emotional awareness of how nature "works"; I do not mean a romanticized image of "our agrarian past."

Considering the long sweep of human history, our patterns of obtaining food have changed remarkably in a comparatively short time. Now, at the beginning of the 21st century, we in this country think nothing of buying pineapple from the Philippines, cocoa from Africa, coffee from Brazil, kiwi from New Zealand, and oranges from Florida; in the middle of winter; at the mall only minutes away. In the U.S. our food travels an average of 1,300 miles before it reaches our home! The "environmental footprint" of such a global food economy is many times greater than that of even our parents' generation. Are there practical steps we can take to mitigate the detrimental impacts of such a vast, complex system?

Yes. One place to begin is to consciously choose where and how we purchase our food. As we examine our choices we will use a model—a framework to organize our thinking about our range of options. This model is presented as a continuum. Harking back to our ancestors, I have called it the Hunter-Gatherer Continuum. In the weekly process of making shopping lists, planning at which stores to stop, anticipating the traffic, and fitting all this into the rest of my schedule, I often feel like a modern-day hunter-gatherer, foraging through the jungle of urban life.

The Continuum

Donning our pith helmets, let's get started. We can envision a spectrum of options for how we shop. The purpose of presenting this continuum is to help us recognize as clearly as possible the *range of choices* we have, and to thoughtfully *consider the larger impacts of these choices* upon our communities and the earth. This simple model is not meant to be exhaustive. You might be aware of other options, and where they might fit in to this simple model. (For a good overview of the interrelated web of our food choices, see the following article by Wendell Berry, "The Pleasures of Eating.")

Culturally Normative						Most Earth Friendly
Supermarket Only	Selective Supermkt.	Some Specialized	Both	Exclusively Specialized	Farmers Market	Subscription Farm

The basic assumption in organizing this continuum is as follows: it begins on the left with the most common options, widely available in our society. As you move along the continuum toward the right, you move progressively away from the culturally normative pathways, towards those which are more earth-friendly, but also rarer. This means that your options will be fewer; therefore choosing these options usually requires more time and often longer commutes. Why then would we want to choose such options? Because these later options are more supportive of our local agricultural community and local food economies, as well as more nutritionally healthful for ourselves and our families. They are also more earth-friendly; that is, they are more likely to sell organically grown and chemically free products, from farmers who are likely to be thoughtful about their impact on the land.

Let us consider for a moment each of the steps along the continuum.

Supermarket Shopping

Perhaps the most common food-purchasing pattern in our society is to simply shop at the closest supermarket, buying the brands we recognize and those items that are on sale. Here, while our choices are vast they are limited to those foods chosen by corporate supermarket chains—almost exclusively products of the vast, global agribusiness complex. Our choosing is often influenced by the constant blitz of advertising, in the media as well as in the store. We are functioning as a consumer within our economic system's most accessible pathway. That system spends considerable time and money to try to shape our awareness. Advertisers will assume that our sole objective is to find the items we want in the freshest (looking) condition, with the widest possible selection of choices, for the lowest price, at the most convenient location (with plenty of accessible parking), from retailers whose names we recognize (from their ads). As far as they go, these are not bad considerations. However, other important factors (e.g., locally produced, organically grown, minimal processing, packaging, and shipping) are of minimal importance in most of these stores. Therefore, while this step on the continuum is culturally most expedient, it is also the least likely to be environmentally friendly, fair to farm laborers, or supportive of the local and regional food economy.

Selective Supermarket Shopping

The next step along this continuum would be to continue to shop at the local supermarket, but to make a concerted effort to shop there as selectively as possible. Buy as many local products and produce as possible. Ask the management to stock local brands and locally grown produce. Seek out minimal and recycled packaging. Buy bulk items in containers you bring from home. Ask about the produce: where was it grown, is it organic, what pesticides were used, how were farm workers treated? Request that the manager stock products you have learned about from other sources, not just ads. In short, use your influence to encourage the supermarket chains to stock more local, earth-friendly goods. In this option you are taking the initiative, both to become a more conscientious consumer and to exert your influence within our mainstream economy. The more people ask for local organic produce, the more likely the store will be to develop a section featuring these choices. Your efforts can make a difference.

However, your influence, and that of other like-minded consumers, is not the only factor which helps to shape the mainstream food economy. Supermarket chains, wholesale distribution systems, and large advertising and marketing organizations are all part of the even larger corporate agribusinesses network. Consumer pressure—even highly organized and orchestrated consumer pressure, such as national boycotts—is only one factor in a much larger field. Corporations have great faith in their ability to mold public opinion. Agribusiness corporations' policies are determined far more by their economic aspirations than by moral pressure. For boycotts to be effective they must involve millions of consumers and last for substantial periods of time. So while you can be a force within the mainstream for change, you should not over-estimate the possible impact of limited efforts. But corporate agribusiness will pay attention to the success of "the competition"—one reason for considering the following options along the continuum.

Occasional Shopping at Specialized Retailers

A next step is to shop occasionally at specialized retailers who focus on local, organic, and earth-friendly products—such as co-ops, natural food stores, and produce stands. As there are far fewer of these retailers than there are supermarkets, you may well have to go out of your way to patronize them. Perhaps you could go there once a month and stock-up. At some specialized retailers, the job of learning about the origin and production of the food has been done for you. More consumer education is incorporated into the organization of these stores. There are still decisions to make, but the whole array of choices is generally much more earth-friendly: produce is more often locally grown, worker conditions considered, pesticide use is minimal. The larger of such retailers (Puget Consumers Co-Op would be a good example, www.pccnaturalmarkets.com) often make available a wide array of educational materials and classes to help you become a more informed consumer. They sometimes offer cooking and nutritional classes to help you learn how to cook healthy dishes with potentially unfamiliar products. These businesses are significantly less tied into the agribusiness economy, more supportive of the local economy and local community efforts towards bioregional self-sufficiency. Products you can't find at these selective retailers, you still buy at the local supermarket on regular shopping trips. You have to plan ahead to shop successfully in this occasional way, or you will find yourself needing to go to two stores every week.

Regular Shopping at Both Specialized Retailers and Supermarkets

The next step along the continuum would be to consciously do just that, shop at both types of stores regularly. On the whole you will probably purchase more food from the specialized stores in this pattern than when you shop there less frequently. Here you need not plan ahead as elaborately. You may well buy more from the specialized store, as you will become more familiar with its options. But, you will be doing more commuting. While the impact on your time and fuel is a factor you will need to consider, you will also exert more "purchasing power" to support the regional food economy, and eating more food which is healthy for you and for the earth.

Buying Almost Exclusively at Specialized Retailers

The next step is to "bite the bullet" and buy as exclusively as you can at such specialized stores. Here your "economic vote" is maximally influencing the local retail economy towards supporting such green businesses. However, your range of choices for products will (most likely) be more limited. These smaller, local retailers simply cannot match the large supermarket chains for their vast array of choices. So, even the most dedicated earth-friendly shoppers often find that they will make occasional forays to the supermarket to pick up some hard-to-find items. In this step the bulk of your consumer power is being used to support the viability of the local food economy and protect your local environment.

Shop (When You Can) at Farmers Markets

A related step—usually available only from late spring through fall—is to buy food at community farmers markets. The bonus here is significant. You get the freshest produce, *all of your money goes directly to the local grower*, and you have an opportunity to get to know the farmer as well. As there are fewer farmers markets than there are specialized retailers, and they are usually open far fewer hours per week, this step increases the complexity of your shopping. However, you are now exerting a much more focused economic influence on your local farming commu-nity, helping to keep small family farming alive in your area—and their land from becoming malls or subdivisions. Many farmers markets are developing a sizable community of support, and often include booths for local crafts people and artists, even strolling musicians, a truly festive atmosphere. So shopping at them can be an enjoyable experience in itself, making the old corporate supermarket seem rather sterile by comparison.

Be a Subscriber to a Community Supported Agriculture Farm

The final step in this continuum, requiring the greatest commitment, is to become a subscriber to a (community supported agriculture) "subscription farm." Here customers contract directly with farmers; they become "subscribers" to that particular farm. You pay a lump sum (in advance of the growing season) for a share of that year's produce. Then regularly, at a designated time each week of the growing season, you pick up your portion of that week's harvest. Your life in some measure will need to be coordinated with the cycles of nature and the farm routine. You will get more food in bulk (i.e., lots of corn at one time, lots of tomatoes at another), much like having your own garden. You might want to put up some of the food for later. Clearly this option requires the most planning, just as in using the produce from your own garden. And, as with your own garden, the food could not be fresher. This step will, of course, require that you continue to purchase (at some retailer) all those other food items which a small farm cannot be expected to produce (staples, dairy, crops not grown in your region, etc.). It is also essentially seasonally limited; in winter you are back at the grocery store full-time.

Another advantage to subscribing to such a farm is that you can maintain a close connection with the grower. Some farms even allow for helping with the harvesting. In using this step on the continuum, you play a significant part in insuring the *continued economic viability* of local organic farms, as the farmer and subscriber both share in the risks of production: in good years you get more produce, in lean years, less. By your participation you have guaranteed that another farmer will not go bankrupt in a bad year and contributed to keeping one more farm an active part of your local economy. You and the farmer have become partners in nutrition, conservation, economics, and social change.

Gardening as an Adjunct to the Continuum

As an auxiliary to the steps along this continuum, you can also cultivate your own vegetable garden. This is not really a step along the continuum itself, as you can garden as an adjunct to your hunting and gathering from any position along the continuum. Here you invest considerable time and effort, but you learn first-hand about the complex issues and joys of "living off the land". It is one thing to read about the complexities of organic farming, the vicissitudes of soil, weather, and sunshine, the foraging habits of numerous insects, and the marvels of composting; it is another to experience them first-hand. In addition, it has been scientifically demonstrated that no corn tastes sweeter, no tomatoes are juicier, no herbs are fresher, and certainly no zucchini more exuberant than your own! You've become a mini-farmer yourself, directly involved in both the labor and the miracle of life sustaining life, a witness to how God's creation works.

The Pleasures of Eating

by Wendell Berry

Berry proposes, "A significant part of the pleasure of eating is in one's accurate consciousness of the lives and the world from which food comes." Like Jim Mulligan's article, this one provides practical steps for shifting our food choices toward realizing that pleasure.

∞

Many times, after I have finished a lecture on the decline of American farming and rural life, someone in the audience has asked, "What can city people do?"

"Eat responsibly," I have usually answered. Of course, I have tried to explain what I meant by that, but afterwards I have invariably felt that there was more to be said than I had been able to say. Now I would like to attempt a better explanation.

I begin with the proposition that eating is an agricultural act. Eating ends the annual drama of the food economy that begins with planting and birth. Most eaters, however, are no longer aware that this is true. They think of food as an agricultural product, perhaps, but they do not think of themselves as participants in agriculture. They think of themselves as "consumers." If they think beyond that, they recognize that they are passive consumers. They buy what they want—or what they have been persuaded to want—within the limits of what they can get. They pay, mostly without protest, what they are charged. And they mostly ignore certain critical questions about the quality and the cost of what they are sold: How fresh is it? How pure or clean is it, how free of dangerous chemicals? How far was it transported, and what did transportation add to the cost? How much did manufacturing or packaging or advertising add to the cost? When the food product has been manufactured or "processed" or "precooked," how has that affected its quality or price or nutritional value?

Most urban shoppers would tell you that food is produced on farms. But most of them do not know what farms, or what kinds of farms, or where the farms are, or what knowledge or skills are involved in farming. They apparently have little doubt that farms will continue to produce, but they do not know how or over what obstacles. For them, then, food is pretty much an abstract idea—something they do not know or imagine until it appears on the grocery shelf or on the table.

The specialization of production induces specialization of consumption. Patrons of the entertainment industry, for example, entertain themselves less and less and have become more and more passively dependent on commercial suppliers. This is certainly true also of patrons of the food industry, who have tended more and more to be mere consumers—passive, uncritical, and dependent. Indeed, this sort of consumption may be said to be one of the chief goals of industrial production. The food industrialists have by now persuaded millions of consumers to prefer food that is already prepared. They will grow, deliver, and cook your food for you and (just like your mother) beg you to eat it. That they do not yet offer to insert it, prechewed, into your mouth is only because they have found no profitable way to do so. We may rest assured that they would be glad to find such a way. The ideal industrial food consumer would be strapped to a table with a tube running from the food factory directly into his or her stomach.

> The industrial eater is, in fact, one who does not know that eating is an agricultural act, who no longer knows or imagines the connections between eating and the land, and who is therefore necessarily passive and uncritical—in short, a victim.

Perhaps I exaggerate, but not by much. The industrial eater is, in fact, one who does not know that eating is an agricultural act, who no longer knows or imagines the connections between eating and the land, and who is therefore necessarily passive and uncritical—in short, a victim. When food, in the minds of eaters, is no longer associated with farming and with the land, then the eaters are suffering a kind of cultural amnesia that is misleading and dangerous. The current version of the "dream home" of the future involves "effortless" shopping from a list of available goods on a television monitor and heating precooked food by remote control. Of course, this implies and depends on a perfect ignorance of the history of the food that is consumed. It requires that the citizenry should give up their hereditary and sensible aversion to buying a pig in a poke. It wishes to make the selling of pigs in pokes an honorable and glamorous activity. The dreamer in this dream home will perforce know nothing about the kind or quality of this food, or where it came from, or how it was produced and prepared, or what ingredients, additives, and residues it contains—unless, that is, the dreamer undertakes a close and constant study of the food industry, in which case he or she might as well wake up and play an active and responsible part in the economy of food.

There is, then, a politics of food that, like any politics, involves our freedom. We still (sometimes) remember that we cannot be free if our minds and voices are controlled by someone else. But we have neglected to understand that we cannot be free if our food and its sources are controlled by someone else. The condition of the passive consumer of food is not a democratic condition. One reason to eat responsibly is to live free.

But if there is a food politics, there are also a food esthetics and a food ethics, neither of which is dissociated from politics. Like industrial sex, industrial eating has become a degraded, poor, and paltry thing. Our kitchens and other eating places more and more resemble filling stations, as our homes more and more resemble motels. "Life is not very interesting," we seem to have decided. "Let its satisfactions be minimal, perfunctory, and fast." We hurry through our meals to go to work and hurry through our work in order to "recreate" ourselves in the evenings and on weekends and vacations. And then we hurry, with the greatest possible speed and noise and violence, through our recreation for what? To eat the billionth hamburger at some fast-food joint hellbent on increasing the "quality" of our life? And all this is carried out in a remarkable obliviousness to the causes and effects, the possibilities and the purposes, of the life of the body in this world.

One will find this obliviousness represented in virgin purity in the advertisements of the food industry, in which food wears as much makeup as the actors. If one gained one's whole knowledge of food from these advertisements (as some presumably do), one would not know that the various edibles were ever living creatures, or that they all come from the soil, or that they were produced by work. The passive American consumer, sitting down to a meal of pre-prepared or fast food, confronts a platter covered with inert, anonymous substances that have been processed, dyed, breaded, sauced, gravied, ground, pulped, strained, blended, prettified, and sanitized beyond resemblance to any part of any creature that ever lived. The products of nature and agriculture have been made, to all appearances, the products of industry. Both eater and eaten are thus in exile from biological reality. And the result is a kind of solitude, unprecedented in human experience, in which the eater may think of eating as, first, a purely commercial transaction between him and a supplier and then as a purely appetitive transaction between him and his food.

And this peculiar specialization of the act of eating is, again, of obvious benefit to the food industry, which has good reasons to obscure the connection between food and farming. It would not do for the consumer to know that the hamburger she is eating came from a steer who spent much of his life standing deep in his own excrement in a feedlot, helping to pollute the local streams, or that the calf that yielded the veal cutlet on her plate spent its life in a box in which it did not have room to turn around. And, though her sympathy for the slaw might be less tender, she should not be encouraged to meditate on the hygienic and biological implications of mile-square fields of cabbage, for vegetables grown in huge monocultures are dependent on toxic chemicals just as animals in close confinement are dependent on antibiotics and other drugs.

The consumer, that is to say, must be kept from discovering that, in the food industry—as in any other industry—the overriding concerns are not quality and health, but volume and price. For decades now the entire industrial food economy, from the large farms and feedlots to the chains of supermarkets and fast-food restaurants, has been obsessed with volume. It has relentlessly increased scale in order to increase volume in order (presumably) to reduce costs. But as scale increases, diversity declines; as diversity declines, so does health; as health declines, the dependence on drugs and chemicals necessarily increases. As capital replaces labor, it does so by substituting machines, drugs, and chemicals for human workers and for the natural health and fertility of the soil. The food is produced by any means or any shortcut that will increase profits. And the business of the cosmeticians of advertising is to persuade the consumer that food so produced is good, tasty, healthful, and a guarantee of marital fidelity and long life.

It is possible, then, to be liberated from the husbandry and wifery of the old household food economy. But one can be thus liberated only by entering a trap (unless one sees ignorance and helplessness as the signs of privilege, as many people apparently do). The trap is the ideal of industrialism: a walled city surrounded by valves that let merchandise in but no consciousness out. How does one escape this trap? Only voluntarily, the same way that one went in: by restoring one's consciousness of what is involved in eating; by reclaiming responsibility for one's own part in the food economy. One might begin with the illuminating principle of Sir Albert Howard's *The Soil and Health*, that we should understand "the whole problem of health in soil, plant, animal, and man as one great subject." Eaters, that is, must understand that eating takes place inescapably in the world, that it is inescapably an agricultural act, and that how we eat determines, to a considerable extent, how the world is used. This is a simple way of describing a relationship that is inexpressibly complex. To eat responsibly is to understand and enact, so far as one can, this complex relationship. What can one do? Here is a list, probably not definitive:

1. Participate in food production to the extent that you can. If you have a yard or even just a porch box or a pot in a sunny window, grow something to eat in it. Make a little compost of your kitchen scraps and use it for fertilizer. Only by growing some food for yourself can you become acquainted with the beautiful energy cycle that revolves from soil to seed to flower to fruit to food to offal to decay, and around again. You will be fully responsible for any food that you grow for yourself, and you will know all about it. You will appreciate it fully, having known it all its life.

2. Prepare your own food. This means reviving in your own mind and life the arts of kitchen and household. This should enable you to eat more cheaply, and it will give you a measure of "quality control": you will have some reliable knowledge of what has been added to the food you eat.

3. Learn the origins of the food you buy, and buy the food that is produced closest to your home. The idea that every locality should be, as much as possible, the source of its own food makes several kinds of sense. The locally produced food supply is the most secure, the freshest, and the easiest for local consumers to know about and to influence.

4. Whenever possible, deal directly with a local farmer, gardener, or orchardist. All the reasons listed for the previous suggestion apply here. In addition, by such dealing you eliminate the whole pack of merchants, transporters, processors, packagers, and advertisers who thrive at the expense of both producers and consumers.
5. Learn, in self-defense, as much as you can of the economy and technology of industrial food production. What is added to food that is not food, and what do you pay for these additions?
6. Learn what is involved in the *best* farming and gardening.
7. Learn as much as you can, by direct observation and experience if possible, of the life histories of the food species.

The last suggestion seems particularly important to me. Many people are now as much estranged from the lives of domestic plants and animals (except for flowers and dogs and cats) as they are from the lives of the wild ones. This is regrettable, for these domestic creatures are in diverse ways attractive; there is much pleasure in knowing them. And farming, animal husbandry, horticulture, and gardening, at their best, are complex and comely arts; there is much pleasure in knowing them, too.

The industrial farm is said to have been patterned on the factory production line. In practice, it looks more like a concentration camp.

It follows that there is great *dis*pleasure in knowing about a food economy that degrades and abuses those arts and those plants and animals and the soil from which they come. For anyone who does know something of the modern history of food, eating away from home can be a chore. My own inclination is to eat seafood instead of red meat or poultry when I am traveling. Though I am by no means a vegetarian, I dislike the thought that some animal has been made miserable in order to feed me. If I am going to eat meat, I want it to be from an animal that has lived a pleasant, uncrowded life outdoors, on bountiful pasture, with good water nearby and trees for shade. And I am getting almost as fussy about food plants. I like to eat vegetables and fruits that I know have lived happily and healthily in good soil, not the products of the huge, bechemicaled factory-fields that I have seen, for example, in the Central Valley of California. The industrial farm is said to have been patterned on the factory production line. In practice, it looks more like a concentration camp.

The pleasure of eating should be an *extensive* pleasure, not that of the mere gourmet. People who know the garden in which their vegetables have grown and know that the garden is healthy will remember the beauty of the growing plants, perhaps in the dewy first light of morning when gardens are at their best. Such a memory involves itself with the food and is one of the pleasures of eating. The knowledge of the good health of the garden relieves and frees and comforts the eater. The same goes for eating meat. The thought of the good pasture and of the calf contentedly grazing flavors the steak. Some, I know, will think it bloodthirsty or worse to eat a fellow creature you have known all its life. On the contrary, I think it means that you eat with understanding and with gratitude. A significant part of the pleasure of eating is in one's accurate consciousness of the lives and the world from which food comes. The pleasure of eating, then, may be the best available standard of our health. And this pleasure, I think, is pretty fully available to the urban consumer who will make the necessary effort.

I mentioned earlier the politics, esthetics, and ethics of food. But to speak of the pleasure of eating is to go beyond those categories. Eating with the fullest pleasure—pleasure, that is, that does not depend on ignorance—is perhaps the profoundest enactment of our connection with the world. In this pleasure we experience and celebrate our dependence and our gratitude, for we are living from mystery, from creatures we did not make and powers we cannot comprehend. When I think of the meaning of food, I always remember these lines by the poet William Carlos Williams, which seem to me merely honest:

> There is nothing to eat,
> seek it where you will,
> but the body of the Lord.
> The blessed plants
> and the sea, yield it
> to the imagination intact.

"The Pleasures of Eating" from What Are People For? by Wendell Berry. © 1990 by Wendell Berry. Reprinted by permission of North Point Press, a division of Farrar, Straus and Giroux, LLC.

Worker Rights,
Animal Rights

It is no accident that those who care about the socially marginalized and the environment are usually people who have spent time experiencing and developing positive relations with oppressed peoples or with the natural world. Intrinsic value cannot be simply asserted; it has to be discovered, and it can be discovered only through such positive experience of others.

—*Carol Johnston*

Introduction

This section's images are particularly memorable: migrant workers' hands making 10,000 knife cuts during an eight-hour slaughterhouse shift; pigs raised in crates so small they often cannot lie down; 25,000 chickens raised in a single poultry house; three top officials from Archer Daniels Midland being sent to prison in 1999 for "conspiring with foreign rivals to control the international market" for a major feed additive; wading through ankle-deep blood on a slaughterhouse floor.

Underlying and creating these images are a handful of large agribusiness corporations, driven by consumer demand for cheap food and stockholder profits. Two excerpts from Eric Schlosser's book *Fast Food Nation* describe worker conditions in slaughterhouses, the challenges small ranchers face, and the power of the fast food industry. Bernard Rollin challenges factory farming practices as unethicial. Poet Pattiann Rogers imagines the myriad conflicting ways in which we relate to animals, while rancher Mike Connelly's story conveys one cow's unique personality.

These stories and images remind us that human rights' abuses and the callous treatment of animals often follow in the wake of the pressure to "get big, or get out."

On the Range

by Eric Schlosser

Eric Schlosser is an award-winning correspondent for the *Atlantic Monthly*. These excerpts come from his best-selling book, *Fast Food Nation*.

The following article is hard to categorize. Schlosser deftly touches on the decline of smaller ranch operations, the consolidation of power in both the beef and poultry "industries," and the "breasts of Mr. McDonald." The common theme in each of these vignettes is the increased market concentration enjoyed and created by large agribusiness firms. A recurring theme to pay attention to: the conditions in which animals are raised.

∞

A New Trust

Ranchers and cowboys have long been the central icons of the American West. Traditionalists have revered them as symbols of freedom and self-reliance. Revisionists have condemned them as racists, economic parasites, and despoilers of the land. The powerful feelings evoked by cattlemen reflect opposing views of our national identity, attempts to sustain old myths or create new ones. There is one indisputable fact, however, about American ranchers: they are rapidly disappearing. Over the last twenty years, about half a million ranchers sold off their cattle and quit the business. Many of the nation's remaining eight hundred thousand ranchers are faring poorly. They're taking second jobs. They're selling cattle at break-even prices or at a loss. The ranchers who are faring the worst run three to four hundred head of cattle, manage the ranch themselves, and live solely off the proceeds. The sort of hard-working ranchers long idealized in cowboy myths are the ones most likely to go broke today. Without receiving a fraction of the public attention given to the northwestern spotted owl, America's independent cattlemen have truly become an endangered species.

Ranchers currently face a host of economic problems: rising land prices, stagnant beef prices, oversupplies of cattle, increased shipments of live cattle from Canada and Mexico, development pressures, inheritance taxes, health scares about beef. On top of all that, the growth of the fast-food chains has encouraged consolidation in the meatpacking industry. McDonald's is the nation's largest purchaser of beef. In 1968, McDonald's bought ground beef from 175 local suppliers. A few years later, seeking to achieve greater product uniformity as it expanded, McDonald's reduced the number of beef suppliers to five. Much like the french fry industry, the meatpacking industry has been transformed by mergers and acquisitions over the last twenty years. Many ranchers now argue that a few large corporations have gained a stranglehold on the market, using unfair tactics to drive down the price of cattle. Anger toward the large meatpackers is growing, and a new range war threatens to erupt, one that will determine the social and economic structure of the rural West.

A century ago, American ranchers found themselves in a similar predicament. The leading sectors of the nation's economy were controlled by corporate alliances known as "trusts." There was a Sugar Trust, a Steel Trust, a Tobacco Trust—and a Beef Trust. It set the prices offered for cattle. Ranchers who spoke out against this monopoly power were often blackballed, unable to sell their cattle at any price. In 1917, at the height of the Beef Trust, the five largest meatpacking companies— Armour, Swift, Morris, Wilson, and Cudahy—controlled about 55 percent of the market. The early twentieth century had trusts, but it also had "trustbusters," progressive government officials who believed that concentrated economic power posed a grave threat to American democracy. The Sherman Antitrust Act had been passed in 1890 after a congressional investigation of price fixing in the meatpacking industry, and for the next two decades the federal government tried to break up the Beef Trust, with little success. In 1917 President Woodrow Wilson ordered the Federal Trade Commission to investigate the industry. The FTC inquiry concluded that the five major meatpacking firms had secretly fixed prices for years, had colluded to divide up markets, and had shared livestock information to guarantee that ranchers received the lowest possible price for their cattle. Afraid that an antitrust trial might end with an unfavorable verdict, the five meatpacking companies signed a consent decree in 1920 that forced them to sell off their stockyards, retail meat stores, railway interests, and livestock journals. A year later Congress created the Packers and Stockyards Administration (P&SA), a federal agency with a broad authority to prevent price-fixing and monopolistic behavior in the beef industry.

For the next fifty years, ranchers sold their cattle in a relatively competitive marketplace. The price of cattle was set through open bidding at auctions. The large meatpackers competed with hundreds of small regional firms. In 1970 the top four meatpacking firms slaughtered only 21 percent of the nation's cattle. A decade later, the Reagan administration allowed these firms to merge and combine without fear of antitrust enforcement. The Justice Department and the P&SA's successor, the Grain Inspection, Packers and Stockyards Administration (GIPSA), stood aside as the large meatpackers gained control of one local cattle market after another. Today the top four meatpacking firms—ConAgra, IBP, Excel, and National Beef—slaughter about 84 percent of the nation's cattle. Market concentration in the beef industry is now at the highest level since record-keeping began in the early twentieth century.

Today's unprecedented degree of meatpacking concentration has helped depress the prices that independent ranchers get for their cattle. Over the last twenty years, the rancher's share of every retail dollar spent on beef has fallen from 63 cents to 46 cents. The four major meatpacking companies now control about 20 percent of the live cattle in the United States through "captive supplies"—cattle that are either maintained in company-owned feedlots or purchased in advance through forward contracts. When cattle prices start to rise, the large meatpackers can flood the market with their own captive supplies, driving prices back down. They can also obtain cattle through confidential agreements with wealthy ranchers, never revealing the true price being paid. ConAgra and Excel operate their own gigantic feedlots, while IBP has private arrangements with some of America's biggest ranchers and feeders, including the Bass brothers, Paul Engler, and J. R. Simplot. Independent ranchers and feedlots now have a hard time figuring out what their cattle are actually worth, let alone finding a buyer for them at the right price. On any given day in the nation's regional cattle markets, as much as 80 percent of the cattle being exchanged are captive supplies. The prices being paid for these cattle are never disclosed.

To get a sense of what an independent rancher now faces, imagine how the New York Stock Exchange would function if large investors could keep the terms of all their stock trades secret. Ordinary investors would have no idea what their own stocks were really worth—a fact that wealthy traders could easily exploit. "A free market requires many buyers as well as many sellers, all with equal access to accurate information, all entitled to trade on the same terms, and none with a big enough share of the market to influence price," said a report by Nebraska's Center for Rural Affairs. "Nothing close to these conditions now exists in the cattle market."

The large meatpacking firms have thus far shown little interest in buying their own cattle ranches. "Why would they want the hassle?" Lee Pitts, the editor of *Livestock Market Digest*, told me. "Raising cattle is a business with a high overhead, and most of the capital's tied up in the land." Instead of buying their own ranches, the meatpacking companies have been financing a handful of large feedlot owners who lease ranches and run cattle for them. "It's just another way of controlling prices through captive supply," Pitts explained. "The packers now own some of these big feeders lock, stock, and barrel, and tell them exactly what to do."

The Breasts of Mr. McDonald

Many ranchers now fear that the beef industry is deliberately being restructured along the lines of the poultry industry. They do not want to wind up like chicken growers—who in recent years have become virtually powerless, trapped by debt and by onerous contracts written by the large processors. The poultry industry was also transformed by a wave of mergers in the 1980s. Eight chicken processors now control about two-thirds of the American market. These processors have shifted almost all of their production to the rural South, where the weather tends to be mild, the workforce is poor, unions are weak, and farmers are desperate to find some way of staying on their land. Alabama, Arkansas, Georgia, and Mississippi now produce more than half the chicken raised in the United States. Although many factors helped revolutionize the poultry industry and increase the power of the large processors, one innovation played an especially important role. The Chicken McNugget turned a bird that once had to be carved at a table into something that could easily be eaten behind the wheel of a car. It turned a bulk agricultural commodity into a manufactured, value-added product. And it encouraged a system of production that has turned many chicken farmers into little more than serfs.

"I have an idea," Fred Turner, the chairman of McDonald's, told one of his suppliers in 1979. "I want a chicken finger-food without bones, about the size of your thumb. Can you do it?" The supplier, an executive at Keystone Foods, ordered a group of technicians to get to work in the lab, where they were soon joined by food scientists from McDonald's. Poultry consumption in the United States was growing, a trend with alarming implications for a fast-food chain that sold only hamburgers. The nation's chicken meat had traditionally been provided by hens that were too old to lay eggs; after World War II a new poultry industry based in Delaware and Virginia lowered the cost of raising chicken, while medical research touted the health benefits of eating it. Fred Turner wanted McDonald's to sell a chicken dish that wouldn't clash with the chain's sensibility. After six months of intensive research, the Keystone lab developed new technology for the manufacture of McNuggets—small pieces of reconstituted chicken, composed mainly of white meat, that were held together by stabilizers, breaded, fried, frozen, then reheated. The initial test-marketing of McNuggets was so successful that McDonald's enlisted another company, Tyson Foods, to guarantee an adequate supply. Based in Arkansas, Tyson was one of the nation's leading chicken processors, and it soon developed a new breed of chicken to facilitate the production of McNuggets. Dubbed "Mr. McDonald," the new breed had unusually large breasts.

Chicken McNuggets were introduced nationwide in 1983. Within one month of their launch, the McDonald's Corporation had become the second-largest purchaser of chicken in the United States, surpassed only by KFC. McNuggets tasted good, they were easy to chew, and they appeared to be healthier than other items on the menu at McDonald's. After all, they were made out of chicken. But their health benefits were illusory. A chemical analysis of McNuggets by a researcher at Harvard Medical School found that their "fatty acid profile" more closely resembled beef than poultry. They were cooked in beef tallow, like McDonald's fries. The chain soon switched to vegetable oil, adding "beef extract" to McNuggets during the manufacturing process in order to retain their familiar taste. Chicken McNuggets, which became wildly popular among young children, still derive much of their flavor from beef additives—and contain twice as much fat per ounce as a hamburger.

The McNugget helped change not only the American diet but also its system for raising and processing poultry. "The impact of McNuggets was so huge that it changed the industry," the president of ConAgra Poultry, the nation's third-largest chicken processor, later acknowledged. Twenty years ago, most chicken was sold whole; today about 90 percent of the chicken sold in the United States has been cut into pieces, cutlets, or nuggets. In 1992 American consumption of chicken for the first time surpassed the consumption of beef. Gaining the McNugget contract helped turn Tyson Foods into the world's largest chicken processor. Tyson now manufactures about half of the nation's McNuggets and sells chicken to ninety of the one hundred largest restaurant chains. It is a vertically integrated company that breeds, slaughters, and processes chicken. It does not, however, raise the birds. It leaves the capital expenditures and the financial risks of that task to thousands of "independent contractors."

A Tyson chicken grower never owns the birds in his or her poultry houses. Like most of the other leading processors, Tyson supplies its growers with one-day-old chicks. Between the day they are born and the day they are killed, the birds spend their entire lives on the grower's property. But they belong to Tyson. The company supplies the feed, veterinary services, and technical support. It determines feeding schedules, demands equipment upgrades, and employs "flock supervisors" to make sure that corporate directives are being followed. It hires the trucks that drop off the baby chicks and return seven weeks later to pick up full-grown chickens ready for slaughter. At the processing plant, Tyson employees count and weigh the birds. A grower's income is determined by a formula based upon that count, that weight, and the amount of feed used.

The chicken grower provides the land, the labor, the poultry houses, and the fuel. Most growers must borrow money to build the houses, which cost about $150,000 each and hold about 25,000 birds. A 1995 survey by Louisiana Tech University found that the typical grower had been raising chicken for fifteen years, owned three poultry houses, remained deeply in debt, and earned perhaps $12,000 a year. About half of the nation's chicken growers leave the business after just three years, either selling out or losing everything. The back roads of rural Arkansas are now littered with abandoned poultry houses.

Most chicken growers cannot obtain a bank loan without already having a signed contract from a major processor. "We get the check first," a loan officer told the *Arkansas Democrat-Gazette*. A chicken grower who is unhappy with his or her processor has little power to do anything about it. Poultry contracts are short-term. Growers who complain may soon find themselves with empty poultry houses and debts that still need to be paid. Twenty-five years ago, when the United States had dozens of poultry firms, a grower stood a much better chance of finding a new processor and of striking a better deal. Today growers who are labeled "difficult" often have no choice but to find a new line of work. A processor can terminate a contract with a grower whenever it likes. It owns the birds. Short of that punishment, a processor can prolong the interval between the departure of one flock and the arrival of another. Every day that poultry houses sit empty, the grower loses money.

The large processors won't publicly disclose the terms of their contracts. In the past, such contracts have not only required that growers surrender all rights to file a lawsuit against the company, but have also forbidden them from joining any association that might link growers in a strong bargaining unit. The processors do not like the idea of chicken growers joining forces to protect their interests. "Our relationship with our growers is a one-on-one contractual relationship," a Tyson executive told a reporter in 1998. "We want to see that it remains that way."

Captives

The four large meatpacking firms claim that an oversupply of beef, not any corporate behavior, is responsible for the low prices that American ranchers are paid for their cattle. A number of studies by the U.S. Department of Agriculture (USDA) have reached the same conclusion. Annual beef consumption in the United States peaked in 1976, at about ninety-four pounds per person. Today the typical American eats about sixty-eight pounds of beef every year. Although the nation's population has grown since the 1970s, it has not grown fast enough to compensate for the decline in beef consumption. Ranchers trying to stabilize their incomes fell victim to their own fallacy of composition. They followed the advice of agribusiness firms and gave their cattle growth hormones. As a result, cattle are much bigger today; fewer cattle are sold; and most American beef cannot be exported to the European Union, where the use of bovine growth hormones has been banned.

The meatpacking companies claim that captive supplies and formula pricing systems are means of achieving greater efficiency, not of controlling cattle prices. Their slaughterhouses require a large and steady volume of cattle to operate profitably; captive supplies are one reliable way of sustaining that volume. The large meatpacking companies say that they've become a convenient scapegoat for ranchers, when the real problem is low poultry prices. A pound of chicken costs about half as much as a pound of beef. The long-term deals now being offered to cattlemen are portrayed as innovations that will save, not destroy, the beef industry. Responding in 1998 to a USDA investigation of captive supplies in Kansas, IBP defended such "alternative methods for selling fed cattle." The company argued that these practices were "similar to changes that have already occurred...for selling other agricultural commodities," such as poultry.

Many independent ranchers are convinced that captive supplies are used primarily to control the market, not to achieve greater slaughterhouse efficiency. They do not oppose large-scale transactions or long-term contracts; they oppose cattle prices that are kept secret. Most of all, they do not trust the meatpacking giants. The belief that agribusiness executives secretly talk on the phone with their competitors, set prices, and divide up the worldwide market for commodities—a belief widely held among independent ranchers and farmers—may seem like a paranoid fantasy. But that is precisely what executives at Archer Daniels Midland, "supermarket to the world," did for years.

Three of Archer Daniels Midland's top officials, including Michael Andreas, its vice chairman, were sent to federal prison in 1999 for conspiring with foreign rivals to control the international market for lysine (an important feed additive). The Justice Department's investigation of this massive price-fixing scheme focused on the period between August of 1992 and December of 1995. Within that roughly three-and-a-half-year stretch, Archer Daniels Midland and its coconspirators may have overcharged farmers by as much as $180 million. During the same period, Archer Daniels Midland executives also met with their overseas rivals to set the worldwide price for citric acid (a common food additive). At a meeting with Japanese executives that was secretly recorded, the president of Archer Daniels Midland preached the virtues of collaboration. "We have a saying at this company," he said. "Our competitors are our friends, and our customers are our enemies." Archer Daniels Midland remains the world's largest producer of lysine, as well as the world's largest processor of soybeans and corn. It is also one of the largest shareholders of IBP.

A 1996 USDA investigation of concentration in the beef industry found that many ranchers were afraid to testify against the large meatpacking companies, fearing retaliation and "economic ruin." That year Mike Callicrate, a cattleman from St. Francis, Kansas, decided to speak out against corporate behavior he thought was not just improper but criminal. "I was driving down the road one day," Callicrate told me, "and I kept thinking, when is someone going to do something about this? And I suddenly realized that maybe nobody's going to do it, and I had to give it a try." He claims that after his testimony before the USDA committee, the large meatpackers promptly stopped bidding on his cattle. "I couldn't sell my cattle," he said. "They'd drive right past my feed yard and buy cattle from a guy two hundred miles further away." His business has recovered somewhat; ConAgra and Excel now bid on his cattle. The experience has turned him into an activist. He refuses to "make the transition to slavery quietly." He has spoken at congressional hearings and has joined a dozen other cattlemen in a class-action lawsuit against IBP. The lawsuit claims that IBP has for many years violated the Packers and Stockyards Act through a wide variety of anticompetitive tactics. According to Callicrate, the suit will demonstrate that the company's purported efficiency in production is really " an efficiency in stealing." IBP denies the charges. "It makes no sense for us to do anything to hurt cattle producers," a top IBP executive told a reporter, "when we depend upon them to supply our plants."

The Threat of Wealthy Neighbors

The Colorado Cattlemen's Association filed an amicus brief in Mike Callicrate's lawsuit against IBP, demanding a competitive marketplace for cattle and a halt to any illegal buying practices being used by the large meatpacking firms. Ranchers in Colorado today, however, face threats to their livelihood that are unrelated to fluctuations in cattle prices. During the past twenty years, Colorado has lost roughly 1.5 million acres of ranchland to development. Population growth and the booming market for vacation homes have greatly driven up land costs. Some ranchland that sold for less than $200 an acre in the 1960s now sells for hundreds of times that amount. The new land prices make it impossible for ordinary ranchers to expand their operations. Each head of cattle needs about thirty acres of pasture for grazing, and until cattle start producing solid gold nuggets instead of sirloin, it's hard to sustain beef production on such expensive land. Ranching families in Colorado tend to be land-rich and cash-poor. Inheritance taxes can claim more than half of a cattle ranch's land value. Even if a family manages to operate its ranch profitably, handing it down to the next generation may require selling off large chunks of land, thereby diminishing its productive capacity.

Along with the ranches, Colorado is quickly losing its ranching culture. Among the students at Harrison High, you see a variety of fashion statements: gangsta wannabes, skaters, stoners, goths, and punks. What you don't see—in the shadow of Pikes Peak, in the heart of the Rocky Mountain West—is anyone dressed even remotely like a cowboy. Nobody's wearing shirts with snaps or Justin boots. In 1959, eight of the nation's top ten TV shows were Westerns. The networks ran thirty-five Westerns in prime time every week, and places like Colorado, where real cowboys lived, were the stuff of youthful daydreams. That America now seems as dead and distant as the England of King Arthur. I saw hundreds of high school students in Colorado Springs, and only one of them wore a cowboy hat. His name was Philly Favorite, he played guitar in a band called the Deadites, and his cowboy hat was made out of fake zebra fur.

The median age of Colorado's ranchers and farmers is about fifty-five, and roughly half of the state's open land will change hands during the next two decades—a potential boon for real estate developers. A number of Colorado land trusts are now working to help ranchers obtain conservation easements. In return for donating future development rights to one of these trusts, a rancher receives an immediate tax break and the prospect of lower inheritance taxes. The land remains private property, but by law can never be turned into golf courses, shopping malls, or subdivisions. In 1995 the Colorado Cattlemen's Association formed the first land trust in the United States that is devoted solely to the preservation of ranchland. It has thus far protected almost 40,000 acres, a significant achievement. But ranchland in Colorado is now vanishing at the rate of about 90,000 acres a year.

Conservation easements are usually of greatest benefit to wealthy gentleman ranchers who earn large incomes from other sources. The doctors, lawyers, and stockbrokers now running cattle on some of Colorado's most beautiful land can own big ranches, preserve open space with easements, and enjoy the big tax deductions. Ranchers whose annual income comes entirely from selling cattle usually don't earn enough to benefit from that sort of tax break. And the value of their land, along with the pressure to sell it, often increases when a wealthy neighbor obtains a conservation easement, since the views in the area are more likely to remain unspoiled.

The Colorado ranchers who now face the greatest economic difficulty are the ones who run a few hundred head of cattle, who work their own land, who don't have any outside income, and who don't stand to gain anything from a big tax write-off. They have to compete with gentleman ranchers whose operations don't have to earn a profit and with part-time ranchers whose operations are kept afloat by second jobs. Indeed, the ranchers most likely to be in financial trouble today are the ones who live the life and embody the values supposedly at the heart of the American West. They are independent and self-sufficient, cherish their freedom, believe in hard work—and as a result are now paying the price.

The Most Dangerous Job

by Eric Schlosser

Take a walk through a slaughterhouse. Picture slaughtering up to 400 cattle per hour. Meet the mainly Latino workers and their Union's leaders. Imagine making 10,000 knife cuts during an eight-hour shift. The stories and images are hard to forget.

∞

One night I visit a slaughterhouse somewhere in the High Plains. The slaughterhouse is one of the nation's largest. About five thousand head of cattle enter it every day, single file, and leave in a different form. Someone who has access to the plant, who's upset by its working conditions, offers to give me a tour. The slaughterhouse is an immense building, gray and square, about three stories high, with no windows on the front and no architectural clues to what's happening inside. My friend gives me a chain-mail apron and gloves, suggesting I try them on. Workers on the line wear about eight pounds of chain mail beneath their white coats, shiny steel armor that covers their hands, wrists, stomach, and back. The chain mail's designed to protect workers from cutting themselves and from being cut by other workers. But knives somehow manage to get past it. My host hands me some Wellingtons, the kind of knee-high rubber boots that English gentlemen wear in the countryside. "Tuck your pants into the boots," he says. "We'll be walking through some blood."

I put on a hardhat and climb a stairway. The sounds get louder, factory sounds, the noise of power tools and machinery, bursts of compressed air. We start at the end of the line, the fabricating room. Workers call it "fab." When we step inside, fab seems familiar: steel catwalks, pipes along the walls, a vast room, a maze of conveyer belts. This could be the Lamb Weston plant in Idaho, except hunks of red meat ride the belts instead of french fries. Some machines assemble cardboard boxes, others vacuum-seal subprimals of beef in clear plastic. The workers look extremely busy, but there's nothing unsettling about this part of the plant. You see meat like this all the time in the back of your local supermarket.

The fab room is cooled to about 40 degrees, and as you head up the line, the feel of the place starts to change. The pieces of meat get bigger. Workers—about half of them women, almost all of them young and Latino—slice meat with long slender knives. They stand at a table that's chest high, grab meat off a conveyer belt, trim away fat, throw meat back on the belt, toss the scraps onto a conveyer belt above them, and then grab more meat, all in a matter of seconds. I'm now struck by how many workers there are, hundreds of them, pressed close together, constantly moving, slicing. You see hardhats, white coats, flashes of steel. Nobody is smiling or chatting; they're too busy, anxiously trying not to fall behind. An old man walks past me, pushing a blue plastic barrel filled with scraps. A few workers carve the meat with Whizzards, small electric knives that have spinning round blades. The Whizzards look like the Norelco razors that Santa rides in the TV ads. I notice that a few of the women near me are sweating, even though the place is freezing cold.

Sides of beef suspended from an overhead trolley swing toward a group of men. Each worker has a large knife in one hand and a steel hook in the other. They grab the meat with their hooks and attack it fiercely with their knives. As they hack away, using all their strength, grunting, the place suddenly feels different, primordial. The machinery seems beside the point, and what's going on before me has been going on for thousands of years—the meat, the hook, the knife, men straining to cut more meat.

On the kill floor, what I see no longer unfolds in a logical manner. It's one strange image after another. A worker with a power saw slices cattle into halves as though they were two-by-fours, and then the halves swing by me into the cooler. It feels like a slaughterhouse now. Dozens of cattle, stripped of their skins, dangle on chains from their hind legs. My host stops and asks how I feel, if I want to go any further. This is where some people get sick. I feel fine, determined to see the whole process, the world that's been deliberately hidden. The kill floor is hot and humid.

It stinks of manure. Cattle have a body temperature of about 101 degrees, and there are a lot of them in the room. Carcasses swing so fast along the rail that you have to keep an eye on them constantly, dodge them, watch your step, or one will slam you and throw you onto the bloody concrete floor. It happens to workers all the time.

I see: a man reach inside cattle and pull out their kidneys with his bare hands, then drop the kidneys down a metal chute, over and over again, as each animal passes by him; a stainless steel rack of tongues; Whizzards peeling meat off decapitated heads, picking them almost as clean as the white skulls painted by Georgia O'Keeffe. We wade through blood that's ankle deep and that pours down drains into huge vats below us. As we approach the start of the line, for the first time I hear the steady *pop, pop, pop* of live animals being stunned.

Now the cattle suspended above me look just like the cattle I've seen on ranches for years, but these ones are upside down swinging on hooks. For a moment, the sight seems unreal; there are so many of them, a herd of them, lifeless. And then I see a few hind legs still kicking, a final reflex action, and the reality comes hard and clear.

For eight and a half hours, a worker called a "sticker" does nothing but stand in a river of blood, being drenched in blood, slitting the neck of a steer every ten seconds or so, severing its carotid artery. He uses a long knife and must hit exactly the right spot to kill the animal humanely. He hits that spot again and again. We walk up a slippery metal stairway and reach a small platform, where the production line begins. A man turns and smiles at me. He wears safety goggles and a hardhat. His face is splattered with gray matter and blood. He is the "knocker," the man who welcomes cattle to the building. Cattle walk down a narrow chute and pause in front of him, blocked by a gate, and then he shoots them in the head with a captive bolt stunner—a compressed-air gun attached to the ceiling by a long hose—which fires a steel bolt that knocks the cattle unconscious. The animals keep strolling up, oblivious to what comes next, and he stands over them and shoots. For eight and a half hours, he just shoots. As I stand there, he misses a few times and shoots the same animal twice. As soon as the steer falls, a worker grabs one of its hind legs, shackles it to a chain, and the chain lifts the huge animal into the air.

I watch the knocker knock cattle for a couple of minutes. The animals are powerful and imposing one moment and then gone in an instant, suspended from a rail, ready for carving. A steer slips from its chain, falls to the ground, and gets its head caught in one end of a conveyer belt. The production line stops as workers struggle to free the steer, stunned but alive, from the machinery. I've seen enough.

I step out of the building into the cool night air and follow the path that leads cattle into the slaughterhouse. They pass me, driven toward the building by workers with long white sticks that seem to glow in the dark. One steer, perhaps sensing instinctively what the others don't, turns and tries to run. But workers drive him back to join the rest. The cattle lazily walk single-file toward the muffled sounds, *pop, pop, pop*, coming from the open door.

The path has hairpin turns that prevent cattle from seeing what's in store and keep them relaxed. As the ramp gently slopes upward, the animals may think they're headed for another truck, another road trip and they are, in unexpected ways. The ramp widens as it reaches ground level and then leads to a large cattle pen with wooden fences, a corral that belongs in a meadow, not here. As I walk along the fence, a group of cattle approach me, looking me straight in the eye, like dogs hoping for a treat, and follow me out of some mysterious impulse. I stop and try to absorb the whole scene: the cool breeze, the cattle and their gentle lowing, a cloudless sky, steam rising from the plant in the moonlight. And then I notice that the building does have one window, a small square of light on the second floor. It offers a glimpse of what's hidden behind this huge blank facade. Through the little window you can see bright red carcasses on hooks, going round and round.

Sharp Knives

Knocker, Sticker, Shackler, Romper, First Legger, Knuckle Dropper, Navel Boner, Splitter Top/Bottom Butt, Feed Kill Chain—the names of job assignments at a modern slaughterhouse convey some of the brutality inherent in the work. Meatpacking is now the most dangerous job in the United States. The injury rate in a slaughterhouse is about three times higher than the rate in a typical American factory. Every year about one out of three meatpacking workers in this country— roughly forty-three thousand men and women—suffer an injury or a work-related illness that requires medical attention beyond first aid. There is strong evidence that these numbers, compiled by the Bureau of Labor Statistics, understate the number of meatpacking injuries that occur. Thousands of additional injuries and illnesses most likely go unrecorded.

Despite the use of conveyer belts, forklifts, dehiding machines, and a variety of power tools, most of the work in the nation's slaughterhouses is still performed by hand. Poultry plants can be largely mechanized, thanks to the breeding of chickens that are uniform in size. The birds in some Tyson factories are killed, plucked, gutted, beheaded, and sliced into cutlets by robots and machines. But cattle still come in all sizes and shapes, varying in weight by hundreds of pounds. The lack of a standardized steer has hindered the mechanization of beef plants. In one crucial respect meatpacking work has changed little in the past hundred years. At the dawn of the twenty-first century, amid an era of extraordinary technological advance, the most important tool in a modern slaughterhouse is a sharp knife.

Lacerations are the most common injuries suffered by meatpackers, who often stab themselves or stab someone working nearby. Tendinitis and cumulative trauma disorders are also quite common. Meatpacking workers routinely develop back problems, shoulder problems, carpal tunnel syndrome, and "trigger finger" (a syndrome in which a finger becomes frozen in a curled position). Indeed, the rate of these cumulative trauma injuries in the meatpacking industry is far higher than the rate in any other American industry. It is almost thirty-five times higher than the national average in industry. Many slaughterhouse workers make a knife cut every two or three seconds, which adds up to about 10,000 cuts during an eight-hour shift. If the knife has become dull, additional pressure is placed on the worker's tendons, joints, and nerves. A dull knife can cause pain to extend from the cutting hand all the way down the spine.

Workers often bring their knives home and spend at least forty minutes a day keeping the edges smooth, sharp, and sanded, with no pits. One IBP worker, a small Guatemalan woman with graying hair, spoke with me in the cramped kitchen of her mobile home. As a pot of beans cooked on the stove, she sat in a wooden chair, gently rocking, telling the story of her life, of her journey north in search of work, the whole time sharpening big knives in her lap as though she were knitting a sweater.

The "IBP revolution" has been directly responsible for many of the hazards that meatpacking workers now face. One of the leading determinants of the injury rate at a slaughterhouse today is the speed of the disassembly line. The faster it runs, the more likely that workers will get hurt. The old meatpacking plants in Chicago slaughtered about 50 cattle an hour. Twenty years ago, new plants in the High Plains slaughtered about 175 cattle an hour. Today some plants slaughter up to 400 cattle an hour—about half a dozen animals every minute, sent down a single production line, carved by workers desperate not to fall behind. While trying to keep up with the flow of meat, workers often neglect to resharpen their knives and thereby place more stress on their bodies. As the pace increases, so does the risk of accidental cuts and stabbings. "I could always tell the line speed," a former Monfort nurse told me, "by the number of people with lacerations coming into my office." People usually cut themselves; nevertheless, everyone on the line tries to stay alert. Meatpackers often work within inches of each other, wielding large knives. A simple mistake can cause a serious injury. A former IBP worker told me about boning knives suddenly flying out of hands and ricocheting off of machinery. "They're very flexible," she said, "and they'll spring on you...zwing, and they're gone."

Much like french fry factories, beef slaughterhouses often operate at profit margins as low as a few pennies a pound. The three meatpacking giants—ConAgra, IBP, and Excel—try to increase their earnings by maximizing the volume of production at each plant. Once a slaughterhouse is up and running, fully staffed, the profits it will earn are directly related to the speed of the line. A faster pace means higher profits. Market pressures now exert a perverse influence on the management of beef plants: the same factors that make these slaughterhouses relatively inefficient (the lack of mechanization, the reliance on human labor) encourage companies to make them even more dangerous (by speeding up the pace).

The unrelenting pressure of trying to keep up with the line has encouraged widespread methamphetamine use among meatpackers. Workers taking "crank" feel charged and self-confident, ready for anything. Supervisors have been known to sell crank to their workers or to supply it free in return for certain favors, such as working a second shift. Workers who use methamphetamine may feel energized and invincible, but are actually putting themselves at much greater risk of having an accident. For obvious reasons, a modern slaughterhouse is not a safe place to be high.

In the days when labor unions were strong, workers could complain about excessive line speeds and injury rates without fear of getting fired. Today only one-third of IBP's workers belong to a union. Most of the nonunion workers are recent immigrants; many are illegals; and they are generally employed "at will." That means they can be fired without warning, for just about any reason. Such an arrangement does not encourage them to lodge complaints. Workers who have traveled a great distance for this job, who have families to support, who are earning ten times more an hour in a meatpacking plant than they could possibly earn back home, are wary about speaking out and losing everything. The line speeds and labor costs at IBP's nonunion plants now set the standard for the rest of the industry. Every other company must try to produce beef as quickly and cheaply as IBP does; slowing the pace to protect workers can lead to a competitive disadvantage.

Again and again workers told me that they are under tremendous pressure not to report injuries. The annual bonuses of plant foremen and supervisors are often based in part on the injury rate of their workers. Instead of creating a safer workplace, these bonus schemes encourage slaughterhouse managers to make sure that accidents and injuries go unreported. Missing fingers, broken bones, deep lacerations, and amputated limbs are difficult to conceal from authorities. But the dramatic and catastrophic injuries in a slaughterhouse are greatly outnumbered by less visible, though no less debilitating, ailments: torn muscles, slipped disks, pinched nerves.

If a worker agrees not to report an injury, a supervisor will usually shift him or her to an easier job for a while, providing some time to heal. If the injury seems more serious, a Mexican worker is often given the opportunity to return home for a while, to recuperate there, then come back to his or her slaughterhouse job in the United States. Workers who abide by these unwritten rules are treated respectfully; those who disobey are likely to be punished and made an example. As one former IBP worker explained, "They're trying to deter you, period, from going to the doctor."

From a purely economic point of view, injured workers are a drag on profits. They are less productive. Getting rid of them makes a good deal of financial sense, especially when new workers are readily available and inexpensive to train. Injured workers are often given some of the most unpleasant tasks in the slaughterhouse. Their hourly wages are cut. And through a wide variety of unsubtle means they are encouraged to quit.

Not all supervisors in a slaughterhouse behave like Simon Legree, shouting at workers, cursing them, minimizing their injuries, always pushing them to move faster. But enough supervisors act that way to warrant the comparison. Production supervisors tend to be men in their late twenties and early thirties. Most are Anglos and don't speak Spanish, although more and more Latinos are being promoted to the job. They earn about $30,000 a year, plus bonuses and benefits. In many rural communities, being a supervisor at a meatpacking plant is one of the best jobs in town. It comes with a fair amount of pressure: a supervisor must meet production goals, keep the number of recorded injuries low, and most importantly, keep the meat flowing down the line without interruption. The job also brings enormous power. Each supervisor is like a little dictator in his or her section of the plant largely free to boss, fire, berate, or reassign workers. That sort of power can lead to all sorts of abuses, especially when the hourly workers being supervised are women.

Many women told me stories about being fondled and grabbed on the production line, and the behavior of supervisors sets the tone for the other male workers. In February of 1999, a federal jury in Des Moines awarded $2.4 million to a female employee at an IBP slaughterhouse. According to the woman's testimony, coworkers had "screamed obscenities and rubbed their bodies against hers while supervisors laughed." Seven months later, Monfort agreed to settle a lawsuit filed by the U.S. Equal Employment Opportunity Commission on behalf of fourteen female workers in Texas. As part of the settlement, the company paid the women $900,000 and vowed to establish formal procedures for handling sexual harassment complaints. In their lawsuit the women alleged that supervisors at a Monfort plant in Cactus, Texas, pressured them for dates and sex, and that male coworkers groped them, kissed them, and used animal parts in a sexually explicit manner.

The sexual relationships between supervisors and "hourlies" are for the most part consensual. Many female workers optimistically regard sex with their supervisor as a way to gain a secure place in American society, a green card, a husband—or at the very least a transfer to an easier job at the plant. Some supervisors become meatpacking Casanovas, engaging in multiple affairs. Sex, drugs, and slaughterhouses may seem an unlikely combination, but as one former Monfort employee told me: "Inside those walls is a different world that obeys different laws." Late on the second shift, when it's dark outside, assignations take place in locker rooms, staff rooms, and parked cars, even on the catwalk over the kill floor.

Farm Factories

by Bernard E. Rollin

Bernard E. Rollin is University Distinguished Professor of Philosophy, Physiology and Animal Sciences at Colorado State University in Fort Collins, Colorado.

A young man fired for caring for pigs on his own time; pigs raised in crates so small they often cannot lie down; calves confined in stalls so narrow they cannot turn around; 25,000 chickens raised in a single poultry house. Factory farming, Rollin believes, violates core biblical ethical principles. In this brief essay Rollin not only discusses these principles, but also compares such confinement farming with the art of animal husbandry.

∞

A young man was working for a company that operated a large, total-confinement swine farm. One day he detected symptoms of a disease among some of the feeder pigs. As a teen, he had raised pigs himself and shown them in competition, so he knew how to treat the animals. But the company's policy was to kill any diseased animals with a blow to the head—the profit margin was considered too low to allow for treatment of individual animals. So the employee decided to come in on his own time, with his own medicine, and cured the animals. The management's response was to fire him on the spot for violating company policy. Soon the young man left agriculture for good: he was weary of the conflict between what he was told to do and how he believed he should be treating the animals.

Consider a sow that is being used to breed pigs for food. The overwhelming majority of today's swine are raised in severe confinement. If the "farmer" follows the recommendations of the National Pork Producers, the sow will spend virtually all of her productive life (until she is killed) in a gestation crate 2 1/2 feet wide (and sometimes 2 feet wide) by 7 feet long by 3 feet high. This concrete and barred cage is often too small for the 500- to 600-pound animal, which cannot lie down or turn around. Feet that are designed for soft loam are forced to carry hundreds of pounds of weight on slotted concrete. This causes severe foot and leg problems. Unable to perform any of her natural behaviors, the sow goes mad and exhibits compulsive, neurotic "stereotypical" behaviors such as bar-biting and purposeless chewing. When she is ready to birth her piglets, she is moved into a farrowing crate that has a creep rail so that the piglets can crawl under it and avoid being crushed by the confined sow.

Under other conditions, pigs reveal that they are highly intelligent and behaviorally complex animals. Researchers at the University of Edinburgh created a "pig park" that approximates the habitat of wild swine. Domestic pigs, usually raised in confinement, were let loose in this facility and their behavior observed. In this environment, the sows covered almost a mile in foraging, and, in keeping with their reputation as clean animals, they built carefully constructed nests on a hillside so that urine and feces ran downhill. They took turns minding each other's piglets so that each sow could forage. All of this natural behavior is inexpressible in confinement.

Factory farming, or confinement-based industrialized agriculture, has been an established feature in North America and Europe since its introduction at the end of World War II. Agricultural scientists were concerned about supplying Americans with sufficient food. After the Dust Bowl and the Great Depression, many people had left farming. Cities and suburbs were beginning to encroach on agricultural lands, and scientists saw that the amount of land available for food production would soon diminish significantly. Farm people who had left the farm for foreign countries and urban centers during the war were reluctant to go back. "How you gonna keep 'em down on the farm now that they've seen Paree?" a song of the '40s asked. Having experienced the specter of starvation during the Great Depression, the American consumer was afraid that there would not be enough food.

At the same time, a variety of technologies relevant to agriculture were emerging and American society began to accept the idea of technologically based economies of scale. Animal agriculture begin to industrialize. This was a major departure from traditional agriculture and its core values. Agriculture as a way of life, and agriculture as a practice of husbandry, were replaced by agriculture as an industry with values of efficiency and productivity. Thus the problems we see in confinement agriculture are not the result of cruelty or insensitivity, but the unanticipated by-product of changes in the nature of agriculture. Confinement-based agriculture contradicts basic biblical ethical teachings about animals. Yet despite the real problems in these farm factories, few Jewish and Christian leaders, theologians or ethicists have come forward to raise moral questions about them or the practices characteristic of this industry.

The Old Testament forbids the deliberate, willful, sadistic, deviant, purposeless, intentional and unnecessary infliction of pain and suffering on animals, or outrageous neglect of them (failing to provide food and water). Biblical edicts against cruelty helped Western societies reach a social consensus on animal treatment and develop effective laws. The Massachusetts Bay colony, for example, was the first to prohibit animal cruelty, and similar laws exist today in all Western societies.

The anticruelty ethic served two purposes: it articulated concern about animal suffering caused by deviant and purposeless human actions, and it identified sadists and psychopaths who abuse animals before sometimes "graduating" to the abuse of humans. Recent research has confirmed this correlation. Many serial killers have histories of animal abuse, as do some of the teens who have shot classmates.

Biblical sources deliver a clear mandate to avoid acts of deliberate cruelty to animals. We humans are obliged, for example, to help "raise to its feet an animal that is down even if it belongs to [our] enemy" (Exod. 23:12 and Deut. 22:4). We are urged not to plow an ox and an ass together because of the hardship to the weaker animal (Deut. 22:10), and to rest the animals on the sabbath when we rest (Exod. 20:10 and Exod. 23:12). Deuteronomy 25:4 forbids the muzzling of an ox when it is being used to thresh grain, for that would cause it major suffering—the animal could not partake of its favorite food, and allowing it to graze would cost the farmer virtually nothing (also in 1 Cor. 9:9 and 1 Tim. 5:18). We are to save "a son or an ox" that has fallen into a well even if we must violate the sabbath (Luke 14:5), and to avoid killing an ox because that would be like killing a man (Isa. 66:3).

Other passages encourage humans to develop a character that finds cruelty abhorrent. We are to foster compassion as a virtue, and prevent insensitivity to animal suffering. The injunction against "boiling a kid in its mother's milk" (Exod. 23:19; Exod. 34:26; Deut. 14:21) is supported by Leviticus 22:26-33, which commands us not to take a very young animal from its mother, and not to slaughter an animal along with its young. The strange story of Balaam and his ass counsels against losing one's temper and beating an animal (Num. 22) and Psalm 145 tells us that God's mercy extends over all creatures. Surely humans are being directed to follow that model.

As one of my colleagues put it, "The worst thing that ever happened to my department is the name change from Animal Husbandry to Animal Science." The practice of husbandry is the key loss in the shift from traditional to industrialized agriculture. Farmers once put animals into the environment that the animals were biologically suited for, and then augmented their natural ability to survive and thrive by providing protection from predators, food during famine, water during drought, help in birthing, protection from weather extremes, etc. Any harm or suffering inflicted on the animal resulted in harm to the producer. An animal experiencing stress or pain, for example, is not as productive or reproductively successful as a happy animal. Thus proper care and treatment of animals becomes both an ethical and prudent requirement. The producer does well if and only if the animal does well. The result is good animal husbandry: a fair and mutually beneficial contract between humans and animals, with each better off because of the relationship. Psalm 23 describes this concept of care in a metaphor so powerful that it has become the vehicle for expressing God's ideal relationship to humans.

In husbandry agriculture, individual animal productivity is a good indicator of animal well-being; in industrial agriculture, this link between productivity and well-being is severed. When productivity as an economic metric is applied to the whole operation, the welfare of the individual animal is ignored. Husbandry agriculture "put square pegs in square holes and round pegs in round holes," extending individualized care in order to create as little friction as possible. Industrial agriculture, on the other hand, forces each animal to accept the same "technological sanders"—antibiotics (which keep down disease that would otherwise spread like wildfire in close surroundings), vaccines, bacterins, hormones, air handling systems and the rest of the armamentarium used to keep the animals from dying.

Furthermore, when crowding creates unnatural conditions and elicits unnatural behaviors such as tailbiting in pigs or similar acts of cannibalism in poultry, the solution is to cut off the tail (without anesthetics) or debeak the chicken, which can cause lifelong pain.

There are four sources of suffering in these conditions:
- violation of the animals' basic needs and nature;
- lack of attention to individual animals;
- mutilation of animals to fit unnatural environments;

- an increase in diseases and other problems caused by conditions in confinement operations.

A few years ago, while visiting with some Colorado ranchers, I observed an example of animal husbandry that contrasts sharply with the experience described at the beginning of this article. That year, the ranchers had seen many of their calves afflicted with scours, a diarrheal disease. Every rancher I met had spent more money on treating the disease than was economically justified by the calves' market value. When I asked these men why they were being "economically irrational," they were adamant in their responses: "It's part of my bargain with the animal." "It's part of caring for them." This same ethical outlook leads ranchers to sit up all night with sick, marginal calves, sometimes for days in a row. If they were strictly guided by economics, these people would hardly be valuing their time at 50 cents per hour—including their sleep time.

Yet industrialized swine production thrives while western cattle ranchers, the last large group of practitioners of husbandry agriculture, are an endangered species.

Confinement agriculture violates other core biblical ethical principles. It is clear that the biblical granting of "dominion" over the earth to humans means responsible stewardship, not the looting and pillaging of nature. Given that the Bible was addressed to an agrarian people, this is only common sense, and absolutely essential to preserving what we call "sustainability."

Husbandry agriculture was by its very nature sustainable, unlike industrialized animal agriculture. To follow up on our swine example: When pigs (or cattle) are raised on pasture, manure becomes a benefit, since it fertilizes pasture, and pasture is of value in providing forage for animals. In industrial animal agriculture, there is little reason to maintain pasture. Instead farmers till for grain production, thereby encouraging increased soil erosion. At the same time, manure becomes a problem, both in terms of disposal and because it leaches into the water table. Similarly, air quality in confinement operations is often a threat to both workers and animals, and animal odors drive down real property value for miles around these operations.

Another morally questionable aspect of confinement agriculture is the destruction of small farms and local communities. Because of industrialization and economy of scale, small husbandry-based producers cannot compete with animal factories. In the broiler industry, farmers who wish to survive become serfs to large operators because they cannot compete on their own. In large confinement swine operations, where the system rather than the labor force, is primary migratory or immigrant workers hired because they are cheap, not because they possess knowledge of or concern for the animals. And those raised in a culture of husbandry, as our earlier story revealed, find it intolerable to work in the industrialized operations.

The power of confinement agriculture to pollute the earth, degrade community and destroy small, independent farmers should convince us that this type of agriculture is incompatible with biblical ethics. Furthermore, we should fear domination of the food supply by these corporate entities.

It is not necessary to raise animals this way, as history reminds us. In 1988 Sweden banned high confinement agriculture; Britain and the EU ban sow confinement. If food is destined to cost more, so be it—Americans spend an average of only 11 percent of their income on food now, while they spent more than 50 percent on food at the turn of the century. We are wrong to ignore the hidden costs paid by animal welfare, the environment, food safety and rural communities and independent farmers, and we must now add those costs to the price of our food.

If we take biblical ethics seriously, we must condemn any type of agriculture that violates the principles of husbandry. John Travis reported the following comments made by the Vatican last December:

> Human dominion over the natural world must not be taken as an unqualified license to kill or inflict suffering on animals...The cramped and cruel methods used in the modern food industry, for example, may cross the line of morally acceptable treatment of animals...Marie Hendrickz, official of the Congregation for the Doctrine of the Faith, said that in view of the growing popularity of animal rights movements, the church needs to ask itself to what extent Christ's dictum, "Do to others whatever you would have them do to you," can be applied to the animal world.

It is a radical mistake to treat animals merely as products, as objects with no intrinsic value. A demand for agriculture that practices the ancient and fair contract with domestic animals is not revolutionary but conservative. As Mahatma Gandhi said, a society must ultimately be morally judged by how it treats its weakest members. No members are more vulnerable and dependent than our society's domestic animals.

Animals and People: The Human Heart in Conflict with Itself

By Pattiann Rogers

Pattiann Rogers has published ten books of poetry. The most recent, *Song of the World Becoming, New and Collected Poems, 1981-2001* (Milkweed Editions), was a finalist for the LA Times Book Award and an Editor's Choice, Top of the List, from *Booklist*. She has received two NEA Grants, a Guggenheim Fellowship, a Lannan Poetry Fellowship, five Pushcart Prizes, three prizes from *Poetry*, two from *Poetry Northwest* and two from *Prairie Schooner*. The mother of two grown sons, she lives with her husband in Colorado.

Barry Lopez has written of Rogers' poetry, "If this is not poetry in service to humanity, I do not know what is." Here Rogers turns her eye to humanity's complex, and often conflicting, relationships with animals, finally concluding, "How can we hope to receive honor if we give no honor? How can we believe in grace if we cannot bestow grace?"

∞

Some of us like to photograph them. Some of us like to paint pictures of them. Some of us like to sculpt them and make statues and carvings of them. Some of us like to compose music about them and sing about them. And some of us like to write about them.

Some of us like to go out and catch them and kill them and eat them. Some of us like to hunt them and shoot them and eat them. Some of us like to raise them, care for them and eat them. Some of us just like to eat them.

And some of us name them and name their seasons and name their hours, and some of us, in our curiosity, open them up and study them with our tools and name their parts. We capture them, mark them and release them, and then we track them and spy on them and enter their lives and affect their lives and abandon their lives. We breed them and manipulate them and alter them. Some of us experiment upon them.

We put them on tethers and leashes, in shackles and harnesses, in cages and boxes, inside fences and walls. We put them in yokes and muzzles. We want them to carry us and pull us and haul for us.

And we want some of them to be our companions, some of them to ride on our fingers and some to ride sitting on our wrists or on our shoulders and some to ride in our arms, ride clutching our necks. We want them to walk at our heels.

We want them to trust us and come to us, take our offerings, eat from our hands. We want to participate in their beauty. We want to assume their beauty and so possess them. We want to be kind to them and so possess them with our kindness and so partake of their beauty in that way.

And we want them to learn our language. We try to teach them our language. We speak to them. We put *our* words in *their* mouths. We want *them* to speak. We want to know what they see when they look at us.

We use their heads and their bladders for balls, their guts and their hides and their bones to make music.

We skin them and wear them for coats, their scalps for hats. We rob them, their milk and their honey, their feathers and their eggs. We make money from them.

We construct icons of them. We make images of them and put their images on our clothes and on our necklaces and rings and on our walls and in our religious places. We preserve their dead bodies and parts of their dead bodies and display them in our homes and buildings.

We name mountains and rivers and cities and streets and organizations and gangs and causes after them. We name years and time and constellations of stars after them. We make mascots of them, naming our athletic teams after them. Sometimes we name ourselves after them.

We make toys of them and rhymes of them for our children. We mold them and shape them and distort them to fit our myths and our stories and our dramas. We like to dress up like them and masquerade as them. We like to imitate them and try to move as they move and make the sounds they make, hoping, by these means, to enter and become the black mysteries of their being.

Sometimes we dress them in our clothes and teach them tricks and laugh at them and marvel at them. And we make parades of them and festivals of them. We want them to entertain us and amaze us and frighten us and reassure us and calm us and rescue us from boredom.

We pit them against one another and watch them fight one another, and we gamble on them. We want to compete with them ourselves, challenging them, testing our wits and talents against their wits and talents, in forests and on plains, in the ring. We want to be able to run like them and leap like them and swim like them and fly like them and fight like them and endure like them.

We want their total absorption in the moment. We want their unwavering devotion to life. We want their oblivion.

Some of us give thanks and bless those we kill and eat, and ask for pardon, and this is beautiful as long as they are the ones dying and we are the ones eating.

And as long as we are not seriously threatened, as long as we and our children aren't hungry and aren't cold, we say, with a certain degree of superiority, that we are no better than any of them, that any of them deserve to live just as much as we do.

And after we have proclaimed this thought, and by so doing subtly pointed out that we are allowing them to live, we direct them and manage them and herd them and train them and follow them and map them and collect them and make specimens of them and butcher them and move them here and move them there and we place them on lists and we take them off of lists and we stare at them and stare at them and stare at them.

We track them in our sleep. They become the form of our sleep. We dream of them. We seek them with accusation. We seek them with supplication.

And in the ultimate imposition, as Thoreau said, we make them bear the burden of our thoughts. We make them carry the burden of our metaphors and the burden of our desires and our guilt and carry the equal burden of our curiosity and concern. We make them bear our sins and our prayers and our hopes into the desert, into the sky, into the stars. We say we kill them for God.

We adore them and we curse them. We caress them and we ravish them. We want them to acknowledge us and be with us. We want them to disappear and be autonomous. We abhor their viciousness and lack of pity, as we abhor our own viciousness and lack of pity. We love them and we reproach them, just as we love and reproach ourselves.

We will never, we cannot, leave them alone, even the tiniest one, ever, because we know we are one with them. Their blood is our blood. Their breath is our breath, their beginning our beginning, their fate our fate.

Thus we deny them. Thus we yearn for them. They are among us and within us and of us, inextricably woven with the form and manner of our being, with our understanding, and our imaginations. They are the grit and the salt and the lullaby of our language.

We have a need to believe they are there, and always will be, whether we witness them or not. We need to know they are there, a vigorous life maintaining itself without our presence, without our assistance, without our attention. We need to know, we *must* know, that we come from such stock so continuously and tenaciously and religiously devoted to life.

We know we are one with them, and we are frantic to understand how to actualize that union. We attempt to actualize that union in our many stumbling, ignorant and destructive ways, in our many confused and noble and praiseworthy ways.

For how can we possess dignity if we allow them no dignity? Who will recognize our beauty if we do not revel in their beauty? How can we hope to receive honor if we give no honor? How can we believe in grace if we cannot bestow grace?

We want what we cannot have. We want to give life at the same moment we are taking it, nurture life at the same moment we light the fire and raise the knife. We want to live, to provide, and not be instruments of destruction, instruments of death. We want to reconcile our "egoistic concerns" with our "universal compassion." We want the lion and the lamb to be one, the lion and the lamb *within* finally to dwell together, to lie down together in peace and praise at last.

From *Song of the World Becoming* by Pattiann Rogers, © 2001 by Pattiann Rogers. Published by Milkweed Editions. Reprinted by permission of the author.

Swinger Goes to Town: Why It's a Good Thing Environmentalism Is Dying

by Mike Connelly

Mike Connelly and his wife, Sandy, raise herefords, hay and two kids on the Lost River in Eastern Oregon.

This is a beautifully woven story of one rancher's relationship to one of his cows. The particularity—one rancher, one cow—of the relationship embodies the honor Pattiann Rogers seeks in the preceding poem. Connelly is not sentimental; in the end his cow meets the same fate as others in the herd. And he joins his fellow ranchers in their disdain for "goddamn environmentalists," while at the same time agreeing with environmentalists that our planet is "getting screwed as a result of our collective obsession with greed and convenience." Connelly asks for empathy from us, an empathy built on relationships with specific places, places "you can walk across."

∞

I live near a small town, about three hundred people. In that town is a café that has one good-sized, well-lit dining room. Around the edges are tables for two and four with silk flowers in vases or, in season, holiday decorations. And right in the middle of that room is a big, long table, long enough that it needs three of those little wire racks that hold the napkins and the ketchup and the salt and pepper. There are never any flowers on it.

When you walk into this room for the first time, something tells you that there is a politics attached to this table. Less clear, even to locals, is what the actual rules are as far as who sits there and who doesn't. But at the very least, people know that it is possible to be unwelcome at this table, and that being either unwelcome or welcome is something that gets earned.

A common trait of those who sit at this table is that they have been unable to discover any redeeming qualities in what we like to call the "goddamn environmentalists." You almost never hear just the word "environmentalist." It's always "goddamn environmentalists" or sometimes "mother-fucking environmentalists" or even "goddamn mother-fucking environmental hippie sons of bitches." The café's owner has a cussbucket she puts on the table every time talk turns to environmentalism. She claims that, at twenty-five cents a word, she can buy a week's cigarettes with a morning's proceeds.

Myself, I'm kind of an odd bird in that I happen to agree with environmentalists that the planet is getting screwed as a result of our collective obsession with greed and convenience. I speak up as often as I can without wearing out my welcome at the table, but I should also say that I think my neighbors are entitled to the hostility they feel toward environmentalists. In fact, I would probably have to say that I feel pretty much the same degree of hostility. Increasingly, I'm having a lot of trouble saying the word "environmentalist" without putting "goddamn" in front of it.

"Hey, Mike, how the hell you been?" says Alden.

Alden is ninety-years-old and about as much a part of the decor of that café as the pie case and the milkshake machine. When I walked in he had just torn too much off the side of his packet of Sweet & Low and was trying to spill at least most of it into his cup of coffee.

"Oh, all right I guess. It's slicker than snot out there this morning."

"You shipping cattle?" he asks, lifting his cup with both hands.

"Yessir. Brought a bunch of cull cows just down here to the Klamath yard. I don't mind telling you, the calves I don't mind sending, but there were some cows in that bunch I've had for a hell of a long time."

"Don't tell me you finally sent that old bitch Swinger?"

Carol waved her hand from back in the kitchen and yelled, "Biscuits?"

"Yes, ma'am, if it's not too much trouble."

Alden was still waiting, although I could see he could already tell. "I guess that would be a hard one to load up."

I pulled my napkin out from under my silverware. "Well, she's gone now."

"She come up open?"

"Yessir. First time in fourteen years she hasn't come up bred. Hell of a calf every damn year, too."

Alden fiddled with his cup, tilting it enough to let the waitress know it was empty. I was looking down at my biscuits, but I could feel him looking at me, trying to figure how I felt about shipping Swinger.

Swinger got her name from the way she behaved in a device called a squeeze chute, which is used to restrain cattle for close-up work. I've never met a cow that actually liked to be in a squeeze chute, which makes sense considering that what happens there generally involves some form of discomfort for the cow in question. But I think Swinger, if she didn't actually like it, at least recognized that it was one of the few opportunities a cow gets to get back at the guy with the hat.

Cows remember the chute. Most will hesitate, maybe bawl once or twice, and then reluctantly step in. Swinger, on the other hand, walked firmly and confidently into place, stopping with her head right where it belongs. When I stepped to the front of the chute she would pivot her head toward me and snort in a way that reminded me of the velociraptors in *Jurassic Park* when they hear the kids whimpering in the corner. She shook and twisted her head ever so slightly, snorting lightly, like she was doing her warm-ups. When I moved in, pressing my knee against the side of her head and wrapping my arm around her neck, she went suddenly calm and limp, lowering her head as low as it would go.

You only fall for this once. The first time I had her in the chute, I had noticed how the older cowboys had all crept up from their posts to watch. Swinger went limp and lowered her head. I bent over with the balling gun and the next thing I knew I was bouncing off a wall about six feet away, my feet completely off the ground and already feeling the broken nose.

I wanted to kill Swinger. I wanted to go get a gun, shoot her between the eyes, cut her into pieces, cook her in a pan, and eat her. It's the ultimate greenhorn's solace: no matter how unruly the animal gets, no matter how miserable they make your life, we always know who eats who in the end. I say "greenhorn" because any real cowboy knows that someday some ungulate will be grazing grass built from his bones. The old-timers who had stopped to watch seemed to be both amused and mildly annoyed by my fury, and turned back toward their posts as I cussed and kicked and made excuses.

Quite some time later I came to a dead halt when I remembered that, as I had been picking myself and my pride up off the ground, Swinger had stood calmly while one of the old-timers slid the balling gun down her throat. Somehow, over the years before I showed up, these men and that cow had worked out some kind of deal that they weren't letting me in on.

It was a strange sensation. I didn't really resent the men, since their deliberate abuse is a tradition both ancient and, ultimately, practical. I think what I resented was how obvious it was all of a sudden that my status as a human being did not necessarily guarantee me a spot above this cow on the social ladder. And I resented the cow, for Pete's sake, a cow who I liked to think lived and died as per my wishes. But I haven't been able to avoid calling what I felt that day "jealousy." There was just no way around it: She knew the rules, and I didn't. She was one of them, and I wasn't.

I know it's just a cow, and I know I'm just a farmer. But I think that what we're talking about here points us toward a dilemma that American environmentalism has never quite had the nerve to confront, a set of questions it has always been afraid to answer:

What exactly is it that causes a human being to "respect" nature?

More important, how does a community of human beings, bound together by story, blood, and lifestyle, get to the point where it feeds and clothes and houses itself in a way that doesn't defeat the purpose?

What exactly is "respect," anyway, and how is it different from mere idolatry or fetishism?

And what exactly are "communities" anyway, and how are they different from mere nations or market segments?

Finally, how can we live so that we experience our dependency upon the nonhuman world as a matter of "plain thusness"—as just a run-of-the-mill, everyday stinky, ecstatic, painful, beautiful, and depressing reality instead of the perfumy and saccharine pabulum oozing from our calendars and coffee-table books?

Now, I realize that many of the more clever environmentalists out there have been willing to at least ask these questions. But all too many of us have stopped at the asking simply because the answers are just too disturbing, too threatening to all we hold dear, too corrosive to the revered institutions of American Environmentalism.

I need to distinguish the kind of environmental zealotry that is litigious, large-scale, and institutionalized from environmentalism that is collaborative, small-scale, and organic to particular communities and landscapes. Part of what I'm trying to argue here is that the first kind is starting to be more trouble than it's worth, and that the second kind deserves a lot more attention and energy from people interested in saving this planet. While I'm willing to acknowledge that there is an important role for large-scale environmentalism, it seems to me the time has come for environmentalists to get crystal clear about what that role is, and to figure out what sorts of situations call for an approach that is more site-specific, more tolerant, less brutalistic.

While I'm willing to acknowledge that there is an important role for large-scale environmentalism, it seems to me the time has come for environmentalists to get crystal clear about what that role is, and to figure out what sorts of situations call for an approach that is more site-specific, more tolerant, less brutalistic.

For about six years now the Oregon Natural Resources Council (ONRC) has maintained a "field office" here in our part of Oregon, and over those years they have established a substantial reputation as "uncompromising" (read: obnoxious and confrontational) defenders of the basin's nonhuman resources. The ONRC is a good example of old-style "litigate and legislate" organizations that are having trouble adapting to a world where the most important and durable environmental advocacy is being done small-scale, at the nuts-and-bolts level of local communities.

The ONRC has recently announced the "Oregon Wild Campaign." The public outreach segment of this campaign is the "Adopt a Wilderness" program, whereby individual supporters become "parents of place" by helping with the assessment, mapping, interpretation, monitoring, and advocacy for a particular tract of land. The ultimate goal is to "protect Oregon's remaining wild lands" by transferring them to federal ownership under the Wilderness Act.

The program's emphasis on individuals committing to particular places sounds nice, and I am sure it has inspired many to get their checkbooks out. But it seems to me that the Oregon Wild Program is rooted more in the institutionalized separation of humans and nature than in an acknowledgment of interconnectedness and interdependence. How else could the ONRC see a solution to the problem of "mankind's alienation from nature" in the bureaucratic designation of wilderness areas? How else could they see the systematic exclusion of human communities from certain landscapes as the only way to foster a sense of respect for those landscapes?

They are able to come to these conclusions because, frankly, they live in cities and suburbs where the suppression of wildness is so basic that even members of the ONRC don't notice how thoroughly it influences their lifestyles. Whether or not they like to think so, they have bracketed off their own lifestyles—relentless wonderlands of technological artifice and corporate insinuation—as "the norm." They resign themselves to the fact that their own "places" are sort of industrial sacrifice areas, beyond hope. They recognize that the human animal needs a closer connection with nature than urban life provides, so they resolve to make sure there is some wilderness out there "somewhere."

I suppose it is possible to "love" a federally designated wilderness area, but as seems clear from the "Adopt a Wilderness" program, it will be the "protective" love of a parent for a child. Or it will be a kind of puppy love that focuses on the "simple pleasures," rather than a living, breathing, grown-up love which reminds us that, as Gary Snyder put it, "there is no death that is not somebody's food, and no life that is not somebody's death."

A year after Swinger sent me flying, I was calving the herd out by myself. Any new calf gets a round of shots and is weighed, tagged, and tattooed, all while a furiously protective mother cow literally breathes down your neck. But after surviving a few hundred such encounters, you grow comfortable with the fact that the cow is almost always more scared of you than you are of her.

So it was, on that bitterly cold February morning, as I approached Swinger and her calf. When Swinger saw me coming she walked quickly away from her calf, which is what most cows do for the same reason that killdeers act like their wings are broken. I figured I had better get it done before she realizes I'm not fooled and starts back.

I had left the fourwheeler running, so I didn't hear the hoofbeats until just before she hit me. Instead of throwing me this time, she took advantage of the fact that this particular spot was a jagged and rock-hard cheesegrater of deep hoofprints in frozen mud. She pushed me over into and then under the fourwheeler, where I stayed until she went back to her calf. To this day I have dark scars on my forearms where mud got ground up under the skin.

It was stage two of my initiation.

She was showing me the rules—not *how* to learn, but that learning as I understood it really didn't apply here. It wasn't a matter of her knowing something and then one way or another passing it on to me. It wasn't about her being better than me or me being better than her or either one of us being a subset or a function of the other. It was about a spontaneous, visceral detachment from anything that wasn't right here and right now. An unsaid and mutual surrender to The Land and its demands. From each, to each other, to both our bones underground. A slow-growing focus onto something that wasn't me and wasn't her but both of us—really more than both since it was both and then whatever we had between us, too. She would die and so would I: to someday feed what's coming.

As I crawled out from under the fourwheeler my dog walked up low, apologizing for having let it happen, and I said to him, "Don't worry about it, dog. That there is one hell of a mother cow."

The first people to start talking like environmentalists had figured out that we, as a nation, were far too obsessed with ourselves as individuals, so much so that we had come to believe that we did not have to balance our desire for material wealth with a respect for the natural systems that originally produced that wealth.

These people were trying to find some way to get human beings to think more about the nonhuman world, to consider that world in our decision-making in a way that we hadn't previously, or at least not since around the start of the industrial revolution. But what is it, exactly, that could bind us to nature in such a way that nature ends up with greater respect? How can obligations be built between humans and nonhumans that are so deep, so integral, so organic that it no longer makes sense to even make the distinction?

The almost-universal approach of American environmentalists has been to get laws passed that establish more centralized control over resources they feel are endangered, or that bring the power of the state to bear upon those who are not behaving as environmentalists think they ought.

Most environmentalists, I'm guessing, would like to think that their efforts to pass regulatory laws, to designate wilderness areas, establish wildlife refuges and otherwise transfer land and resources into government ownership have all been geared toward overcoming the problems caused by our heritage of excluding the nonhuman world from moral consideration. But if we take a good, honest look at where most of environmentalism is today, it seems clear that we have been unduly preoccupied with "getting it in writing," and that we have been unwilling or unable to let go of the one artifact of the industrial revolution that made nature morally invisible to us in the first place: The Written Law. There is another way, much harder to talk about, for people to feel morally obligated to nature: I'll call it *empathy*.

Empathy is not sympathy and it's not pity. It is not the same as "goodwill." We feel empathy for another when we get inside their heads or hearts. We encounter empathy by way of metaphor. It's about an identification based on a similarity. It can be a material similarity, like the facial features of brothers, but it can also be a function of experience, like the feeling of brotherhood between lifelong friends. It is a source of irresistible moral obligations. But unlike written laws or contracts, these bonds are at home in the heart, they have not been spoken or written out onto a table somewhere and turned into a document. They must be lived, not "enacted."

Empathy can be turned into words, even into writing, without turning it into Law. We call these stories, and the best ones are allowed to change over time. They are an ongoing, open-ended negotiation. These stories, if they are allowed to work, become the boat we're all floating in. I don't mean "all" like "all humanity." But all of us who live in this place, this particular, tangible, seeable, knowable, lovable place. The place you can walk across.

Environmentalists need to tell more stories, not pass more laws. And they need to listen more closely to the stories of those they hope to change, and realize that people who are forced to change don't stay changed any longer than they have to. People can, and will, change themselves by the stories they tell, and by the subtle changes they make to stories they have inherited. We will not replace their stories. We have no business replacing their stories. We should show our manners, and be grateful to have a place around their fire, and a turn to speak.

It was raining hard again this year, this day as we sat having coffee at the café. Not since '64, the old-timers said, had they seen the Lost River this high. We joked about plowing with motorboats. A local real-estate agent came in with some clients, a family from California that had had it with the city. The agent always sat his clients at the big table, which bothered most of us since his specialty was subdividing farm ground. Whenever he would leave, someone would joke about running out the moneychangers. When he heard we were talking about Swinger he asked me to tell about that time the water was high at Harpold.

Harpold Dam is this pretty good-sized check dam down at the tail end of the irrigation district. I've got a little pasture down next to it where I keep a few animals, and this year Swinger was down there. Limbs and trash and such had been built up against the pilings, and it was raising the river even higher. Some folks upstream were starting to worry about flooding.

Two local men, middle-aged and overweight, floated out to the dam in a boat, trying to dislodge the debris. One of them leaned too far over the side of the boat, and over it tipped. I happened to be down at my barn and I heard their partner on the shore yelling for help. Both men went under long enough that we started wondering if we were watching someone die, but then one of them climbed up out of the water onto the steel channel between two pilings. After he inched his way to a small flat spot on top of the piling, he yelled to the other guy, who was pinned between a piling and a big limb, part of his bleeding face just above water, his arms bloody and wrapped around the steel channel.

My neighbor, a team roper, happened to be driving by just then. He jumped out of his truck and slid down the bank with his rope in his hand. He waited for the guy to bob up some and threw his rope and caught him, first try. We all grabbed the rope and pulled with all we had but we couldn't bust him loose.

We cussed not having a horse. Then I looked over at my bunch of cows, who had all come over to see what was going on. Swinger was right out in front. My neighbor, knowing Swinger, thought of it at the same time I did. We knotted another rope to the one we were pulling on. I got the dog to bring Swinger in close enough to throw at and my neighbor nailed her, first throw.

Swinger jumped and jerked and spun and then popped the man right up onto the shore. Someone jumped on the rope and cut it just before she tore him in half.

As I finished the story, I noticed that the father from California had stopped eating about halfway through. Then he remembered and began to butter his toast.

"And you said you sold this cow today?"

"Yessir."

"Why?"

I never did really answer his question. I'm pretty sure the only answer I had would have been one he wouldn't want to hear.

Some stories we save for our own folk, and for good reason. The best stories—living stories, working stories—don't mean something to everyone and I can't think why they should. They are not part of the land: they are the land. Not any land but this land right here. They are the faint trails in the underbrush. They are the stag-scratched treebark. They are the cat piss in the cave. They are under our feet like groundwater. They are less portable than we'd like to believe, and they matter more than anything.

It was almost lunchtime when I finally left the café. The sun had come out strong. I went home and got on the horse and rode up into the hills. I just let the horse go where it would. The sun was warm on my face. I might have fallen asleep.

I thought of Swinger in the auction ring with everybody yelling and prodding. I thought of her climbing up the slick ramp into a livestock semi full of cows she'd never seen. I thought of her walking onto the kill floor and slumping down as she was shot or shocked unconscious. I thought of her getting cut across the throat, drained and skinned and hooked and hung.

I felt for her. I felt it for her. Not instead of her but what I imagined her to feel. Not shame and not regret, not pain and not injustice, but an unthinkable knowing that this is what is asked of us, an unprayable faith that this is just what must happen, or else everything falls apart, everything spins away to nothing. This is where we find respect. This is how we'll save things.

She will die for us.

I will die for you.

You will die for me.

Feeding what's coming.

This article originally appeared in *Orion* (Summer 1999). 187 Main Street, Great Barrington, MA 01230. www.oriononline.org.

Genetically Modified Organisms

As we learned from experience with DDT, nuclear power, and CFCs, we only discover the costs of new technologies after they are extensively used. We should apply the Precautionary Principle with any new technology, asking whether it is needed and then demanding proof that it is not harmful. Nowhere is this more important than in biotechnology because it enables us to tamper with the very blueprint of life.

—*David Suzuki*

It's not the nature of genetic engineering itself that's the problem; it is the way genetic engineering has evolved. Early on, it came under the control of the private sector....By definition, the private sector's goal is to make money. It will not focus its attention on the needs of the poor, except as a way to sell its products.

—*Tewolde Egziabher*

Introduction

Myriad questions surround genetically modified (GM) foods. Are they safe for human consumption? Will they cause ecological damage? Are they the key to "feeding the world?" What sort of policies and agricultural systems lead to food security? Who benefits—large farmers, small farmers, corporations, the hungry—when food is genetically modified? Is it ethical to take genetic material from a flounder and insert it into a tomato? Well-meaning people answer these questions differently. Let's look at two examples.

First, we will consider different ideas about food security. Food security refers to a region or nation's ability to predictably maintain access to a nutritious, sufficient and safe supply of food for its population. What does food security entail, or how might food security be achieved? Here are two different perspectives:

C. Ford Runge and Benjamin Senauer, Professors of Applied Economics at the University of Minnesota, answer:

> ...it [food security] involves improving a developing nation's access to cheaper food from comparatively advantaged exporting countries. It is generally more efficient and cheaper than self-sufficiency, in which a nation tries to produce all crops that its population needs... Finally, the drive for food security should tap the potential of GM technology for developing countries to both enhance nutrition and boost agricultural output (*Foreign Affairs*, May/June 2000, pp. 39-40).

On the other hand, Tewolde, Ethiopian Environmental Minister, states:

> The biotech industry is suggesting that food security will come through the farmer's loss of control of essential agricultural inputs. Do you see the lie? This is food insecurity...Without local control, local availability of food can never be certain. It would be far better to develop a system that would enable the farmer himself to be in charge (see Marilyn Snell's interview, p. 192).

Notice that the former definition of food security assumes access to cheap energy for the transportation of food across the globe. When Runge and Senauer claim that self-sufficiency is more expensive and less efficient than relying on foreign production of foodstuffs, their economic accounting does not include the costs of certain externalities (see Redefining Progress's article on p. 112 for further elaboration). And in supporting GM food as an important element of food security, they ignore the fact that farmers using GM technology have less and less control over their farming practices. Loss of control makes farmers more vulnerable to political upheaval. During times of such upheaval, it is especially important to food security that a country/region have the ability to grow its own food, not be dependent upon international markets.

For a second example of how differently people approach GM foods, consider the application of the precautionary principle. The precautionary principle states: "When an activity raises threats of harm to human health or the environment, precautionary measures should be taken even if some cause and effect relationships are not fully established scientifically" (from the Wingspread Conference, Racine, Wisconsin, 1998). Anthony Trewavas, a plant biologist at the University of Edinburgh, states:

> When people say to me they do not need GM, I am astonished at their prescience, their ability to read a benign future in a crystal ball that I cannot. Now is the time to experiment...When the climate is changing in unpredictable ways, diversity in agricultural technology is a strength and a necessity not a luxury...We have heard much of the Precautionary Principle in recent years; my version of it is 'be prepared' (from "GM Food Is the Best Option We Have," p. 199).

Geneticist David Suzuki, on the other hand, states:

> As we learned from experience with DDT, nuclear power, and CFCs, we only discover the costs of new technologies after they are extensively used. We should apply the Precautionary Principle with any new technology, asking whether it is needed and then demanding proof that it is not harmful. Nowhere is this more important than in biotechnology because it enables us to tamper with the very blueprint of life (see "Experimenting with Life," p. 183).

Trewavas's version of the principle is "be prepared," while Suzuki advises more caution. At Earth Ministry we side more with Suzuki than Trewavas, and support Tewolde's perspectives on food security more than Runge's and Senauer's. However, we acknowledge that there are very diverse opinions. GM foods are so new that many in the United States (Europeans are more solidly anti-GM) are undecided about their relative merits. We therefore included Trewavas's "pro-GM food" essay. (To read more "pro-GM" essays, see Gregory Pence's *Designer Food,* and *The Ethics of Food,* edited by Pence.)

Two fundamental principles guide our work at Earth Ministry: first, creation is good, a revelation of God; second, God has special concern and care for the poor and dispossessed. Two questions flow naturally from these principles. First, does the action/technology/decision under consideration honor and maintain the inherent integrity of creation? Second, does the action/technology/decision under consideration pay attention to and meet the needs of the poor? With respect to the issues surrounding GM food, we believe both questions must be answered "no." Ecologically speaking, we do not believe that the precautionary principle's standards— is the new technology needed, and is it proven safe?—have been met in relationship to GM food. Socially and economically speaking, we find it appalling when corporations like Monsanto promote GM food and technology because of the possibility that GM crops may require fewer chemicals, while at the same time profiting more and more from sales of the world's most popular herbicide, Roundup. Similarly, we are concerned when the Monsantos of the world represent themselves as primarily interested in feeding the hungry when the seeds they develop and promote do not in subsequent years reproduce well (in the case of hybrid seeds) or at all (in the case of Terminator seeds), thereby ensuring farmers' continuing dependence on the company's supplies of seeds. These are our biases; we may be wrong in our conclusions. We offer these articles for your consideration.

Experimenting with Life
by David Suzuki

David Suzuki is an award-winning scientist, environmentalist and broadcaster.

As a geneticist, Suzuki argues we should be cautious when considering genetically modified (GM) food, asking whether we need it and demanding proof that it is not harmful. He reminds us that "we only discover the costs of new technologies after they are extensively used" and cites as examples our experiences with DDT, nuclear power, and CFCs.

∞

I am a geneticist by training. At one time, I had one of the largest research grants and genetics labs in Canada. The time I spent in this lab was one of the happiest periods of my life and I am proud of the contribution we made to science. My introductory book is still the most widely used genetics text in the world.

When I graduated as a geneticist in 1961, I was full of enthusiasm and determined to make a mark. Back then we knew about DNA, genes, chromosomes, and genetic regulation. But today when I tell students what our hot ideas were in '61, they choke with laughter. Viewed in 2000, ideas from 1961 seem hilarious. But when those students become professors years from now and tell their students what was hot in 2000, their students will be just as amused.

At the cutting edge of scientific research, most of our ideas are far from the mark—wrong, in need of revision, or irrelevant. That's not a derogation of science; it's the way science advances. We take a set of observations or data, set up a hypothesis that makes sense of them, and then we test the hypothesis. The new insights and techniques we gain from this process are interpreted tentatively and liable to change, so any rush to apply them strikes me as downright dangerous.

No group of experts should be more aware of the hazards of unwarranted claims than geneticists. After all, it was the exuberance of geneticists early in this century that led to the creation of a discipline called eugenics, which aimed to improve the quality of human genes. These scientists were every bit as clever, competent, and well-meaning as today's genetic engineers; they just got carried away with their discoveries. Outlandish claims were made by eminent geneticists about the hereditary nature of traits such as drunkenness, nomadism, and criminality, as well as those judged "inferior" or "superior." Those claims provided scientific respectability to legislation in the US prohibiting interracial marriage and immigration from countries judged inferior, and allowed sterilization of inmates of mental institutions on genetic grounds. In Nazi Germany, geneticist Josef Mengele held peer-reviewed research grants for his work at Auschwitz. The grand claims of geneticists led to "race purification" laws and the Holocaust.

Today, the leading-edge of genetics is in the field of biotechnology. The basis of this new area is the ability to take DNA (genetic material) from one organism and insert it into a different species. This is truly revolutionary. Human beings can't normally exchange genes with a carrot or a mouse, but with DNA technology it can happen.

However, history informs us that though we love technology, there are always costs, and since our knowledge of how nature works is so limited, we can't anticipate how those costs will manifest. We only have to reflect on DDT, nuclear power, and CFCs, which were hailed as wonderful creations but whose long-term detrimental effects were only found decades after their widespread use.

Now, with a more wise and balanced perspective, we are cutting back on the use of these technologies. But with genetically modified (GM) foods, this option may not be available. The difference with GM food is that once the genie is out of the bottle, it will be difficult or impossible to stuff it back. If we stop using DDT and CFCs, nature may be able to undo most of the damage—even nuclear waste decays over time. But GM plants are living organisms. Once these new life forms have become established in our surroundings, they can replicate, change, and spread; there may be no turning back. Many ecologists are concerned about what this means to the balance of life on Earth that has evolved over millions of years through the natural reproduction of species.

Genomes are selected in the entirety of their expression. In ways we barely comprehend, the genes within a species are interconnected and interact as an integrated whole. When a gene from an unrelated species is introduced, the context within which it finds itself is completely changed. If a taiko drum is plunked in the middle of a symphony orchestra and plays along, it is highly probable the resultant music will be pretty discordant. Yet based on studies of gene behavior derived from studies *within* a species, biotechnologists assume that those rules will also apply to genes transferred *between* species. This is totally unwarranted.

As we learned from experience with DDT, nuclear power and CFCs, we only discover the costs of new technologies after they are extensively used. We should apply the Precautionary Principle with any new technology, asking whether it is needed and then demanding proof that it is not harmful. Nowhere is this more important than in biotechnology because it enables us to tamper with the very blueprint of life.

Since GM foods are now in our diet, we have become experimental subjects without any choice. (Europeans say if they want to know whether GMOs are hazardous, they should just study North Americans.) I would have preferred far more experimentation with GMOs under controlled lab conditions before their release into the open, but it's too late.

We have learned from painful experience that anyone entering an experiment should give informed consent. That means at the very least food should be labeled if it contains GMOs so we each can make that choice.

This article originally appeared in YES! A *Journal of Positive Futures*, Summer 2000. Reprinted with permission of David Suzuki.

*W*orldview of *Abundance*

by Vandana Shiva

Environmental thinker and activist Vandana Shiva is director of the Research Foundation for Science, Technology and Natural Resource Policy. Her books include *Biopiracy: The Plunder of Nature and Knowledge*. This article from *Orion* (Summer 2000) is adapted from her most recent book *Stolen Harvest: The Hijacking of the Global Food Supply* (South End Press, 2000).

Shiva, a leading opponent of GMOs, summarizes here her major concerns about genetically modifying plants and the efforts by multi-national companies to control and patent seed varieties developed over the millennia by farmers around the world. She argues for a "nonviolent agriculture," based on "compassion for all species and the protection of biodiversity."

∞

In 1987 I was invited to a meeting in Geneva on biotechnology. There were people like myself who had done environmental work on agriculture, people from the United Nations, and people from the major seed and agrochemical corporations. Two things an executive from the Sandoz corporation said had sent a chill down my spine. He mentioned a genetically engineered bacteria that had been released in the Congo River as a cure for river blindness. I asked if they had done any ecological trials, and he said, "We can't afford to stop to do ecological trials." The second thing he said was, "By the turn of the century there will only be five corporations that control health and food, and we have to be one of those five. Otherwise we won't survive."

In the press conference that followed that meeting, a journalist asked me, how will you be able to respond when this is the kind of power you are dealing with? I shut my eyes and reflected for a moment. I said, there was another moment in history, when eighty-five percent of the planet was controlled by one island nation. When an old man pulled out a spinning wheel people said, how can you defeat the British Empire with this spinning wheel? And he said, it's precisely because it looks so small, because it can be in the hands of everyone, that it is a powerful instrument. In that period of the Industrial Revolution, what was being colonized was textiles. In today's world what is being colonized is food and biodiversity. And I realized, the seed is the metaphor of transformation in our times.

Food is our most basic need, the very stuff of life. Of the 250,000 to 300,000 species of plants alive today, at least 10,000 to 50,000 are edible. Seven thousand species have been farmed and used for food. For more than ten thousand years, farmers have worked with nature to evolve crop varieties to suit diverse climates and cultures. Andean farmers have bred more than 3,000 varieties of potatoes. Traditionally, 10,000 wheat varieties were grown in China. In Papua New Guinea, more than 5,000 varieties of sweet potatoes are cultivated. This tremendous diversity has been the basis of our food supply.

Local markets and local cultures have allowed crop diversity to thrive in our fields, enabling farmers to continue evolving diverse breeds and conserving seeds and plant varieties. Seed is the first link in the food chain. Farmers select and save the best seeds from a good crop to plant them again the next season. Free exchange of seed among farmers has been the primary means of maintaining biodiversity as well as food security.

As global markets replace local markets, new intellectual-property-rights regimes, which are being universalized through the World Trade Organization, allow corporations to usurp the knowledge of the seed and claim it as their private property. Over time, this results in corporate monopolies over the seed itself.

Here, I focus on India to tell the story of how corporate control of food and globalization of agriculture are robbing millions of their livelihoods and their right to food. I do this because I am an Indian and because Indian agriculture is being especially targeted by global corporations. However, this phenomenon is not unique to India. It is being experienced in every society, as small farms and small farmers are pushed to extinction, as monocultures replace biodiverse crops, as farming is transformed from the production of nourishing and diverse foods into the creation of markets for genetically engineered seeds, herbicides, and pesticides.

In India, rice is identified with *prana*, or life breath. Before the Green Revolution introduced monocultures in the 1960s, Indian farmers had developed 200,000 varieties of rice through their innovation and breeding. These indigenous rice varieties had evolved to survive floods and droughts, to thrive in uplands and coastal ecosystems, and to offer enhanced taste and medicinal value. Farmers bred red rice and brown rice and black rice. They bred rice that grew eighteen feet tall in the Gangetic floodwaters, and saline-resistant rice that could be grown in the coastal waters.

Basmati rice has been grown for centuries and is referred to in ancient text, folklore, and poetry. This naturally perfumed variety of rice has always been treasured and eagerly coveted by foreigners. Years of research on Basmati strains by Indian and Pakistani farmers have resulted in a diverse range of Basmati varieties. Today, there are twenty-seven distinct, documented varieties of Basmati grown in India. Their superior qualities are an outcome of these farmers' informal breeding and innovation. And this innovation by farmers has not stopped. Farmers involved in the movement dedicated to conserving native seed diversity are still breeding new varieties.

In recent years, Basmati rice has been one of India's fastest-growing export items. Every year, India exports between 400,000 and 500,000 tons of Basmati annually. At $850 a ton, Indian Basmati is the most expensive rice imported by the European Union.

In 1997, the U.S. Patent Office granted Texas-based RiceTec, Inc. patent number 5663484 on Basmati rice lines and grains. The patent will allow RiceTec to sell internationally what it claims to be a new variety of Basmati. RiceTec's patented Basmati variety was derived from farmers' varieties bred over centuries on the Indian subcontinent. RiceTec's method of crossing different varieties to mix strains is a very commonplace method of breeding.

RiceTec's Basmati patent illustrates the problem inherent in patenting living resources. Claiming invention for plant varieties denies the creativity of nature on the one hand, and of farmers on the other. If this false claim to invention is maintained, it could be used to penalize Basmati farmers for infringing on the RiceTec patent. Indian farmers who grow Basmati would be forced to pay royalties to RiceTec, and the costs to Indian agriculture would be huge. Further, seed legislation forces farmers to use only "registered" varieties. Since farmers' varieties are not registered, and individual small farmers cannot afford the costs of registration, they are slowly pushed into dependence on the seed industry.

The piracy of Basmati is just one example of how corporations are claiming intellectual property rights to the biodiversity and indigenous innovations of the Third World, thereby robbing the poor of the last resources that allow them to survive outside the global marketplace. The perverse system that treats plants and seeds as corporate inventions is transforming farmers' highest duties—to save seed and exchange seed with neighbors—into crimes.

Today ten corporations control thirty-two percent of the commercial seed

market, valued at $23 billion, and one hundred percent of the market for geneti-
cally engineered seeds. These corporations also control the global agrochemical
and pesticide market. As corporations claim intellectual property rights on seeds
and plants, centuries of collective innovation by farmers and peasants are being
hijacked. Just five corporations control the global trade in grain. Monocultures and
monopolies are destroying the rich harvest of seed given to us over millennia by
nature and farming cultures.

Food is necessary for all living species. That is why an ancient Hindu text, the
Taittreya Upanishad, calls on humans to feed all beings in their zone of influence.
In ecological agricultural cultures, technologies and economies are based on an
integration between crops and animal husbandry. The wastes of one provide nutrition for the other, in mutual and reciprocal ways. Crop byproducts feed cattle, and
cattle waste feeds the soils that nourish the crops. Crops do not just yield grain,
but also straw, which provides fodder and organic matter. Crops are thus food for
humans, animals, and the many organisms in the soil.

It is often said that the so-called miracle varieties of the Green Revolution
prevented famine because they had higher yields. However, these higher yields
disappear in the context of *total yields* of crops on farms. Green Revolution varieties
produced more grain by diverting production away from straw. However, less straw
means less fodder for cattle and less organic matter for the soil. Since cattle and
earthworms are our partners in food production, stealing food from them makes it
impossible to maintain food production over time, and means that the partial yield
increases were not sustainable. The gain in "yields" of industrially produced crops
is thus based on a theft of food from other species and the rural poor in the Third
World.

During the debate about the entry of the global seed organization Cargill into
India in 1992, a Cargill executive stated, "We bring Indian farmers smart technologies, which prevent bees from usurping the pollen." During the United Nations
Biosafety Negotiations, Monsanto circulated literature that claimed that "weeds
steal the sunshine." A worldview that defines pollination as "theft by bees" and
claims that diverse plants "steal" sunshine is one aimed at stealing nature's harvest,
by replacing open, pollinated varieties with hybrids and sterile seeds, and destroying biodiverse flora with herbicides.

This is a worldview based on scarcity. A worldview of abundance is the worldview of women in India who leave food for ants on their doorstep, even as they
create the most beautiful art in *kolams* and *mandalas* with rice flour. Abundance is
the worldview of peasant women who weave designs of paddy to hang up for birds
when the birds do not find grain in the fields. This view of abundance recognizes
that, in giving food to other beings and species, we maintain conditions for our
own food security. In the *Isho Upanishad* it is said, "The universe is the creation
of the Supreme Power meant for the benefits of [all] creation. Let not any one
species encroach upon others' rights."

Global corporations are stealing nature's harvest not only through patents on life forms but also through genetic engineering. Crops that are genetically engineered to be resistant to herbicides can create highly invasive "superweeds" by transferring the genes for herbicide resistance to weeds. Crops designed to be pesticide factories, and genetically engineered to produce toxins and venom with genes from bacteria, scorpions, snakes, and wasps, can threaten nonpest species and contribute to the emergence of resistance in pests and hence the creation of "superpests." In every application of genetic engineering, food is being stolen from other species for the maximization of corporate profits.

The Green Revolution, although it displaced diverse nutritious food grains and spread monocultures of rice, wheat, and maize did, however, focus on staple foods and their yields. The genetic engineering revolution is undoing the narrow gains of the Green Revolution by not only neglecting the diversity of staples, but also by focusing on herbicide resistance, not higher yields. According to Clive James, transgenic crops are not engineered for higher yields. Fifty-four percent of the increase in transgenic crops is for those engineered for herbicide resistance, not increased food. Worldwide, 40 percent of the land under cultivation by genetically engineered crops is under soybean cultivation, 25 percent under corn, 13 percent under tobacco, 11 percent under cotton, 10 percent under canola, and 1 percent each under tomato and potato.

Tobacco and cotton are nonfood commercial crops, and crops such as soybeans are not food staples for most cultures outside East Asia. Soybeans will not provide food security for dal-eating Indians, and corn will not provide security in the sorghum belt of Africa. Food security is not just having access to adequate food. It is also having access to culturally appropriate food. Vegetarians can starve if asked to live on meat diets. I have watched Asians feel totally deprived on bread, potato, and meat diets in Europe.

The trend toward the cultivation of genetically engineered crops indicates a clear narrowing of the genetic basis of our food supply. Currently, there are only two commercialized staple-food crops. In place of hundreds of legumes and beans eaten around the world, there is soybean. In place of diverse varieties of millets, wheats, and rices, there is only corn. In place of the diversity of oil seeds, there is only canola. As the biotechnology industry globalizes, these monoculture tendencies will increase, thus further displacing agricultural biodiversity and creating ecological vulnerability.

In Indian agriculture, women use up to 150 different species of plants as medicine, food, or fodder. For the poorest, this biodiversity is the most important resource for survival. In West Bengal, 124 "weed" species collected from rice fields have economic importance for local farmers. In a Tanzanian village, over eighty percent of the vegetable dishes are prepared from uncultivated plants. Herbicides such as Roundup and the transgenic crops engineered to withstand them therefore destroy the economies of the poorest, especially women. What is a weed for Monsanto is a medicinal plant or food for rural people.

As criticism of biotechnology's emphasis on herbicide-resistant crops and crops that produce toxins grows, the biotechnology industry has started to talk of engineering crops for nitrogen fixing, salinity tolerance, and high nutrition instead. However, all these traits already exist in farmers' varieties and farmers' fields. Biodiversity already holds the answers to many of the problems for which genetic engineering is being offered as a solution.

In the mountain farming systems of the Garhwal Himalaya, there is a particular cropping pattern called *baranaja*, which means literally "twelve seeds." The seeds of twelve or more different crops are mixed and then randomly sown in a field fertilized with cow dung and farmyard manure. After sowing, the farmer transplants crops from one area of the field to another area in order to maintain an even distribution. As in other cultivation practices, constant weeding is necessary. The crops are all sown in May, but are harvested at different times, from late August to early November, thus ensuring a continuous food supply for the farmer during this period and beyond.

The different crops have been selected by the farmers over the ages by observing certain relationships between plants, and between plants and soil. For example, the *rajma* creeper will climb only on the *marsha* plant and on no other plant in the fields. The symbiotic relationships between different plants contribute to the increased productivity. When farmers cultivate *baranaja*, they get higher yields, diverse outputs, and a better market price for their produce than when they cultivate a monoculture of soybeans.

Cultivating diversity can therefore be part of a farming strategy for high yields and high incomes. But since these yields and incomes are from diverse crops, centralized commercial interests are not interested in them. They demand uniformity and monocultures.

What we are seeing is the emergence of food totalitarianism, in which a handful of corporations control the entire food chain and destroy alternatives so that people do not have access to diverse, safe foods produced ecologically. The right of corporations to force-feed citizens of the world with culturally inappropriate and hazardous foods has been made absolute under the new trade rules. The right to food, the right to safety, the right to culture are all being treated as trade barriers that need to be dismantled.

This food totalitarianism can only be stopped through major citizen mobilization for democratization of the food system. In periods of injustice and external domination, reclaiming economic and political freedom requires peaceful noncooperation with unjust laws and regimes. This peaceful noncooperation has been the democratic tradition of India and was revived by Mohandas Gandhi as *satyagraha*. Literally, *satyagraha* means "the struggle for truth." The salt *satyagraha* embodied India's refusal to cooperate with the unjust salt laws.

On March 5, 1998, the anniversary of Gandhi's call for the salt *satyagraha*, a coalition of more than two thousand groups started the *bija satyagraha*, a noncooperation movement against patents on seeds and plants. These groups refuse to accept the colonization of life through patents and perverse technologies, and the destruction of food security by the free trade rules of the World Trade Organization. The *bija satyagraha* is an expression of the quest for freedom for all people and all species, and an assertion of our food rights.

Another attempt to reclaim food democracy has been through reclaiming the seed from the destructive control of corporations. For more than a decade, Indian environmentalists and farmers have built *Navdanya*—the movement for saving seed. *Navdanya* has started sixteen community seed banks in six states in India. Thousands of members practice chemical-free agriculture and have taken a pledge to continue to save and share the seeds and biodiversity they have received as gifts from nature and their ancestors.

Ecological and organic agriculture is often referred to in India as *ahimsic krishi*, or "nonviolent agriculture," because it is based on compassion for all species and hence the protection of biodiversity. In India, ARISE, the national network for organic agriculture, holds village-level courses throughout the country to support farmers wanting to give up chemical addiction. While organic agriculture is a low-input, low-cost option, and hence an option for the poor, it is often presented as a "luxury of the rich." This is not true. The cheapness of industrially produced food and expensiveness of organic foods do not reflect their cost of production but rather the heavy subsidies given to industrial agriculture.

Millions of people from across the world have been putting the principles of ecological agriculture into practice. The post-Seattle challenge is to change global trade rules and national food and agricultural policies so that these practices can be nurtured and spread, and so that ecological agriculture, which protects small farms and peasant livelihoods and produces safe food, is not marginalized and criminalized. The time has come to reclaim the stolen harvest and celebrate the growing of good food as the highest gift and the most revolutionary act.

Movements for food democracy have begun to gain momentum. Globally, we have seen citizens' movements against genetic engineering and corporate control over agriculture move concerns about genetic engineering from the fringe to the center stage of trade and economics. In Britain in 1999, an alliance of farmers, consumers, development groups, and environmentalists launched a campaign for a five-year freeze on genetic engineering. Throughout Europe, similar bans and moratoriums are increasing. Opposition to genetic engineering is building broad-based alliances—between scientists and the people, between producers and consumers, between the people of the North and South. Solidarity and synergy between diverse groups is necessary because the corporate push for genetic engineering raises issues of democracy at many levels.

Public-interest scientists who have worked on the science of ecological impact have been an important part of this movement. The team of scientists who gathered for the meeting hosted by the Third World Network in Penang in 1994—Mae Wan Ho, Christine von Weiszacker, Beatrix Tappeser, Peter Wills, and Jose Lutzenberger, along with others—has played a key role in raising ecological and safety issues. Without the solidarity of such scientists with citizens' movements, industry's attempts to polarize the debate, as if it were between "informed scientists" and "un-informed citizens," or between "reason" and "emotion," might have been successful. The protests would have been brushed aside, and the commercialization of geneti-cally engineered organisms would have continued without any question or pause.

Solidarity between producers and consumers is also necessary. Since most people of the countries of the South are farmers, and only two percent of the world's farm-ers survive in the North, movements for food democracy will take the shape of con-sumer movements in the North, and both farmers' and consumer movements in the South.

The democratization of the food system is based in the movements for the recov-ery of biodiversity and the intellectual commons. On the one hand, refusal to regard life's diversity as corporate inventions and property is a recognition of the intrinsic value of all species and their self-organizing capacity. On the other hand, the refusal to allow privatization of living resources through patents is a defense of the right to survival of the two-thirds majority that depends on nature's capital. It is also a de-fense of cultural diversity, since the majority of the world's cultures do not see other species and plants as "property," but as kin. This larger democracy of life, based on the earth democracy, or what we call *vasudhaiva kutumbakam*, is the real force of resistance against the brute power of the so-called "life sciences industry," which is pushing millions of species to extinction and millions of people to the edge of survival.

Reclaiming democracy in food production implies reclaiming the rights of all species to their share of nutrition, and, through this ecological step, reclaiming the right of all people to food, including future generations. A food democracy that is inclusive in this way can feed us abundantly.

This article originally appeared in *Orion* (Summer 1999). 187 Main Street, Great Barrington, MA 01230. www.oriononline.org.

Against the Grain : An Interview with Tewolde Egziabher

by Marilyn Berlin Snell

Marilyn Berlin Snell is *Sierra*'s writer/editor. Here she interviews Tewolde, Ethiopia's Environmental Minister, about his opposition to genetically engineered agricultural crops. His perspectives are important as we often hear that GMO foods will benefit developing countries and feed the world's hungry.

∞

Biotechnology has been heralded as a boon to developing countries, where the lion's share of the world's hungry dwell. Its breakthroughs—food crops genetically engineered to resist disease, pests, and drought, or to contain vitamins and nutrients severely lacking in the diets of the poor—are seen as a 21st-century version of the Green Revolution of the 1960s and '70s, when hybrid crop varieties and heavy use of fertilizers and irrigation boosted yields 20 to 30 percent. The promise of more abundant and more nutritious food appears to hold out the hope that hunger and disease can be alleviated. With potential like this, who wouldn't be in favor of genetically engineered crops?

For starters, many of the people they are supposed to help. One of the strongest and most articulate voices to emerge in opposition to biotechnology is Tewolde Berhan Gebre Egziabher (formally addressed, as is Ethiopian custom, as Tewolde). Born to a peasant farming family in northern Ethiopia in 1940, Tewolde worked as a plant ecologist and university president before becoming the head of Ethiopia's Environment Protection Authority in 1995. Concerned with the impact that unregulated biotech products could have on the rich biodiversity of the developing world, and also with how the plight of hungry people was being used to promote genetic engineering, Tewolde has been a key international negotiator on issues of biotech safety and accountability. He helped hammer out the United Nations Convention on Biological Diversity and draft the Biosafety Protocol, which if ratified will set international standards for trade in and use of biotech products. During the protocol talks, the U.S. delegation heavily influenced the discussion—often bolstered by agricultural allies like Canada and Australia. The meetings were heated and often acrimonious, with the United States and its friends at one end of the spectrum, arguing that genetically modified organisms do not need special regulations, while Tewolde and the majority of participating nations argued that they most certainly do.

Since 1999, Tewolde has represented what has come to be called the Like-Minded Group—made up of most developing nations plus China—in protocol negotiations and at World Trade Organization meetings. Two of the most important issues debated at these meetings have been whether a country has a right to know what it is importing, and whether a government has a right to refuse an import it believes endangers its population. As drafted, the Biosafety Protocol now states that nations have such rights. The next step is ratification by at least 50 nations and ensuring that the WTO or other international bodies cannot overrule the protocol.

In April Tewolde spoke with *Sierra* about his ongoing fight on behalf of the environment and the poor, and how it feels to butt heads with a superpower.

Sierra: Biotechnology proponents argue that biotech crops that resist pests and increase yields provide a solution to grave problems such as hunger and malnutrition. How do you respond?

Tewolde: First, to my knowledge there has not been one commercially grown transgenic crop that out-yields all other varieties of that crop. Genetic engineering
may live up to this promise, but we will have to see. What the transgenic crops
have done so far is tie the farmer to specific chemicals and a specific company.

That said, this notion that genetically engineered crops will save developing
countries misses the real point. The world has never grown as much food per
capita as it is doing now, yet the world has also never had as many hungry. The
problem is not the amount of food produced, but how it is both produced and
distributed. For example, farmers in developing countries who buy genetically
engineered seeds that cannot reproduce—and so can't be saved and used for
next year's crop—become tied to transnational companies like Monsanto.

As it stands, the political and economic problems within our developing countries prevent us from using existing technologies that are under our control. For
example, in 1981, the Lonrho Company was allowed to freely plant trees in
Swaziland while the people had to get a special permit to plant any tree. And it
continues to be the case that in many countries of the South, individual landowners keep big tracts of land uncultivated while many hungry citizens cannot
grow food because of lack of land.

How much more difficult is it going to be to use technology that is controlled
from another country? Let me give an example: Ethiopia just had a war with
Eritrea that provoked a trade embargo. I'm not complaining about the embargo;
I wish we had never made any war. But suppose we had become dependent on
some crop variety from the United States, Japan, or Kenya? What if, during this
political fracas, our trading partners had said, "No more seed"? What then?

The biotech industry is suggesting that food security will come through the
farmer's loss of control of essential agricultural inputs. Do you see the lie? This
is food insecurity. Even if genetic engineering managed to double, triple, or
quadruple food production, it would still remain an irrelevance. Genetic engineering can't help here, unless we can engineer people who can think straight
and be decent.

I don't trust the government. I don't mean particularly the Ethiopian government—I mean any government. Without local control, local availability of food
can never be certain. It would be far better to develop a system that would enable
the farmer himself to be in charge. I know it sounds remote in the United States
to think of a breakdown of law and order, but in Africa there are many politically
unstable countries. If every time there was a breakdown of law and order, the
system of food production were to suffer, it could mean death to millions.

Sierra: It sounds almost as though you see genetic engineering as the seed of something evil.

Tewolde: It's not the nature of genetic engineering itself that's the problem; it is the way genetic engineering has evolved. Early on, it came under the control of the private sector and is now being developed almost solely by that sector. By definition, the private sector's goal is to make money. It will not focus its attention on the needs of the poor, except as a way to sell its products.

Sierra: Beyond the political and economic issue of who controls the products of biotechnology, do you see any other threats to the South?

Tewolde: Let me begin by stressing that the threat is not only to the South; it is to life as a whole. The major threat is that we are combining genes that have not previously been combined. We are creating new traits and we simply don't know what could happen. We must be careful not to make major mistakes.

There are, however, some threats that are more specifically amplified in the South, arising from three factors. One is that there is a lot more biodiversity toward the equator, which means that the variables and possible complications increase. The second factor has to do with the ambient temperature: In the tropics, the temperature outside is nearer to the temperature of containment in laboratories. This means that those transgenic organisms that accidentally escape to the open environment have a greater chance of survival. The third factor relates to genetic engineering's current emphasis on crops. The gene pool of most of these modified crops exists in unadulterated form in tropical and sub-tropical areas. Take barley, for example. Ethiopia has the largest gene pool for cultivated barley anywhere in the world. Canada grows barley, but there is no native barley there. Should a genetically engineered variety go wrong and escape into the environment, Canada can start over again and develop a new variety—forgetting about all the varieties it has contaminated and destroyed. But if that were to happen in Ethiopia, the native gene pool—including wild relatives of crop plants—could be polluted. Such mistakes could never be undone.

There is an additional element that is not biological in nature. Economically, the countries closer to the equator are much poorer than the industrialized countries, and therefore lack the resources to deal with these sorts of mistakes.

Sierra: How did you first get involved in issues relating to biotechnology?

Tewolde: In the 1980s I was president of a university and also in charge of a few research projects. In 1989, I started leading a project to identify environmental problems and to suggest strategies to try to harmonize environment and development in Ethiopia. Around this time, the Rio Conference was gearing up, so I became involved in negotiating the proposed text of the 1992 biodiversity convention. Then, at the Earth Summit, two other issues came to the fore that really helped galvanize my thinking.

The first was the insistence of the U.S. delegation on intellectual property rights, while refusing to see that communities—indigenous communities that are not well versed in biological theory—have rights that must be respected as well. The second had to do with the U.S. delegation's insistence that genetic engineering is the same as any old sexual reproduction, and therefore did not need to be regulated. This came to be known as "substantial equivalence," in which sexual reproduction—where a man and a woman meet, mate, and their genes mix—is essentially the same as mixing genes from a tobacco plant and a firefly.

I opposed this idea of substantial equivalence. There was a lot of arguing about this in the convention negotiations. Finally, it was agreed that the parties would examine *if* there were a need for a protocol on safety in modern biotechnology. That's where we had to start, because opposition to regulation was so fierce. Most nations wanted a biosafety protocol, but a few powerful nations were totally opposed. I was part of the group that wrote what was called a majority report, saying that there was a need for a protocol. The minority report, that of the U.S. delegation, essentially said there was no need at all. Many of its delegates even used the argument that the majority report came from developing countries whose science is dubious. Fortunately, we had U.S. scientists from various universities testify that there *is* a risk.

Sierra: It's difficult to imagine that the U.S. delegation would challenge your science in such a way.

Tewolde: But that's the usual argument! The delegates don't say it in the meetings. Most of these negotiations happen in the corridors anyway. You lobby some delegation and say "You know what? So and so was saying that the other side's data is rubbish." It's standard negotiating practice.

Even so, after we presented the majority group report, our battle was won. At that point, the ad hoc working group said that there should be a protocol, and the next phase of the negotiations began.

Sierra: Because the U.S. Congress in the end refused to ratify the Rio Convention on Biological Diversity, it now has only "observer status" in negotiations on how to implement the protocol, correct?

Tewolde: That's right. However, the United States does claim to support the convention. So presumably the United States would continue to be supportive of the protocol as well—but for practical reasons now: If its laws on genetic engineering do not conform to the protocol, countries will refuse to trade with it in genetically modified organisms.

When the protocol comes into force, the first issue it will handle is the labeling of all genetically modified organisms. At the moment, all the document says is that if a country is exporting genetically modified organisms, it must say "it may contain," which is not very informative. That was a point on which the protocol negotiations nearly collapsed at the Montreal meeting in January 2000. The degree of labeling is an issue that is still unresolved.

Sierra: Some observers have noted that even with the Biosafety Protocol in place, refusing genetically modified imports will be significantly more difficult for developing countries because they have much more to lose in financial aid and other arrangements. What are the costs for a country like Ethiopia in saying no to these types of imports?

Tewolde: If the United States were to disregard the Biosafety Protocol and intimidate poor countries into accepting genetically modified organisms, quite a few of them would probably accept. But one expects that a respectable government, such as the one in the United States, will honor laws—even if they are not their laws.

This will sort itself out. In the transition period though, products that wouldn't sell in Europe or Japan will probably be pushed on us. Especially with regard to food aid, I expect this is already happening. Obviously, it is an extremely difficult situation if you know people are dying from lack of food and the only food you are offered is genetically engineered. [*According to the U.S.-based Institute for Food and Development Policy, more than 2 million tons of genetically modified organisms are sent directly by U.S. foreign assistance to developing countries each year, while the World Food Program distributes another 1.5 million tons of transgenic crops donated by the U.S. government. The food is typically sent with no labeling. —Sierra Ed.*]

Sierra: The Like-Minded Group, which you represent in international negotiations, has championed the "precautionary principle" as a way to address issues of biosafety. How would you define this principle?

Tewolde: The simplest way to state it is that you must evaluate risks before you take them. That does not mean "do not take any risks at all," though this is very often what people who want to distort its meaning suggest. It means, rather, that if you must take a risk in the absence of knowledge you should err on the side of caution and say, "until I know, I won't do this."

Sierra: How do you respond to critics who say the precautionary approach is little more than technophobia?

Tewolde: I'm not saying that there are not people who use it in that way. But, as a scientist, I take it to mean that if I am making a decision I should not make one from a position of "not knowing." In our daily lives, most of us operate from this perspective. If you want to jump into a pool, for example, you first estimate how deep it is so that you don't break your neck. You always observe and evaluate before you take that fateful step. That, in essence, is the precautionary principle.

Sierra: It sounds like a good idea. Why is it so difficult to adhere to at the global level?

Tewolde: At the global level, the principle is invoked to protect society, not the individual. Society and the individual are not necessarily the same. Often, the individual—and here I include corporations—has to be tamed to make society possible. That's why we have the law. One problem with the present push toward globalization is that it is focused only on the rights of the individual or the state—both of which are capable of somewhat capricious actions. I hope you will pardon me, but I'd also add that the more influential governments are now really largely run by individuals who represent corporate interests. I think genetic engineering is really going wild because it is not controlled by society but by selfish individual interests.

Sierra: That was actually my next question—what you thought the preeminent motives driving the U.S. delegation have been.

Tewolde: I'm glad you asked, because I was a bit apprehensive to talk about what I see as the corporate control of government. When I am in negotiations with the United States, Canada, and Australia, though, corporate control is clear.

Sierra: You're suggesting that in these negotiations you're essentially dealing with a multinational corporation rather than a government?

Tewolde: No. It is a government but corporate interest is top on its agenda. Given the arguments put forward by these governments, this conclusion is the only one that makes sense. I know the individuals who are making these arguments. They have deep scientific knowledge. But then they argue that genetic engineering and sexual reproduction are essentially the same. The only explanation I have is that they don't want to regulate genetic engineering. And, if they don't want to regulate genetic engineering, one must ask why. Who benefits?

Sierra: How has it been for you to go up against the United States in negotiations?

Tewolde: If you mean do I get intimidated, I don't. I have nothing vested that I have to protect. I have only my conscience to negotiate with. I have been insulted. I have been threatened. I just shrug my shoulders. It doesn't matter. Let me be clear here, though: I'm not referring to the negotiators. I have never had any negative reaction from the negotiators, American or otherwise. I am refer- ring to corporate representatives who come into those meetings. They come as observers and we meet and interact informally. They don't negotiate, though sometimes governments name people from various corporations as members of their delegations.

Sierra: What role has public opposition to genetic engineering played in these high-level negotiations?

Tewolde: Public opinion has played a most critical role in the negotiations on biosafety. In 1999, in Cartagena, Colombia, the group led by the United States refused outright to consider any form of regulations of commodities that are genetically modified. The next move by this group was the United States and Canada tried to introduce the issue about genetically modified commodity regulation into the WTO negotiations in Seattle in December 1999. But, as you know, public opposition and opposition from within by developing countries forced that effort to collapse. It was only because that happened in Seattle that the negotiations in Montreal last year succeeded. The U.S. group felt it had to back down on most of the issues.

Sierra: Whose voice will ultimately prevail on this issue?

Tewolde: The people's voice. If the people are convinced it is important, they will refuse to buy corporate products that have been genetically engineered. If corporations want a market, then they will have to go along with what the public requests.

Reprinted with permission from the July/August 2001 issue of SIERRA magazine.

GM Food Is the Best Option We Have

by Anthony J. Trewavas

Anthony Trewavas is a professor at the Institute of Cell and Molecular Biology at the University of Edinburgh in Scotland. He earned a Ph.D. in biochemistry from University College, London, in 1964 and was a postdoctoral fellow in the School of Biological Sciences at the University of East Anglia from 1964 to 1970. He joined the University of Edinburgh in 1970, where he has taught and done research for thirty years.

Trewavas is known as a defender of biotechnology and GM food in England, where it is not easy to champion such a view. In this essay, Trewavas argues that the GM golden rice is a wonderful opportunity to help the poor of the world and that we must embrace scientific advances in plant technology, not fear them. Citing several examples, he dismisses fears about "superweeds" and "frankensteinfood" and he argues that GM plants hold the key to a better agricultural future for everyone.

While Trewavas does "share in the general distrust of GM commercialization," he says if that is the problem, "change the economics, don't demean the knowledge," associated with GM technology. The introduction to this section (p. 181) provides the reasons for Earth Ministry's opposition to GM food.

∞

I have been a plant biologist for 40 years. What drew me to the subject was love of the organism. All those that deal with plants will know this feeling of pleasure and peace that comes from contact. We use plants in many different ways; for food, clothes, timber, cooking and drugs and to beautify our environment. To improve these uses for human benefit we must first gain better understanding of the way such complex organisms work. My respect has grown the more I have come to understand the beautiful and intricate way in which plants function. Our role on this planet is to act the good gardener. Like all such gardeners or stewards we seek to provide a planetary garden which survives in harmony with itself. But this garden can only be in harmony when all our fellow men and women, the other stewards of this planet, can enjoy a complete and fulfilling life enabling the full flowering of the potential in all of us.

There are some people in this country [United Kingdom] that stereotype scientists without ever knowing any of them; that ascribe ulterior motives to scientific endeavour and surround themselves with acolytes of similar limited experience. These people commonly rate the wisdom of nature as superior to human ingenuity and survival.

But we investigate nature so that we can stop the natural things that destroy our lives and curtail our stewardship. I am talking about natural things like child death, leprosy, disease-ridden water, starvation or floods that are clearly part of nature and nature's wisdom. Human ingenuity, which our opponents cast so easily aside, has given us antibiotics, anaesthetics and warm houses to prolong and protect life, security of food supply, transport to places so that we can share in the pride and glory of human achievements in arts, music and architecture; and has even taken us to the moon. All these ingenuities derive from knowledge of the world in which we live and result from experimentation and improvement of nature, the "good gardening" which opponents denigrate. There is a desire by some to reverse history, to recover some mythical golden age when life expectancy was under half what it is now; when people died needlessly and painfully from a variety of unknown causes (some most certainly from diseases in their poor quality food) and when, for example in the UK, half the young men called up for the Boer war were refused on the grounds of serious underweight, height and poor health identified as resulting from malnourishment. When problems develop we must continue to rise to the challenge to tackle them as we have done in the past with nobility and intellect. Do not listen to the siren voices that say "stop the world I want to get off." There are many such voices in the UK at present.

A decade ago, as a university plant biologist, I thought that genetic manipulation, GM, would be publicly funded and used for the benefit of mankind. Indeed I share in the general distrust of GM commercialisation and I know this is a major complication in the UK. But this is the world we live in; if you don't like it, change the economics, don't demean the knowledge. We can't eliminate knowledge simply because someone makes a profit out of it.

Two recent reports of publicly funded, university GM research now indicate its true potential. US scientists in collaboration with Japanese workers have genetically improved (GM) rice to increase seed yield of each plant by 35%. Why is this important?

One of the most certain facts about the human population is that it is increasing. By 2025 there will be 2.3 billion extra souls on mother earth, 50 times the current population of the UK, and they will have to be fed. Our current numbers of some six billion have already placed dangerous burdens on the ecosystems of spaceship earth and threaten our biodiversity on which we are all interdependent. Global warming may indeed be global warning. So ploughing up wilderness to feed these extra people is no option. We can also eliminate organic farming as a meaningful solution. Organic farmers rely ultimately and only on soil nitrogen fixation to provide the essential nitrate and ammonia for crop growth and yield. Rainwater provides the other minerals. Since the maximum yields of fixed nitrogen have been measured numerous times we can estimate that by taking another 750 million ha [1 hectare = 10,000 sq. meters or 2.471 acres—Ed.] of wilderness under the plough we could feed just three billion. When Greenpeace tells us to "go organic" I ask myself which three billion will live and which three billion will die; perhaps they can enlighten us when they have finished tangling with the courts.

Clever plant breeding in the early 60's produced rice and wheat plants with well over double their previous yield; such progress enabled a parallel doubling of mankind, without massive starvation. But this option is now exhausted. Ignoring the problem, leaving billions to starve in misery, the worst of all tortures according to Amnesty International, is not an option either. "Every man's death diminishes me because I am part of mankind; ask not for whom the bell tolls..." is a philosophy I know many here will share with John Donne. So where one grain grew before, we now again have to ensure that two will grow in the future. Currently GM is our best option to achieve this difficult task. This first report is very encouraging.

Critics say to me there is enough food to feed the world and they may well be right, at present. We produce sufficient to feed 6.4 billion people but the excess is largely in the West, and it is far easier for scientists to conjure more food from the plants we grow than to persuade the West to share its agricultural bounty with its poorer neighbors. But the excess will not last long; our population increases by 1.3% a year, current annual cereal increases are only 1.1%. We live on the residual excess produced by the green revolution. At some point catastrophe beckons.

Our second report deals with a problem that kills one million young children in the third world every year and leaves many millions permanently blind. For a variety of reasons, babies can be prematurely weaned off breast milk. It's not a problem in the West, a variety of other foods and milk is available. But in the backwoods of the Far East, the usual option is rice gruel. Rice however contains no vitamin A and such babies rapidly become deficient. Either eye development is permanently damaged (we all need vitamin A for sight), or they succumb to childhood diseases that any western baby shrugs off in a week. Scientists in a Swiss university in a "tour de force" have genetically improved rice to make vitamin A. This golden rice has been given to the International Rice Institute in the Philippines for distribution to help ameliorate this serious problem and ensure a better life for parents and children....

But these are foreign examples; global warming is the problem that requires the UK to develop GM technology. 1998 was the warmest year in the last one thousand years. Many think global warming will simply lead to a wetter climate and be benign. I do not. Excess rainfall in northern seas has been predicted to halt the Gulf Stream. In this situation, average UK temperatures would fall by 5 degrees centigrade and give us Moscow-like winters. There are already worrying signs of salinity changes in the deep oceans. Agriculture would be seriously damaged and necessitate the rapid development of new crop varieties to secure our food supply. We would not have much warning. Recent detailed analysis of arctic ice cores has shown that the climate can switch between stable states in fractions of a decade. Even if the climate is only wetter and warmer, new crop pests and rampant disease will be the consequence. GM technology can enable new crops to be constructed in months and to be in the fields within a few years. This is the unique benefit GM offers. The UK populace needs to be much more positive about GM or we may pay a very heavy price.

In 535 A.D. a volcano near the present Krakatoa exploded with the force of 200 million Hiroshima A bombs. The dense cloud of dust so reduced the intensity of the sun that for at least two years thereafter, summer turned to winter and crops here and elsewhere in the Northern hemisphere failed completely. The population survived by hunting a rapidly vanishing population of edible animals. The after-effects continued for a decade and human history was changed irreversibly. But the planet recovered. Such examples of benign nature's wisdom, in full flood as it were, dwarf and make minuscule the tiny modifications we make upon our environment. There are apparently 100 such volcanoes around the world that could at any time unleash forces as great. And even smaller volcanic explosions change our climate and can easily threaten the security of our food supply. Our hold on this planet is tenuous. In the present day an equivalent 535 A.D. explosion would destroy much of our civilisation. Only those with agricultural technology sufficiently advanced would have a chance at survival. Colliding asteroids are another problem that requires us to be forward-looking, accepting that technological advance may be the only buffer between us and annihilation.

When people say to me they do not need GM, I am astonished at their pre-science, their ability to read a benign future in a crystal ball that I cannot. Now is the time to experiment; not when a holocaust is upon us and it is too late. GM is a technology whose time has come and just in the nick of time. With each billion that mankind has added to the planet have come technological advances to increase food supply. In the 18th century, the start of agricultural mechanisation; in the 19th century, knowledge of crop mineral requirements, the eventual Haber Bosch process for nitrogen reduction. In the 20th century, plant genetics and breeding, and later the green revolution. Each time population growth has been sustained without enormous loss of life through starvation even though crisis often beckoned. For the 21st century, genetic manipulation is our primary hope to maintain developing and complex technological civilisations. When the climate is changing in unpredictable ways, diversity in agricultural technology is a strength and a necessity not a luxury. Diversity helps secure our food supply. We have heard much of the precautionary principle in recent years; my version of it is "be prepared."

But how do these examples compare with the scepticism shown by the UK public over GM food; doesn't it harm human health? What about those apocalyptic visions of damage to the environment propounded by green organisations? If these views had any real substance I would share them, but they are totally contrary to all experience.

The testing of GM food is exemplary in its detail and takes at least four years. Sir John Krebs, head of our new Food Standards Agency, concluded that GM food is as safe as its non-GM counterpart. If eating foreign DNA and protein is dangerous we have been doing so for all of our lives with no apparent effects. Each GM food will be considered by regulatory authorities on its own merit.

As for GM environmental effects, many countries provide us with details of reduced use of herbicides and pesticides of 15-100%, of increased crop yields, less insect damage, a return of non-target insects to fields and reductions in fungal toxins in food. Even the flurry over the Monarch butterfly has been capped by record numbers on migration last year. Over 20 laboratories have now shown the original Monarch fears were groundless. Within five years, vaccines against the killer E. coli, hepatitis B, cholera and other diseases will all come in GM food. Even now they are in human trials. These vaccines will be very stable, be easily distributed world-wide, need no refrigeration or injection, merely consumption. The great campaign to eliminate world-wide disease, as we have with smallpox, will be well under way. Apocalypse now? Hardly.

Many of you may think that environmentalists are synonymous with ecologists. You would be mistaken. Let me read out for you extracts from what has become known as the Aachen declaration made by a large number of ecologists.

"Today's campaign against gene technology has no base in ecologically sound science. In the case of gene technology there is substantial evidence for positive environmental effects with decreased pesticide use and healthier food. The campaign neglects the beneficial effects of these plants for the environment. Unfortunately many environmental activists have chosen to publicise only potential adverse effects of GM crops during their campaign, natural phenomena like gene transfer or pollen movement between organisms are declared as a phenomenon related only to GM crops although this happens throughout nature." Patrick Moore, a founding member of Greenpeace, has said the present Greenpeace campaign is junk science and pagan myth.

We have in recent years been treated to flag wavers like "superweeds," "genie out of the bottle" and "frankenstein food"; statements as empty of meaning and content as those who mouth them. Superweeds are merely herbicide resistant weeds. There are over 100 weeds world-wide with resistance to some 15 different herbicides. There are even four crops with natural herbicide resistance from conventional breeding. These include rapeseed oil and are used by farmers.

If you sow a rape crop with natural herbicide resistance, only marginal regulations apply and the crop could be grown alongside an organic farm without objection. The herbicide resistant genes would spread to surrounding weedy relatives by so-called gene flow, although as we now know at a very low rate. Furthermore pollen from this crop could be spread by bees up to a kilometre away although it would probably not be viable at this distance. The chances of such pollen successfully competing with local sources and producing seed would be extremely remote. Perhaps more important there would be no objections from green organisations.

However in one case this natural herbicide resistant gene has been isolated and inserted back into rapeseed oil by GM. Planting this GM crop necessitates satisfying 50 pages of regulations, four years of safety tests, 3-4 committees for approval with detailed examination and at the end of the day the likelihood of getting your crop trampled by unthinking activists. You would also get objections from organic farmers miles in every direction. Yet the spread of resistance genes to weedy relatives would be identical between the two crops and spraying both fields with herbicide would lead to identical ecological effects. Common sense is called for here, and there is certainly a lack of common sense in current attitudes with supposed contamination by GM.

If rape is removed from the field, the herbicide resistance gene in feral weedy relatives would disappear within a few years. If the cultivated field is left fallow, both GM and non-GM rapes would disappear within a few years. Like any other crop plant, domesticated rape cannot compete with weeds. The genes we put into crops are for our benefit and not for survival in the wild. Crops last no longer than a domesticated chiuhuahua would last in the company of wolves. Populations of weeds are a sea of natural mutant variants. I am unable to think of any gene they could acquire from our efforts that would improve their weediness. Certainly in ten thousand years of plant breeding and gene flow into weedy relatives none has ever been discovered....

The main goal we are told by GM opponents is to "go organic." Was this a thought-through policy or made up on the hoof? It is quite clear to me it was the latter.

Experts tell us that cancers that occur under the age of 65 are avoidable. Thirty percent of these cancers are thought to result from poor diet. Over 200 detailed investigations have shown that a diet high in fruit and vegetables cuts all cancer rates by at least half. But only 10% of us eat the recommended fruit and vegetable requirements. Increasing the price of these essential foods will reduce consumption, particularly in the poorest families for which the food bill is a much higher proportion of their weekly wage. The consequence, higher avoidable cancer rates, premature death and soaring health bills. Organic food, whatever its supposed environmental merits (and incidentally these merits are shared by many conventional farms), is less efficient and more wasteful of land. For a variety of reasons it comes at a much higher price and will continue to do so. Any attempt to "go organic," to thus increase the price of fruit and vegetables and thereby reduce consumption, will have the consequences on cancer and death I have listed above. Let us hope it is not your child. My fear is that unsubstantiated claims and incorrect assumptions about organic food will lead those who strive upwards on weak incomes to buy organic but eat less fruit and vegetables because of the expense. The only justification left for buying organic food is that farmers apply less pesticide in its production. But that is precisely what the current GM crops offer us but at conventional food prices or even lower! Whose food is the real benefit now?

I am often asked what do I want to see in agriculture. Variety is probably the spice of stability. My own preference is for Integrated Crop Management (ICM), a sustainable but efficient technology organised in the UK by LEAF and CWS farming systems among others. ICM requires the farmer to use his intelligence while delivering on the so-called environmentally friendly front. In fact ICM with its emphasis on crop rotation, integrated pest management, zero tillage and precisely timed manure and mineral application is nicely placed between two extremes. The organic farmer who does what he is told by the Soil Association (something I tell students is best described as authoritarian farming), and the conventional farmer who merely does what he is told on the instruction leaflets by companies. As for many of our students with lecture information, the instructions and rules pass through, without stopping in the brains of either. The goal must be to train the farmer to view his farm as an ecosystem and then leave it to the individual and his particular circumstance to construct his own farming system. Advantageously a variety of agricultural styles would result which should improve the stability of food supply in the uncertain years ahead.

Reprinted by permission of the author. Excerpted from *The Ethics of Food: A Reader for the Twenty-First Century* by Gregory E. Pence, editor.

Addressing Hunger: Political and Economic Perspectives

Hunger is a social disease linked to poverty, and thus any discussion of hunger is incomplete without a discussion of economics....People are hungry because they are too poor to buy food. There is a shortage of purchasing power, not a shortage of food.

—*Anuradha Mittal*

Introduction

Hunger—"830 million people worldwide without adequate access to food"—is a distant reality for most of us. But it is a shocking reality. For many years people of faith have responded by both feeding the hungry and seeking to address hunger's systemic causes. The interview with Anuradha Mittal points to poverty as perhaps the most important cause of hunger. As my colleague at Earth Ministry says, "Do you know any rich, hungry people?" Mittal describes the pressure developing countries face to service their debt. In order to do so, they often must grow crops for export rather than food for their own people. She points out the hypocrisy of transnational corporations using hunger to promote biotechnology. While acknowledging that the Green Revolution increased food production, she disputes the claim that it reduced hunger. In the final reading, George McGovern discusses the monetary costs involved in eradicating hunger. His is a positive message because he believes that, with the political and financial backing of the world's wealthier nations, ending hunger is a genuine possibility.

On the True Cause of World Hunger: An Interview with Anuradha Mittal

by Derrick Jensen

Trained as a political scientist, Anuradha Mittal has extensive experience in food-related activism in the U.S. and in the Third World. She's editor of two books, *America Needs Human Rights* and *The Future in the Balance: Essays on Globalization and Resistance* (both Food First Books). She has also written numerous articles on global trade and human rights for the *Wall Street Journal*, the *New York Times*, the *Washington Post* and other publications. Prior to coming to the U.S. in 1994, she worked with the Society for Participatory Research in Asia on issues of people's access to land and natural resources. She is interviewed here by journalist Derrick Jensen.

∞

Food First (www.foodfirst.org) was started more than twenty-five years ago by Joseph Collins and Frances Moore Lappé, author of *Diet for a Small Planet*. Designed to be a people's think tank—more than half of its funding comes from individual donors—the organization seeks to establish access to food as a basic human right.

By now, we're all familiar with the images of hungry people in Ethiopia, Somalia, India, Bangladesh. But how has it come to pass that so many people are without food? Is it because there simply is not enough food to go around? Food First works to answer these questions, educating the public about the root causes of hunger and debunking the myths put forward by corporations and the governments that serve them.

Mittal, a native of India, once believed those myths. "When I was a little girl," she says, "I was taught in school that India had become independent through a long struggle, and that if we wanted to maintain our independence, the country had to move forward with development: building dams, investing in high technology. I remember how, before movies, we'd see a newsreel about the prime minister christening a new dam, after which they'd play the national anthem. I would get tears in my eyes."

When she went to college at the University of Delhi and became involved in student activism, she realized that she hadn't been taught the whole truth: "The dams were actually death centers that displaced millions from their land with no restitution, and those in power didn't care about the thousands of people they dispossessed or killed. I suddenly realized that human beings have a great capacity for making decisions that intentionally starve others. I wanted to know why." Mittal set out to reeducate herself.

As Mittal is quick to point out, the problem of hunger is not restricted to India and other Third World nations. "The forces that are oppressing and colonizing people overseas," she says, "are the same forces that are oppressing working Americans in this country."

Jensen: What is the scope of world hunger?

Mittal: The United Nations estimates that around 830 million people in the world do not have adequate access to food. Numbers, though, distance us from the real pain felt by the hungry. Hunger is a form of torture that takes away your ability to think, to perform normal physical actions, to be a rational human being. There are people in my own country, India, who for months have not had a full stomach, who have never had adequate nutrition. This sort of hunger causes some to resort to eating anything to numb the pain: cats, monkeys, even poisonous roots.

When we think about hunger, we often picture dark brown faces, black faces, naked children with thin legs and bloated stomachs. This is the image of hunger the media have given us, but it is crucial to remember that hunger exists not only in Asia, Africa, and Latin America, but right here in the United States, the richest nation on earth. Thirty-six million Americans do not have enough to eat, and that number is growing. Nearly half of those lining up outside soup kitchens have one or more family members employed, but most of them are simply too poor to buy food. They are the people who scavenge in dumpsters outside restaurants. They're the schoolchildren who cannot pay attention in class because they did not have dinner or breakfast. They're people like Katherine Engels, a grandmother who testified at a Congressional hearing on hunger that she often drinks a cup of tea for dinner, then rolls up some white bread and eats it, because that gives her the sense that her stomach is full.

Hunger is a social disease linked to poverty, and thus any discussion of hunger is incomplete without a discussion of economics. Often, when we see a person asking for money for food, we think, *Why don't you get a job?* How many of us realize that, of the people removed from the welfare rolls by welfare reform in 1996, only one out of ninety-seven will ever get a job that pays a living wage? At the minimum wage of $5.15 per hour, even if you work fifty hours a week, you earn little more than $13,000 dollars per year. There's no way a family living in a city could survive on that. They couldn't pay rent *and* put food on the table, to say nothing of clothes and other necessities.

If we're going to speak meaningfully about hunger, we need to understand the true causes of hunger. For example, hunger is not caused by shortage of food. According to our research over the last twenty-six years at Food First, the world's farmers produce 4.3 pounds of food per person, per day. This includes vegetables, cereals, fish, meat, and grains.

Jensen: If there is enough food, then why is there hunger?

Mittal: People are hungry because they are too poor to buy food. There is a shortage of purchasing power, not a shortage of food.

Of the 830 million hungry people worldwide, a third of them live in India. Yet in 1999, the Indian government had 10 million tons of surplus food grains: rice, wheat, and so on. In the year 2000, that surplus increased to almost 60 million tons—most of it left in the granaries to rot. Instead of giving the surplus food to the hungry, the Indian government was hoping to export the grain to make money. It also stopped buying grain from its own farmers, leaving them destitute. The farmers, who had gone into debt to purchase expensive chemical fertilizers and pesticides on the advice of the government, were now forced to burn their crops in their fields.

At the same time, the government of India was buying grain from Cargill and other American corporations, because the aid India receives from the World Bank stipulates that the government must do so. This means that today India is the largest importer of the same grain it exports. It doesn't make sense—economic or otherwise.

This situation is not unique to India. In 1985, Indonesia received the gold medal from the UN Food and Agriculture Organization for achieving food self-sufficiency. Yet by 1998, it had become the largest recipient of food aid in the world. I participated in a fact-finding mission to investigate Indonesia's reversal of fortune. Had the rains stopped? Were there no more crops in Indonesia? No, the cause of the food insecurity in Indonesia was the Asian financial crisis. Banks and industries were closing down. In the capital of Jakarta alone, fifteen thousand people lost their jobs in just one day. Then, as I traveled to rural areas, I saw rice plants dancing in field after field, and I saw casava and all kinds of fruits. There was no shortage of food, but the people were too poor to buy it. So what did the U.S. and other countries, like Australia, do? Smelling an opportunity to unload their own surplus wheat in the name of "food aid," they gave loans to Indonesia upon the condition that it buy wheat from them. And Indonesians don't even eat wheat.

Jensen: In some South American countries, the governments grow and export coffee while their citizens starve. Have India and Indonesia begun converting agricultural lands to growing cash crops for export?

Mittal: Yes, as in other developing countries, we have seen an emphasis on export agriculture. Around three-quarters of the countries that report child malnutrition are exporting food. Remember the much-publicized famine in Ethiopia during the 1980s? Many of us don't realize that, during that famine, Ethiopia was exporting green beans to Europe.

In 1999, a UN Population Fund report predicted that India would soon become one of the world's largest recipients of food aid. The report went on to blame the increasing population for the problem. What it did not mention is that the state of Punjab, also known as "the granary of India," grows abundant food even today, but most of it is being converted into dog and cat food for Europe. Nor did the report mention that the neighboring state of Haryana, also traditionally a fertile agricultural state, is today one of the world leaders in growing tulips for export. Increasingly, countries like India are polluting their air, earth, and water to grow products for the Western market instead of growing food to feed their own people. Prime agricultural lands are being poisoned to meet the needs of the consumers in the West, and the money the consumers spend does not reach the majority of the working poor in the Third World.

Jensen: I'm not sure it's Westerners' *needs* that are being met. More like their desires.

Mittal: Yes, luxuries are being construed as necessities, and freedom has come to mean the ability to choose from twenty different brands of toothpaste.

Jensen: You've mentioned U.S. aid a few times. What's wrong with U.S. aid? I mean, isn't it commendable that we're willing to help out?

Mittal: I hear that a lot. I've been on radio talk shows where people have called in to accuse me of being arrogant and ungrateful: "Here we are, sending your people food aid, and you just complain!" I wish it were true that U.S. aid came from a generosity of spirit, but it has always been a political tool used to control the behavior of Third World countries, to forge dubious alliances, and to buy cooperation during the Cold War. With the end of the Cold War, aid turned into a scheme for finding new markets for U.S. agribusiness, and now for dumping foods containing genetically modified organisms (GMOs), which are being rejected by consumers in the West because we know so little about their long-term effects on humans and the environment.

But the deeper issue here has to do with the fact that food aid is not usually free. It is often loaned, albeit at a low interest rate. When the U.S. sent wheat to Indonesia during the 1999 crisis, it was a loan to be paid back over a twenty-five-year period. In this manner, food aid has helped the U.S. take over grain markets in India, Nigeria, Korea, and elsewhere.

I don't entirely reject the notion of food aid. Although I think that most countries can be food self-sufficient, there might be a few that need assistance. But aid has to follow certain principles. First, the food should be delivered when the people need it: i.e., right away. Second, it should not be used as a political tool, as in North Korea, where famine was allowed to bring the country to its knees before food assistance was provided. Third, the food should be procured locally or regionally, insofar as possible. And fourth, it should be culturally sensitive: the aid should consist of food that the people actually eat, and not just what a donor country wants to dump....

Jensen: You mentioned GMOs. How does biotechnology fit into all of this?...

Mittal: I am deeply disturbed by the way hunger has been used to promote biotechnology. Suddenly, transnational corporations like DuPont, Monsanto, Novartis, and Syngenta, which have already caused so much misery, are casting themselves as do-gooders. Monsanto gave us Agent Orange, yet it's presented by the U.S. government and the corporate media as a good corporate citizen, concerned for the poor and hungry in the Third World. The U.S. government is "combating hunger" by allocating money from development-assistance programs to promote biotechnology in the Third World. And the civic groups that are opposing the corporate takeover of our food system and challenging genetic engineering—because we do not know its environmental and health consequences—are portrayed as selfish people who want to deny the Third World the benefits of biotechnology.

For years, oil companies have used "greenwashing" as a public-relations strategy, professing environmental concern to cover up their environmentally destructive activities. The biotech corporations are now using "poorwashing": faking concern for the burgeoning, hungry population of the developing world while exploiting those populations in order to reap greater profits.

Jensen: Let's talk about the debt the Third World owes to the World Bank and industrialized nations. U.S.-foreign policy critic Noam Chomsky says, in essence, that the debt should be repaid, but it should be repaid by the people who actually received the loans, by which he means U.S.-imposed dictators, who siphoned off billions to their private bank accounts. But it should not be repaid by the citizens of the countries, who never got any of the money in the first place.

Mittal: But when the so-called aid has been given for, say, a large dam, who actually ended up with the money? It wasn't a dictator, but the German, French, or American corporation that built the dam. Its investors are the ones who got paid. And the people of the nation got a dam they neither wanted nor needed.

I've been involved in this struggle for a very long time. So much of it revolves around the notion of debt relief, which is just another version of the white man's burden. These backward people, the argument goes, just can't seem to figure out how to run their countries or their economies, and we need to keep perpetually giving them food and money.

But I'm not interested in debt relief. I'm interested in reparations. The Third World does not owe anyone anything. In fact, the industrialized nations owe *us* money.

Jensen: How so ?

Mittal: Take the case of my country, India—although any other country would provide just as good an example. Why did Columbus try to find a new route to India? Because it was a land of spices and wealth and gold, a country of grandeur. But when the Europeans came in—the East India Company, to be precise, which soon turned into the governing body for India and its people— my country saw the end of a golden age and the beginning of more than a hundred years of exploitation by the British. By the time India gained independence in 1947, this ancient civilization had become, at best, a "developing" country. There were many famines in India under British rule, in which millions died. And all the while, British India was being forced to export coffee, tea, rice, and wheat.

Jensen: Just like today.

Mittal: And famines and starvation continue. After India gained independence, the Western powers once again found a way to colonize the country, first through the World Bank, and now through what I call the "unholy trinity" of the World Bank, the International Monetary Fund, and the World Trade Organization. Third World countries were—and are—given bad loans, loans the people did not and do not want, loans about which we have never been consulted, loans for projects, such as large dams, that we protested and continue to protest....

In country after country, the money has been funneled through the puppet governments and returned to the Western transnationals, all on the bent backs of the poor. Meanwhile, the poor nations have been compelled to slash their health and education programs, privatize the service sector, and cut down on jobs traditionally filled by women. Nurses, primary teachers: who needs them? Get rid of them.

And why do we have to do this? Because we have to service a debt that did not make a damn bit of difference in the day-to-day lives of ordinary people, working-class people, middle-class people. If you calculate how much money was given as a loan and how much has flowed back out, you'll understand why I say that the colonization has continued. The extraction of resources from these countries has, if anything, increased. The flow is always toward the rich, industrialized nations. We have not only repaid the loans made to corrupt regimes; we have overpaid them. And that overpayment did not start in the 1950s. This extraction has gone on for centuries, through various forms of colonization. It's time to give people in the Third World their fair due. It's time for reparations *now*.

The philosophy behind demanding reparations is that it says we are no longer victims, but people demanding our basic human rights, which have been violated for too long. And it's about accountability. Increasingly, we are beginning to hear about accountability for Third World leaders, such as Chilean dictator Augusto Pinochet, who was almost put on trial in Spain. It's time for that sort of accountability to be brought to the Western governments for what they have done to other cultures—and to their own people. It is time to try the Kissingers and McNamaras of the U.S.

Jensen: Years ago, I asked a Tupac Amaru rebel what his group wanted for the people of Peru. His answer has haunted me ever since: "We want to be able to grow and distribute our own food. We already know how to do that. We merely need to be allowed to do so." In three sentences, he cut to the heart of colonialism, the heart of the problem we face.

Mittal: I couldn't agree more. Food is both personal and political. Food unites families and communities; across cultures, festivals based around harvest seasons are about sharing and strengthening communities. And food is political: The French Revolution wasn't driven just by the ideals of liberty, freedom, and egalitarianism. It was driven by the fact that there wasn't enough bread in Paris.

Jensen: They could always eat cake.

Mittal: Or, today, tulips.

Over the last three decades we have seen protests, rebellions, uprisings, and revolutions against this new colonialism, and these movements have often been centered around food. In the seventies, there were riots in Peru because the World Bank stipulated an increase in the price of bread. In the 1990s, the Zapatista uprising and the protests in Bolivia were spurred by food unavailability and privatization of the basic necessities of life. The same has been true in Pakistan and India. In 1995, villagers in Mexico stopped trains to loot them—not for gold, but for corn.

When we look at the growing discontent around the world, we find that many rebels have the same demand: the basic human right to be able to feed oneself. This is what the landless people's movement in Brazil wants, and the Poor People's Assembly in Thailand, and Jose Bove—the French farmer who drove his tractor through a McDonald's—and the farmers in India who burned the Cargill building and Monsanto's trial fields, and the small farmers in the U.S. These groups don't want power or wealth. They only want to be able to feed themselves and their families, and to live with dignity.

Jensen: Why is it so central to Western civilization—and, more recently, to capitalism—to colonize and dispossess other peoples?

Mittal: I, too, wonder about this all the time. Is it intentional? Is it human nature to colonize and wreak havoc upon the poor? One thing I do know when the rich are getting richer and the poor are getting poorer, these two things do not happen in a vacuum. The rich get richer at the expense of the poor. This mechanism is built into the capitalist system, around which our societies and our economies are organized. You know capitalism's "golden rule": whoever has the gold makes the rules. This system rewards greed and a complete lack of accountability on the part of CEOs, investors, and transnational corporations.

This is not a result of human nature. Nor is it something that just happens. It is a matter of power being exercised without any social, political, or environmental concerns. It is the planned exploitation of the poor on the part of those who stand to profit from it. And it is deeply ingrained in our society, because the powerful have built an entire economic and governmental structure to support it.

Jensen: It seems pretty clear that access to land is central to everything we're talking about. Deny people that access, and you deny them self-sufficiency. Deny them self-sufficiency, and you can force them to work in your factories.

Mittal: The elites make a big mistake when they dispossess the working poor. They seem to believe that further dispossession will kill the poor people's spirit. But dispossessed people are angry people. Think about the courage of the poor who continue to occupy the land that the rich have stolen from them, even in the face of severe repression by private armies and police forces and death squads. We call them the "landless," but they are the ones who have earth in the cracks of their heels and under their fingernails. Their smell is of the land, and their blood washes the land for which they are killed. Look at them and tell me who has a right to the land.

What sustains these communities in the face of repression is the fact that they have nothing more to lose. When you have been beaten, tortured, and have seen your loved ones killed, there's only one thing to do: fight back...

Jensen: A few years ago, a family farmer said to me, "Cargill gives me two choices: either I can cut my own throat, or they'll do it for me." The same could be said by farmers in any number of countries.

Mittal: In the south of India, you can go to village after village and not find a farmer who has both kidneys: they've all sold a kidney to feed their family. And there have been reports of farmers taking their own lives by consuming the same pesticides, the same poisons, they were told to use on their fields. They use this "gift" of industrial agriculture, which has cost them so much money and so much hope already, to end their own life.

In the U.S., farmers are killing themselves and trying to make it look like an accident so their families can get life insurance money. Forced out of their profession and unable to make a livelihood, they see no other way out.

At the World Food Summit in 1996, Dan Glickman, then the head of the USDA, claimed that U.S. farmers would feed the world. He did not tell the summit that in the last few census polls, the category of "farmer" as a profession has been removed. According to the U.S. Census Bureau, farmers are not endangered; they're extinct. When Glickman talks about farmers, he really means corporations such as Cargill and Archer Daniels Midland—self-styled "Supermarket to the World." (Or, as I call it, Super*markup* to the World.) They aren't U.S. farmers. They're agribusinesses.

Jensen: But aren't they the ones who brought us the Green Revolution, which improved agricultural yields and thus saved millions of lives?

Mittal: This is one of the big myths. When I mention that India has a grain surplus, people often say to me that the Green Revolution—which is based on the use of chemical fertilizers and pesticides—is responsible for that. But we need to examine this claim closely.

From 1970 to 1990, the two main decades of the Green Revolution, the total food available per person in the world rose by 11 percent. This much is true. At the same time, the estimated number of hungry people fell by more than 150 million. So you might think there's a correlation between the increase in food due to the Green Revolution and the decrease in hunger. But if you eliminate China from the analysis, the number of hungry people in the world actually *increased* by 60 million. And it was not population growth that made for more hungry people. Remember, the total food available per person increased everywhere. What created more hunger was the absence of land reform and living-wage jobs. The remarkable change in China, where the number of hungry people was more than cut in half, was the result of broad-based land reforms, which improved living standards. This is the little-known truth about the Green Revolution. Yes, food production increased, but did it have an impact on hunger? No...

Jensen: And there is currently an attempt to start a second Green Revolution based around GMOs.

Mittal: The same companies that benefited from the Green Revolution are now promoting genetic engineering. They recognize that the seed is the most important link in the food chain. Whoever controls the seed controls the food system. With genetic engineering, they can now patent the seeds. DuPont bought Pioneer Hybrid, a major seed company, for $8.5 billion; Monsanto has spent more than $7 billion on seed companies. The chemical companies are attempting to control the food system more than ever before.

This article originally appeared in *The Sun* Magazine, February 2002. Reprinted with permission of the author. Derrick Jensen is the author of A *Language Older than Words*, and most recently *The Culture of Make Believe*.

Hunger Is a Political Condition
by George McGovern

As a senator from South Dakota, George McGovern was the Democratic candidate for president of the United States in 1972. He earned a Ph.D. in history at Northwestern University and was elected to the U. S. House of Representatives in 1956. As a protégé of Sen. Hubert Humphrey, McGovern was appointed director of the Food for Peace Program by President Kennedy. He was elected to the Senate in 1962 and ran for President as an opponent of the Vietnam war.

His essay considers how much it would cost for the nations of the world to end hunger. Like Mittal, McGovern recognizes that addressing hunger is a political and economic issue and includes the need to improve education for girls and women (especially in the two-thirds world), wiser use of water and "improved farming methods." Unlike Mittal, McGovern sees the Green Revolution as a success in staving off hunger.

∞

Hunger is a political condition. The earth has enough knowledge and resources to eradicate this ancient scourge. Hunger has plagued the world for thousands of years. But ending it is a greater moral imperative now than ever before, because for the first time humanity has the instruments in hand to defeat this cruel enemy at a very reasonable cost. We have the ability to provide food for all within the next three decades. Consider just one encouraging statistic. When I ran for the presidency in 1972, 35 percent of the world's people were hungry. By 1996, while the global population had expanded, only 17 percent of the earth's people were hungry—half the percentage of three decades ago. This is an impressive fact, particularly in view of the gloomy prophecies of the 1960s that population growth was racing ahead of food production. Widespread famines across the Third World were also predicted. Clearly the gains in food production from scientific farming, including the Green Revolution, plus the slowing of population growth have reduced hunger in the developing countries.

Here are some other encouraging statistics: The world now produces a quantity of grain that, if distributed evenly, would provide everyone with 3,500 calories per day, more than enough for an optimal diet. This does not even count vegetables, fruits, fish, meat, poultry, edible oils, nuts, root crops, or dairy products. Despite the dire predictions that the world's population would soon outstrip food production, it has been the other way around: food production has risen a full 16 percent above population growth.

The American Association for the Advancement of Science has noted that 78 percent of the world's malnourished children live in countries with food surpluses. Clearly, this condition indicates a need for a keener social conscience and better political leadership.

A 1996 United Nations survey that is regarded as the most accurate forecast available estimated that world population will peak and then level off near the year 2050 at just under 10 billion—an increase of 4 billion over the present total. Population may then decline somewhat, because of lower birthrates. Such predictions are uncertain. It may be that advances in medicine and health care will enable people to live longer, thus offsetting declining birth rates Although a population of 10 billion will tax some resources, projected increases in food production indicate that the world can feed that many people a half-century from now...

Having grappled for years with the global hunger challenge and the American domestic condition, I am sure that we have the resources and the knowledge to end hunger everywhere. The big question is, do we have the political leadership and the will to end this scourge in our time?

One of my admired friends of long standing was the late Archbishop Dom Helder Camara of Brazil. He once observed: "When I give food to the poor, they call me a saint. When I ask why the poor have no food, they call me a communist." I learned much about the burdens and hurts of the poor from this good man. Following his example, I have tried...to ask the hard questions and then to seek the sometimes difficult answers...

Two questions need to be considered together in a treatise about world hunger: (1) What would it cost for the nations of the world, acting through the United Nations, to end hunger? and (2) What will be the cost if we permit hunger to continue at its present level? Of the scores of experts with the UN agencies in Rome chiefly involved in the global hunger issue, I have yet to meet a single one —conservative, liberal, or mugwump—who doesn't believe that the cost to the world of hunger is vastly greater than the cost of ending it. I can think of no investment that would profit the international community more than erasing hunger from the face of the earth.

So what will it cost? Beyond what the United States and other countries are now doing, it will take an estimated $5 billion a year, of which $1.2 billion would come from the United States. If this annual allocation were continued...until 2015, we could reduce the 800 million hungry people by half. To erase hunger for the remaining 400 million would cost about the same if it were to be accomplished in the 15 years leading up to the year 2030.

The U.S. Agency for International Development puts the cost at $2.6 billion annually, whereas the UN Food and Agriculture Organization estimates the cost higher at $6 billion. My figure of $5 billion annually—which is based on my own judgment of the cost of some of the steps I would like to see taken, including especially a universal school lunch program for every child in the world—is $2.4 billion higher than USAID's but still a billion below the United Nations figure. I concur with the estimate of the respected Bread for the World Institute in Silver Spring, Maryland, that it would take another $5 billion—largely in updating our food stamp program—to meet the needs of the 31 million inadequately fed Americans. Thus, the total American cost internationally and domestically would be an additional $6.2 billion a year—a fraction of what we now spend on cigarettes, beer, or cosmetics. If we decided to enact a modest increase in the minimum wage, we could cut the increase in food stamps in half.

What will it cost if we *don't* end the hunger that now afflicts so many of our fellow humans? The World Bank has concluded that each year malnutrition causes the loss of 46 million years of productive life, at a cost of $16 billion annually, several times the cost of ending hunger and turning this loss into productive gain.

Of course it is impossible to evaluate with dollars the real cost of hunger. What is the value of a human life? The twentieth century was the most violent in human history, with nearly 150 million people killed by war. But in just the last half of that century nearly three times as many died of malnutrition or related causes. How does one put a dollar figure on this terrible toll silently collected by the Grim Reaper? What is the cost of 800 million hungry people dragging through shortened and miserable lives, unable to study, work, play, or otherwise function normally because of the ever-present drain of hunger and malnutrition on body, mind, and spirit? What is the cost of millions of young mothers breaking under the despair of watching their children waste away and die from malnutrition? This is a problem we can resolve at a fraction of the cost of ignoring it. We need to be about that task now. I give you my word that anyone who looks honestly at world hunger and measures the cost of ending it for all time will conclude that this is a bargain well worth seizing. More often than not, those who look at the problem and the cost of its solution will wonder why humanity didn't resolve it long ago...

But victory over hunger will not come without [American leadership and] the assistance of those countries able to help, including the European nations, Japan, Canada, Australia, Argentina, and the OPEC oil states. And before the battle is over, perhaps it can be joined by China, India, and Russia. Of equal or greater importance is the need for reform in the developing countries if hunger is to be ended. This means improved farming methods; the conservation and wiser use of the earth's limited water resources; more rights and opportunities—especially education—for the girls and women of the Third World; a greater measure of democratic government responsive to basic human needs, including food security; and a substitution of common-sense negotiation of differences instead of the murderous civil, ethnic, and nationalistic conflicts that have torn up people, property, and land across the Third World. It is estimated that 10 percent of the world's hungry people are in that condition because of the disruptions of war and other civil strife. People in villages and on farms, including poor women and men, as well as city dwellers, need to be involved in political and economic decisions that affect their lives. Education and democracy may be the most powerful combatants in the war on hunger and poverty.

These are a few of the conditions that need to be confronted to build for the first time the architecture of food security on our planet.

My own experience with these issues probably began when I was a boy growing up on the agricultural and ranching plains of South Dakota...I saw some of the world's best farmers floundering because they could not sell their surplus production for a break-even price. At the same time I read of hunger and starvation in other parts of the world. That cruel paradox bothered me in the 1930s as a teenager; it still does in the year 2000...

Working here in Rome and traveling out from time to time to meet the hungry, poor, and sick around the globe, I recall a Scripture first read to me in childhood by my father: "The Spirit of the Lord is upon me, because he hath anointed me to preach the gospel to the poor; he hath sent me to heal the broken-hearted, to preach deliverance to the captives, and the recovering of sight to the blind, to set at liberty them that are bruised" (Luke 4:18). I can't live up to all the lofty implications of this testimony from Luke, but I'm grateful to...the American people for giving me an opportunity to do the best I can...I pray that in God's good time it may bring some measure of healing to the poor, the bruised, and the broken-hearted of the earth.

Stories of Hope: Promising Directions

Our future rests on our being able to take care of our kids and teach them how to take care of the land, how to nourish themselves, and how to gather at the table. That is where our culture is passed on to the next generation.

—*Alice Waters*

Unless we're willing to pay more for food, relinquish out-of-season produce, and rarely buy anything that comes in a package or is advertised on television, we support the current food system every time we eat a meal. That is why voting with our forks must extend beyond the food choices of individuals to larger political arenas.

—*Marion Nestle*

Introduction

Food and Faith concludes with hopeful stories highlighting ordinary people finding ways to create and support more sustainable agricultural systems. These systems generally do not transport food 1,200 miles to reach our plates. They seek to embed their economies within nature's economies; in economic language, these systems seek to decrease their contributions to externalities in order to maintain ecosystem integrity. They seek to restore relationships between consumers and farmers. They seem to share the belief that providing people access to land and the means to move toward localized food production will lead to food security, rather than a system which relies on corporately owned mega-farms and fossil fuel based fertilizers and transportation. They recognize that fair wages are due those who grow and harvest our food.

Finally, these systems and the communities they support seem to both engender and experience a sense of joy. We hope you will connect with others in your area, and find your own "stories of hope." [The "Organization and Resource Guide" (Appendix B) on p. 286 includes ideas, organizations, web sites, phone numbers, and more that can assist you in your search.]

Taking Action: Voting with Forks

by Marion Nestle

I have argued that one of the most important lessons of antismoking campaigns is that efforts to improve eating habits must be environmental as well as personal, societal as well as individual. A focus on societal determinants does not in any way deny the importance of individual responsibility for food choices. Indeed, there is much that people can do to deal with and counter the lobbying, marketing, and public relations practices of the food industry.

Our overabundant food system, a result as well as a cause of our flourishing economy, gives most of us the opportunity to make a political statement every time we eat—and to make a difference. The questions in Table 38 (see pages 222-223) suggest guidelines for making such decisions. For example, buying locally produced, organically grown food not only improves the taste and nutritional quality of the diet (if for no other reason than that the foods have not traveled so far or been stored so long) but also supports local farmers, promotes the viability of rural communities, and creates greater diversity in agricultural production. In the early 1990s, Oldways Preservation & Exchange Trust (a Boston-based group devoted to incorporating traditional foodways into current dietary choices) recognized the political implications of food choice when it urged chefs and restaurateurs to forge alliances with local food producers and "vote with your fork!"

The value of such alliances is vividly illustrated by the purchasing practices of a small (65-seat) vegan restaurant, Angelica's Kitchen, in New York City's East

Village neighborhood. Among many other products, the restaurant buys 830 pounds of parsley, 2,100 pounds of greens (collards, kale), 3,400 pounds of squash, and 7,800 pounds of carrots every *month*, all of it organically grown and much of it from local suppliers.[1] Another example: The celebrity chef Eberhard Müller and the food consultant Paulette Satur run an organic farm on Long Island that produces 3,000 pounds of organic lettuce every week while the season lasts; they distribute the farm's produce to more than 50 New York restaurants.[2] Such alliances between restaurant owners, chefs, cooks, and farmers hold the promise of economic viability for everyone concerned.

In his book *The McDonaldization of Society*, George Ritzer advocates "subverting the process" by making what he calls "personal irrational choices": Never buy artificial (processed) food products, buy organic, avert your eyes during television commercials, and don't take children to fast-food restaurants.[3] Michael Jacobson and Laurie Ann Mazur argue for downsizing commercialism to a more appropriate role in society. Their advice: Pay attention (count advertisements), declare yourself a personal ad-free zone (don't wear corporate logos), boycott products, turn off the television, get television commercials and soft drinks out of schools, and teach critical media skills so everyone can tell the difference between advertisements and content.[4] The manifesto of the international Slow Food Movement (its logo is a snail) says, "Our defense should begin at the table with Slow Food. Let us rediscover the flavors and savors of regional cooking and banish the degrading effects of Fast Food."[5]

Adopting such actions is one way to apply ethical principles, but the higher cost and inconvenience of doing so are certain to preclude those choices for many (if not most) people. Unless we are willing to pay more for food, relinquish out-of-season produce, and rarely buy anything that comes in a package or is advertised on television, we support the current food system every time we eat a meal. That is why voting with our forks must extend beyond the food choices of individuals to larger political arenas. Countless community, state, and national organizations deal with food issues, and it is not difficult to find one to suit any political viewpoint or taste. As has been demonstrated by the support for creating federal standards for organic food, such groups can join together quickly and effectively when an issue of mutual interest emerges. This ability to exercise democratic power holds much hope for achieving a more equitable balance of interests in matters pertaining to food and health.

Table 38: Ethical questions related to food choice

Production methods
Do they protect and preserve natural resources?
Do they avoid pollution of air, land, and water?
Do they adequately reward producers of basic farm commodities?

Do they ensure food safety?
Do they ensure worker safety and economic benefits?
Do they promote nutritional quality?

Marketing methods

Do they avoid inappropriate targeting of children?
Do they emphasize products of high nutritional quality?
Do they disclose the contents of products?
Do they avoid making inappropriate or misleading health claims?
Do they avoid exerting inappropriate pressure on officials in legislative, judiciary, and executive branches of government?
Do they avoid exerting inappropriate pressure on journalists or their employers?
Do they avoid exerting pressure on nutrition and food professionals to engage in activities that give rise to conflicts of interest?

Advising methods

Do they consider the balance between risks and benefits whenever possible?
Do they take ethical issues into consideration?
Do they promote ethical choices whenever possible?

From *Food Politics: How the Food Industry Influences Nutrition and Health*, by Marion Nestle. © 2002. Reprinted by permission of University of California Press.

Hungry for Change

by Jennifer Bogo

In an unruly plot of land behind the Martin Luther King Jr. Middle School in Berkeley, California, the raspberry bushes shake with activity. A slow rustling that begins at one end quickly picks up speed, rippling down the patch as a dozen hands part the thorny branches, reaching in and out, the vines now thicker with probing fingers than with the bright red berries themselves. Carrots can't seem to hide, either, in this tangle of vegetation. They're yanked up by their green tops, brushed off, and briefly passed under the flow of a tall, spindly faucet. With a splash of water and a resounding crunch, they disappear.

"More raspberries over here!" a young voice hollers. The rustle moves immediately to the left. A teacher walks by, but not a single guilty glance is shot her way. The students at King love to get down and dirty with the earth to reap the fruits of their labor, and here in the Edible Schoolyard, that's encouraged. Founded in 1995 by celebrated chef and restaurateur Alice Waters, this unorthodox program introduces more than 900 sixth, seventh, and eighth graders each year to the finer points of organic gardening and healthy eating.

Waters sits on a bale of hay in a handmade gazebo of acacia branches, an oasis of calm in the bedlam of roving paths, tumbling poppies, and climbing purple peas that surrounds her. She smiles with pride at the wild turn nature has taken in this corner of the King schoolyard, which she first helped transform from its asphalt blanket. Here, even Waters's auburn hair escapes confinement, its silvery streaks wispy in the absence of her signature hat. Though her voice, like her presence, is soft and reserved, the message it presses is clearly not.

Among chefs and diners alike, the name Alice Waters is synonymous with sustainable cuisine. The best-tasting ingredients, she has long held, are also the ones that, grown by local farmers, ensure the future of the land. They are picked ripe from plants that thrive naturally in the climate in which they're grown—without the heavy hand of chemical agriculture—and represent the rich diversity of fruits and vegetables abandoned by corporate growers.

Fresh, seasonal produce, delivered by 75 Bay Area suppliers, makes up every dish at Waters's well-known Berkeley bistro, Chez Panisse, which recently celebrated its 30th anniversary with a homegrown feast written up by *The New York Times* and attended by such luminaries as Francis Ford Coppola, California Senator Barbara Boxer, and Martha Stewart. During the past decade, the James Beard Foundation has lauded Chez Panisse as the Best Restaurant in America, and Waters as the Best Chef in America and Humanitarian of the Year.

It was Waters's daily drive past the dilapidated-looking school that seven years ago inspired the birth of this unique garden—a green space generated not by landscape designers but by the enthusiastic hands of the students themselves—and eventually the conversion of a long-abandoned cafeteria into a kitchen classroom where students could transform their prize crops into delicious and healthy meals. "Our future rests on our being able to take care of our kids and teach them how to take care of the land, how to nourish themselves, and how to gather at the table," says Waters, her blue eyes intense. "Because that is where our culture is passed on to the next generation."

In the Edible Schoolyard, the students build, plant, and cultivate. They turn steaming piles of compost with long pitchforks. They harvest, and, finally, they eat. By doing so, Waters says, they learn a valuable lesson. "The heart of environmentalism is about feeding ourselves and understanding how important those decisions are," she says. "When you don't know where your food comes from, you feel like you don't have to take care of the land or the seas or the air. But as soon as you realize that, you want to do something else about it."

A floppy-brimmed sun hat shades the face of Kelsey Siegel, the garden manager and teacher, as he arms students with full-size shovels and wheelbarrows and then sends them out into the jungle they helped grow. Some will set up fences to support tomatoes. Others will clear more ground to plant corn. In the garden, everyone has a job.

Sixth-grader Ishon Mohindroo, dirt smudged at the hairline of his dark-brown crew cut, leans forward on his shovel, directing exactly where to plant the three different varieties of potatoes. "There," he instructs. "The spud end goes up." Freshly dug trenches are soon punctuated with neatly heaped mounds of soil. From across the neighboring tomato plants float the sounds of an animated game of rock-paper-scissors. "Scissors" wins, and someone—"paper," no doubt—pushes off with the wheelbarrow to go sift some more compost for the plot.

Play is an integral part of the Edible Schoolyard experience. There are no papers and pencils in the King garden, no multiple-choice tests. The students' time in the garden is strictly experiential. The education the land offers is absorbed through constant conversation with the teachers, and with each other, as they work side by side. It is reinforced by field trips to local organic farms and a curriculum that weaves ecology into classroom lessons in science, history, and language arts. "Every time they plant something, they know they are creating more oxygen," says Phoebe Tanner, a sixth-grade math and science teacher, "and repairing a tiny crack in global warming."

After the students carry fresh ingredients from the Edible Schoolyard garden to the kitchen, they learn firsthand the more tangible—and tasty—outcomes as well. Kitchen teacher Esther Cook, with pewter fork and spoon earrings dangling from her ears, holds up a crisp grape leaf and demonstrates how it will soon wrap into a dolma, a tidy little Mediterranean package of pine nuts and rice.

The students, clad in denim aprons, busy themselves stemming leaves and juicing lemons, while seventh-grader Emily Stein leads the way to the compost with the rinds. She opens the pungent bin of food scraps and peers in. "Did you see the pile outside?" she asks. "We add all this to it and then spread it in the garden. Then we bring the food in here that we've grown."

"We have artichokes! A lot of schools don't," Emily says proudly, as she juices another lemon, the citrusy droplets filling the air. "And we once made mayonnaise. Before that I thought it was something you just bought in a jar at the store."

The students' menu—quesadillas, rice pudding, Indian curries—would make a multicultural Betty Crocker proud. Such ethnic diversity distinguishes King, where 22 languages are spoken. Seventh-grader Atte Alho, covered in equal parts by a brown polar fleece and freckles, explains that he eats a lot of smashed potatoes, sausage, and meatballs in his native Finland. When asked to name his favorite food here at King, he hesitates: "What's that really flat bread called again? Oh, yeah—chapati. And I like tortillas!"

At the end of the kitchen hour, red-checkered tablecloths snap in the air and then alight softly on tables, where they're held in place by tall vases of garden flowers. The food, piled high on platters, makes its rounds as the students—some eagerly, some much more tentatively—try their creations. An adult helper at one table raises a glass pitcher full of water into the air. "To the Swedes!" she proclaims.

Her toast is echoed by the enthusiastic voices at the table, all glasses held high. "To the African Americans!" someone yells. "To the Spanish!" The voices are soon drowned out by the table to the left, which breaks into a tribal-culinary rhythm, hands and utensils drumming out the beat.

The Edible Schoolyard program, like the garden itself, is very much still growing, its roots extending beyond the conventional time constraints of class. Produce and recipes make their way home, and home makes its way to the schoolyard—open to anyone who wants to drop by—and to the kitchen as well, where each year families sit down to a meal served by King's sixth-grade class.

Waters shifts on her bale of hay, contemplating the program's most ambitious plan to date: complete integration with the daily school lunch. "In that way," she says, "all of these important values will be washed over every student, every day."

While King has been a pioneer in educating students about a healthy relationship with food, the lesson now seems to stop when the lunch bell rings. The school still lacks full-service meals, or even a cafeteria to eat them in. Students have access only to a snack service that offers such items as prepackaged hamburgers and burritos, which they can eat outside on nice days or in stairwells on rainy ones. Eric Weaver, chair of the City of Berkeley's Child Nutrition Advisory Committee, says that this all-too-typical fast-food model has resulted in a kind of "food apartheid," in which students from wealthier families are sent to school with brown-bag lunches and "poor children who qualify for free meals get garbage."

Waters yearns for an ecologically designed cafeteria at King—soon to be realized through a bond measure passed by the city—a flagship for the entire school district's goals. Berkeley, despite its currently less-than-ideal system, is the first district in the country to pass a food-program policy to ensure that each of its 10,000 students receives a nutritious lunch—a meal healthy not only for students but for Bay Area farms and the environment as well. Already, organic fruits are included in some snacks and lunches, and four of the district's 11 elementary schools have salad bars with ingredients gathered from farmers markets; four more of these salad bars will open this year. All items at King's planned cafeteria, from dairy to meat to vegetables, will be provided by local suppliers who conscientiously maintain the health of their land. And, as in the kitchen class now, students will share ownership in the food they eat by assisting in preparing and serving its daily meals.

"Students need to be aware of the world around them, aware of the consequences of what they eat, aware of our precious natural resources," Waters says. And where could be a more natural place to learn that than in an Edible Schoolyard? After all, she adds, "This is what we all have in common. We all have to eat, and we all go to school."

Houses of Worship Sing Praises of Coffee for a Cause

by Jake Batsell

Coffee is the world's second most heavily traded commodity (next to oil). The next two stories introduce fair trade, shade grown coffees, which promote social justice (through paying farmers a fair price for their coffee) and ecological well-being. The first story highlights churches in the Seattle, Washington area, and why they serve the fair trade brew. The second selection introduces Don Juan, a fair trade coffee grower in the small Mexican village of Nuevo Progreso.

Fair trade coffee is being served all over the country. A number of cities have passed resolutions requiring fair trade coffee be served in all city offices. These include Boston, Berkeley, San Francisco, Oakland, Madison, Santa Cruz, and Cambridge. Over 100 colleges now serve fair trade coffee including: Amherst College, Boston College, Brown University, Columbia University, Duke University, Purdue University, UCLA, University of Chicago, University of Connecticut, University of Delaware, University of Kansas, University of Maryland, University of Minnesota, University of Vermont, University of Wisconsin at Madison, and Western Washington University. Certain denominations (Lutheran, Unitarian, Presbyterian, Methodist) sponsor national fair trade coffee programs; see www.equalexchange.com/interfaith for more information. Global Exchange (*fairtrade@globalexchange.org*; 415-575-5538) and TransFair USA (510-663-5260; www.transfairusa.org) are further sources of good information.

∞

It's a Sunday-morning staple, something to sip during chats with fellow churchgoers after listening to hymns and sermons about serving a higher purpose. But today, coffee itself is playing a larger role in churches' commitment to social justice. More churches are buying organic, "fair-trade" and "shade-grown" gourmet coffee, with profits benefiting environmental and social causes that are in step with congregations' faith-based values.

Independent companies that specialize in selling such coffee are increasingly turning to churches, synagogues and other places of worship, tapping into an audience that is likely to be receptive to an altruistic sales pitch. "It's a natural marriage," said Dan Olmstead, co-owner of Poverty Bay Coffee in Auburn WA, which last year began selling its shade-grown coffee to St. Margaret's Episcopal Church and has since landed three more churches as customers.

"They're there to try to find ways to make a tangible difference, and when you can (make a difference) in the natural course of buying things you need, everybody wins," Olmstead said.

Equal Exchange, a Canton, Massachusetts based coffee company that buys its beans directly from farmers in the developing world, says sales through its Inter-faith Coffee Program have jumped 50 percent in the past year to about $810,000 in 2001. The 4-year-old program has grown to include 3,800 congregations of various denominations and religions, including 155 in Washington state.

"There's a really strong link in communities of faith around social-justice issues," said Erbin Crowell, coordinator of Equal Exchange's interfaith program. "Just by coincidence, right there in front of them is this product that they share on a weekly basis that is perhaps one of the most direct links to communities in the developing world."

Among the array of so-called "coffees with a conscience" are fair-trade certified, organic and shade-grown. With fair-trade coffee, a third party certifies that coffee beans are bought from indigenous farmers for a fair, set price—right now, it's a minimum of $1.26 a pound. The fair-trade movement has gathered momentum this year as world coffee prices have plummeted below 50 cents a pound, worsening the living conditions of many farmers as plantations have shed jobs and cut wages.

Organic and shade-grown coffees have a more environmental focus. Organic farmers avoid use of pesticides, fertilizers and other chemicals. With shade-grown farming, taller trees protect the coffee plants, enrich the soil and provide a habitat for migratory birds.

All of those causes appeal to Rev. Leroy Hedman of South Seattle's Georgetown Gospel Chapel, who said his church became an Equal Exchange customer earlier this year because "we believe in justice and empowerment." Hedman said many of his church's members are blue-collar workers who can relate to the idea that farmers should be paid fairly for their labor.

"We do it for the sake of fairness to the small farmer and their cooperatives and also for a good product that's organic and hopefully shade-grown and a lot better for the environment," he said.

At another Equal Exchange customer, Temple Beth Am in Seattle's Wedgwood neighborhood, Rabbi Jonathan Singer delivered a sermon on Yom Kippur in September that singled out buying fair-trade coffee as a way to combat injustice.

"It fit in very well with the message he wanted to deliver on Yom Kippur: We should not willingly support the oppression of others," said Temple Beth Am member Allan Paulson, who serves on the temple's social-action committee and has worked to bring fair-trade coffee to the temple.

Pura Vida Coffee, a Seattle-based retailer that donates its net profits to children's programs in coffee-growing regions around the world, reports that about half its sales stem from churches, Christian bookstores and religious retreat centers. John Sage, a former Microsoft executive who co-founded Pura Vida, said sales have grown by about 150 percent for three years running.

"We're probably signing up at least two new churches or Christian bookstores a day," Sage said. "Even if the coffee is selling at a premium, the church is willing to pay for it."

Fair-trade, organic and shade-grown coffees generally run somewhere between $8 and $12 a pound, though many churches are considered wholesale customers and receive discounts. While more expensive than the canned coffee that still represents the majority of U.S. coffee sales, it's comparable in price to the products offered by major specialty coffee chains, some of whom sell their own fair-trade and organic blends.

Church coffee, of course, has long had a dubious reputation—as Sage recalled, "Somebody once told me that the only coffee worse than church coffee is military coffee."

"People make jokes about church coffee, and they're all deserved," said Peggy Johnson, business manager for St. Margaret's. "The first thing we wanted was to create a cup of coffee that people would drink, and increase our hospitality.

"Given the opportunity to buy coffee where the benefit accrues to the farmer as opposed to the corporation—and to do it at little or no increase to the price—was almost a no-brainer."

But to be successful in a java mecca like Seattle, coffee that promotes a noble cause has to be backed up by a product that is pleasing to the palate.

"It was really, really important to me that our coffee be of super-high quality for it to stand on its own," Sage said. "It's not enough to be a good cause. That's usually the knockout punch."

Sharon Webb, who discovered Pura Vida coffee two years ago at University Presbyterian Church in Seattle, said she's a fan of the taste and the cause.

"It's excellent coffee, and then I heard that it supports people," Webb said. "I like the idea of being able to use my coffee money to help others."

"Singing Praises of Coffee for a Cause", by Jake Batsell, *Seattle Times* Business Reporter, December 22, 2001, © *The Seattle Times*. Used with permission.

Heart Benefits of Shade Grown Coffee

By Joel Sisolak

Nuevo Progreso is like many small villages in the hills of southern Mexico. The primary industry is agriculture. The primary crop is coffee, destined for foreign markets. But there is a difference evident as one walks out into the groves surrounding the village. A lushness abounds, a spring green that is rapidly disappearing from many coffee regions in Latin America. This is land with heart.

The Tseltales, descendants of the Mayans, believe that everything has heart. Not just humans, but every plant and animal, and every stone and river has heart. This is not a kind of animism, but a worldview that understands all things as living and resting in communion with God. Heart is tied to place, heart is strengthened by good relationships, and it is through heart that God speaks to the Tseltales.

I recently traveled with a delegation to Chiapas, Mexico to learn more about living with heart. We walked the hilly landscape around Nuevo Progreso where we met Don Juan, a third generation Tseltal coffee farmer. He dropped a load of firewood to join us for a tour of his land, land he cooperatively owns with 21 other indigenous families.

Don Juan explained that the farmers in the cooperative are moving away from slash and burn practices and adopting more sustainable, erosion resistant methods. Shade plants are planted with the young coffee bushes, including fruit trees that feed the farmers' families and larger trees that fix nitrogen into the soil and supply firewood. Fallen leaves are gathered for mulching around the coffee bushes. As we walked through Don Juan's land we heard choruses of birdsong in the tree canopy, a sound absent from many "modern" plantations where heavily fertilized coffee is grown in full sunlight.

Coffee will not grow in direct sun unless supported by fertilizers, but with foreign investments, many farms have "technified" because the sun growing process accelerates yield. Unfortunately, this process also poisons the land and rarely benefits small-scale farmers. Within the volatile coffee market, many growers are paid less for the coffee they harvest than what they are forced to pay for the fertilizer to grow it, a form of economic slavery. Compounding the exploitation are intermediaries called "coyotes" who charge farmers exorbitant rates for financing, equipment and transportation.

Through the cooperative, Don Juan's farmers are paid approximately $1.25 per pound for certified organic coffee. This "fair trade" price insures that they can continue to use sustainable farming methods, and that the land will remain healthy for generations to come.

Organic certification takes 5 years for fields formerly treated with pesticides and fertilizers. Don Juan admits that it also takes a lot of work, but once converted to organic methods, the trees are healthier and easier to sustain, and shade-grown coffee simply tastes better. The beans mature more slowly giving them a richer, deeper flavor.

Other farmers near Nuevo Progreso are taking notice of the cooperative's success. They see the healthy green trees that produce far longer than sun grown trees. They also note the good price Don Juan's farmers get by selling to an increasing market for certified organics, and by selling their coffee through the cooperative to avoid the price gouging coyotes. Don Juan is meeting with his neighbors to explain how they too can convert back to more traditional organic, shade grown methods. He explains to them that the traditional methods he learned from his grandfather are best for business, for their homes, and for their hearts.

Don Juan reminded our delegation that "all children of the Earth must care for the Earth, the worms, everything, in order to live peacefully. We come from the land to care for the land." This ethic is critical to the preservation of countless species. The middle-altitude tropical forests of Latin America contain some of the highest levels of biodiversity in the world, providing habitat for many of the planet's animal and plant species. This includes wintering homes for many of the migratory birds Americans are used to seeing in our warmer months: warblers, swallows, and vireos to name a few.

Sadly, Mexico's tropical forests are disappearing. Slash and burn agriculture, much of it for sun grown coffee, is destroying or has destroyed nearly 90 percent of the rain forest in Chiapas, creating full sun coffee groves that are "green deserts" barren of nearly all wildlife. On the other hand, species diversity on well-shaded coffee farms can rival that of tropical forests. From 1990 to 1994 a team from the Smithsonian Migratory Bird Center counted more than 150 bird species on shade grown coffee farms in Chiapas.

When I hear a bird sing outside the window of my Seattle breakfast nook, I imagine that it has migrated from the south, from the shade trees of Nuevo Progreso. I enjoy my coffee in the morning, now more than ever, because I have a relationship with the farmers and the land that produce it. The birdsong gladdens my heart as the coffee jump-starts my day.

With the increasing availability of fair trade, shade-grown coffee, we all are invited to begin our days with heart. Churches have an opportunity to lead this conversion. In many churches, the coffee hour serves as a kind of "second communion." Having first gathered around the common table for the bread and wine of the Eucharist, congregations gather a second time in the social hall. Church coffee hours provide a chance to deepen relationships and catch up on a week's worth of stories. Now, this fellowship hour can also be an act of justice for the poor and the Earth, an extension of communion to the lands and peoples of coffee growing communities in the developing world.

Each year the United States, the leading coffee importer in an $18 billion industry, consumes about a fifth of the world's total, much of it from Mexico. At my church we drink fair trade, shade-grown coffee from Chiapas, and an increasing number of congregants are buying it for their home consumption.

[Editor's Note: To learn how to bring fair trade, shade-grown coffee to your coffee hour and breakfast table, visit *www.equalexchange.com/interfaith* or *www.transfair.usa*; see p. 290 for further information.]

Reprinted by permission of the author.

What is Community Supported Agriculture?

By Michael Schut

The first Community Supported Agriculture (CSA) farm/garden in the United States was established in 1986. Today there are over 600 across the country. CSAs are one of the more exciting ways for individuals, communities and congregations to support local, organic farming and farmers.

CSAs are also called "subscription farms." Here, farmers contract directly with their customers, who are then their "subscribers." For a lump sum (a share-price), paid in advance of the growing season, a subscriber becomes a shareholder. The share entitles subscribers to a given volume of fresh, organically grown produce during the growing season and for winter storage. (Some CSAs include more than vegetables in their share: fruit, honey, eggs, even organically grown meats.) At a designated time each week, shareholders pick up their portion of that week's harvest, either at the farm itself, or at some central in-town location.

There are many advantages to subscribing to such a farm. Subscribers maintain a close connection with "their" grower; many CSAs invite their subscribers to help with the harvesting, a great activity for families. Subscribers play a significant role in ensuring the continued economic viability of local organic farms, as the risks of farming are shared by farmer and customer: in good years, subscribers enjoy bountiful produce, in lean years, less. By participating, shareholders contribute to keeping one more farm and one more farmer an active part of the local food economy. Subscriber and farmer become working partners.

Of course, CSAs are also about health. Freshly harvested organic food grown without herbicides and pesticides which contaminate soil and water form the basis of both a healthy diet and healthy soil. CSAs offer the opportunity to reconnect with the rhythms of nature through eating food in season. Many CSA participants discover a kind of spiritual nourishment previously missing from their lives.

Finally, CSAs are fun! Many sponsor seasonal harvest festivals. Community is built as families meet other subscribing families at "their" farm. Many CSAs produce a newsletter for their subscribers, and include recipes in their weekly produce baskets.

Congregational Supported Agriculture

The CSA model fits very nicely with congregations. Supporting a CSA allows a congregation to embody its recognition that they are called to care for the land, care for the soil and water, care for small farmers struggling to survive in global agricultural markets, and care for their own health. A congregation is obviously already a community. Its members become subscribers; it would be entirely possible for one moderate to large congregation to support one CSA! Imagine the congregation's farmer, delivering shares every Sunday morning during the growing season!

What a fellowship hour that would be—families splitting their shares with each other, people trading zucchinis for tomatoes for cucumbers. What a practical vision of God's care for all of us would be embodied in such a scene.

To receive a list of CSAs in your area contact the Biodynamic Farming and Gardening Association, Inc. at (800) 516-7797 or www.biodynamics.com. They will send you names, addresses, and phone numbers of all CSAs in your state.

Zen, Wheelbarrows, and Collard Greens: Reflections from the Founder of a Give-Away Garden Project

by Dan Barker

The man who helps me would have been a great pioneer; he hates jobs and lawns. He is nearly 50 and has never been able to tolerate employment for longer than three months at a stretch. To him lawns and civilization are the same phenomenon, ass-backwards and fit for no good use. When he and I are working together we are a team; we get it done.

At Ms. Wittingham's, the house looks well kept. She comes out—a cataract clouding her left eye—and says her husband of 40 years used to love to do the garden, but he's now disabled with a stroke. Sorry to hear that, that's why we're here. We shoulder the lumber back to a plot beside the garage, lay out the two-by-eight frames, bang 'em up, the sound of the hammer drums the neighborhood awake. My helper builds the trellis while I line out the frames and knock down lumps of weeds. We set the frames by nailing 12-inch stakes at each corner. My helper does one side, I the other. Work output is divided equally, down to the erg.

We start wheeling in the soil, two wheelbarrows a turn, six to each soil frame. Place and nail the trellis, one man strings while the other rakes the new seedbeds smooth, the zen of the garden, the rest and quiet. While I talk how-to with Ms. Wittingham, my helper cleans up, stows the tools, and plugs in a fresh chaw of Redman, maybe tunes in Paul Harvey.

I teach Ms. Wittingham about planting, seed conservation, composting, watering, and fertilizing and tell her I'll be by again in early May, when the weather warms up, to deliver starts for tomatoes, eggplant, peppers, basil, and flowers. What's a garden without flowers? She says thank you. She's shy about the new gardening techniques; she's never availed herself of a social service before but now she's older and the money is gone. Careful for her dignity, I accept her thanks for making it so easy, one phone call. This is truly a Christian thing you're doing, she says, and I say glad you like it. I think, but don't say, that it's also Buddhist, Taoist, pagan, Dayak. Putting in gardens is a phenomenon 50,000 years deep.

On to the next one. Birdi Johnson has arthritis; she's been into the wine already this morning, doesn't come out of the house much. Neither does her 15-year-old daughter; too much danger lurks out here. We build the second garden of the morning, slipping on the mud and dog shit in the back yard. All she wants to grow is tomatoes, beans, collards, and corn, and I say great, sure, grow what you like to eat, it's your garden. If your hands are too painful to do the planting, I'll send someone by to help you.

On to a burger place that will let us wear rain gear dripping with mud while we eat. Then on to Roger Kerns; he's a paraplegic, an ex-athlete whose back was shattered in a drunken car crash. He's into lecturing high-school kids on the net results of cars and fun. He tries not to show bitterness at being a dupe of some universal force that took him off at the seventh vertebra. This garden is a double high—one frame on top of the other—so he can reach it from his electric wheelchair. He's supervising the placement, wants the overhanging maple branches pruned, the yard debris cleared away; we do what he wants, a little extra work because he can't and we can and we're here.

And on again to Thelma Carson's, she's 88, still going strong, has done for herself all her life. I'm lucky to know her and her example, but the kids from the crack house down the block busted through her door, knocked her down, broke her hip, stole her 13-inch TV, black-and-white to boot, her food stamps. She heard I was a "good man," and that is what I'm trying to be. At least the little punks can't steal the garden. I'll drop by later this summer to see how you're keeping, and I'll call Senior Services for you, have them come and fix that back door like they should have last winter; your life and my life is our life, even this brief meeting, but you get to keep the garden, yes it is yours, a gift. A gift should be well made and leave nothing wanting. Art.

Those last two went fast, on the flat ground, time for one more if you've got the oomph, sure, why not, long way to go and a short time to get there. Let's do Kris S., three kids, three fathers, no men around now, Aid to Dependent Children and food stamps, run out of her last two houses by crank (a drug similar to crack) monsters. She wants to teach her children vegetable gardening to insure that they will never starve. We build it, bang it up square to the world, put it in the sunny spot next to the kitchen door. She wants to be employed as a part-time planter, and I say here's Birdi Johnson's address.

The day is done, we'll do it again tomorrow and tomorrow and tomorrow, all week the same people, the same stories, until two and a half months pass in a kind of hazy, sweaty dream that manifests 125 new gardens this year, renewed lives. On the way back to the operations site where the soil, tractor, and lumber are stored, a BMW misses a stop sign and nearly crunches the truck, our most essential tool; the brothers drinking wine and waiting for customers down on the corner of crack alley stare at us, big dumb white devils.

I invented this work by consolidating my experience working in nurseries, construction, writing poetry, while trying to recover from a divorce and being robbed at gun point in a wino grocery store, knocked unconscious by a blow from a .38 butt, the muzzle pressed against my occipital bone for 10 minutes, the hammer cocked; the gunman's accomplices couldn't figure how to open the computer cash register.

Three months later I see the robber buying primo vegetables at the local gourmet produce store, gutwrenching fear like being back in Vietnam, in a firefight, my only weapon a quarter to call the cops. But they don't want to go to the trouble of busting him and his girlfriend accomplice; he wore a mask, impossible to visually identify him in court, they contend. But I knew, and vowed never again to put myself in the victim's position. Meanwhile the schools are failing, the jails are full. The Dalai Lama tells how to quiet the demons grown from hate and fear and act out of compassion, I and thou are one, like it or not.

In the slums, where the ground has been in turf for a hundred years, or the housing was built on the gravel of an ancient flood plain, it is not enough just to go in and pass out seeds. To be effective it is necessary to bring in the whole garden. Most of the impoverished, elderly, and disabled, in need of additional sustenance, are no longer able to till that depleted soil. They can plant, weed, water, and harvest, though, if they've got a garden to work in. In this city alone there are thousands who need and would use the proceeds from a garden. Any one of us could become any one of them.

You never know how the cards will play: riding high in April, down to the Social Security office in May. If after 20 years of little but bad news, some bozo says, hey, I've got a free vegetable garden for you—that's right, soil frames, weed-free organic soil, seeds, starts, fertilizer, instructions, cooking tips, yes, I'll come to your house and build it for you, no strings—you might be glad to see me coming. Another spark of human joy alive in the soul-stream.

Most of us have little connection to the manipulations that constitute business and government. Many of my clients' more immediate concerns are whether the Meals on Wheels girl is going to show up and if she'll have time to smile, or better, to chat. They worry that the medical department will cut off their diabetically gangrenous legs. Many say the government just wants them to die. And in their defiance they go out to tend their new gardens. All summer, that is where we find them, outside, working, making sure that the gardens are just right, harvesting their evening meals. For some, so alone, it is all they have. The lifespirit is winning.

The work is religious; there are three sides to it. One involves arduous physical labor—building soil frames, wheelbarrowing soil, four gardens a day, four days a week, until the goal is reached or surpassed. A second side absorbs the incessant tales of suffering, sees the misery and despair, the rotted teeth, the heart problems, the amputations, the disfigurements of body and soul. The third side demonstrates the capacity to run a business dedicated to the alleviation of that suffering. The books and the reports must be straight, so I can build a garden where there wasn't one before, and with a bit of work, a new occupation of time and spirit is opened.

Many observers consider giving away complete vegetable gardens—to the poor, the disabled, the single mothers, the aged—to be the best idea they've ever heard. It is real, it works. They tell me so, they bestow their blessings on me. For some of my prospective gardeners, it seems a miracle that another human being would do this work at no cost to them. For others, it is only their due for life having fouled them.

How did getting a vegetable garden become possible? I decided to make the gardens available, and they decided to take them. But no matter the motives or reasons, excuses or philosophies, the result is now 525 new vegetable gardens in this city—real change in the real world. The soul, the well-being of several thousand people, has been substantially enhanced. They are lifted by their practice of self-providence into the greater miracle of life.

Some nationally syndicated columnist recently opined that we live in a world that no longer rewards virtue. No reward, indeed. The first lie is that we live in the world. We are the world, the planet spinning, the galaxy, the universe. We are each other. The aged are our mothers and fathers, the young our children, their mothers our sisters. The reward for doing virtuous work is the same as it has always been: You grow out of your own abyss, dissolving the existential distance betwixt I and thou.

The charitable trusts and foundations who fund my project want to know if the gardens work. Do they dissolve the current anguish ripping the dignity from the impoverished? I can't say with certainty that one gang kid has been deflected from his run toward a violent end or prison, or that I've given shelter to homeless families. But I've saved thousands of people considerable money, time, and trouble, trips to the doctor, despair, sessions with their therapists, longing for death. I tell the gardeners that this is the store you don't have to go to. You get hungry, come on out and pick yourself a meal. When you plant, use three seeds—one for you, one for your neighbor, one for God. They always laugh when I mention God, or silently let the word slide on by. I go home knowing that I've planted the possibility of self-caring. But the doctors want a figure; I tell them each garden is capable of producing at least $500 worth of food a summer, if you don't count gas, time, etc., and that 95 percent of the gardens are productive the first year, 85 percent the second—I don't keep track after that, though often I run across a garden still producing after five or six years. Some people even load their gardens onto trucks when they move.

What is more difficult to convey is the health and joy alive in a 70-year-old woman showing me her beans and tomatoes, or the pride of accomplishment beaming from the face of the 12-year-old son of an ex-prostitute who put him in charge of the garden. Or the envy of the neighbors—I put down a garden, and the next year two or three neighbors will call for theirs. We're strictly word of mouth. I wouldn't know how well it was working otherwise. There's never been a shortage of recipients, only a shortage of money, time, and energy.

The free market/welfare system in which we live is too large, too pervasive to be countered by something so small as a garden, extended metaphor or no. Still, the notion of giving away gardens contains the whole cycle of life, incorporating use of local materials (dairy and racetrack manures, construction subsoil, compost, surplus seed), reducing use of fossil fuels, reconnecting people with life—thus serving all. Everything necessary is already in place: Parks departments have tractors, trucks, working space, and greenhouses, much of the time underused; thousands of people desire to be of service to their neighbors, workers could be recruited from agricultural programs and extension agents. All we have to do is put it together and get it paid for. One announcement on TV and there would be no end to the requests for gardens. People in need need all the help they can get. They will endure and will invite peace from others.

It's taken me seven years to get the project into the black, and it couldn't have happened without the goodwill and generous hearts of my wife and friends. We lift ourselves. Accolades go to the foundations and trusts that have sponsored and believed in the work. They call it charity, but it is simply service, a providence that can even be employed by the recipients, as shown by several older women who wanted—and got—double or triple gardens so they could provide vegetables for the entire neighborhood.

They ask me why I do this, and I say it needs to be done. Don't you need a vegetable garden, one you can get to, one you can use without too much physical effort to maintain? There, now you've got one, good luck, happy to do it. Or, once, when I was tired and being interviewed for a newspaper article, the young reporter asked why, and I said I'm out to change the world. And when she asked, what do you do in real life, my tact left me, and I replied, don't you think giving away gardens is real life? Don't you think trying to lift the weight of suffering by one micron is real? To affirm the good in you, in life, the Tao speaks of neighbors who do not tread on each other, but live their lives in quiet wonder, grow old, and die. And the way to affirm the good life is to deliver it. If such an act challenges the men on the corner, good; shovels are easy to come by.

What is bothersome is not that giving away gardens is so wonderful, but that it is so rare.

Reprinted by permission from the author.

Notes

1. McEachern, L. *The Angelica Home Kitchen.* New York: Roundtable Inc., 2000, 19.

2. Norwich W. "Salad Days." *New York Times Magazine* Aug. 13, 2000: 52-56.

3. Ritzer G. *The McDonaldization of Society: An Investigation into the Changing Character of Contemporary Social Life,* revised edition. Thousand Oaks, CA: Pine Forge Press, 1996.

4. Jacobson, MF, LA Mazur. *Marketing Madness: A Survival Guide for a Consumer Society.* Boulder CO: Westview Press, 1995.

5. Slow Food USA. Taste and Culture (leaflet). New York, 2000 (online: www.slowfood.com).

Food & Faith

justice, joy and daily bread

Study Guide

by Michael Schut

How to Use This Material

This is the study guide designed to accompany *Food and Faith*. We are excited to offer this course and glad for your interest in it. The format and ethos of this course is similar to the study guide in *Simpler Living, Compassionate Life*, an award-winning book also published by Living the Good News in cooperation with Earth Ministry.

We have tried to make this curriculum flexible and easy to use. While going through all eight sessions is, of course, the most comprehensive option, some church and/or small group situations may not allow time for this. We have suggested **optional course lengths of 4 or 6 weeks.** (See page 245.) Another option allowing you to go through all eight sessions is to spread the course out: four sessions in the fall and four in the spring, or meeting monthly rather than weekly.

Before you gather for Meeting One, make sure you have read the readings for that session. (See page 247 under "Read Before Meeting One.")

Course Goals

Your own goals and hopes will surely vary. These goals guided the writing of this course:
- To make connections between faith and food choices
- To celebrate the provision of "our daily bread"
- To build a sense of community and support within the group
- To encourage more healthful eating habits
- To explore the connections between the industrialization of agriculture and ecological degradation
- To explore the connections between the consolidation of power within multi-national agribusinesses, and workers' rights and animal rights
- To encourage the healing of our separation from food and land.

Course Organization

Facilitator: The role of course facilitator rotates each week; the course does not require an experienced leader, expert or teacher. This should contribute a shared sense of ownership, responsibility and community to the participants. The facilitator for Meeting One will most likely be the person who organized the class. Some groups find it helpful to designate a facilitator for each subsequent meeting during Meeting One. Others may choose someone to facilitate the next session at the end of each meeting. The facilitator should read all the material for "their" meeting beforehand, to have an idea about timing, flow and content.

Setting and Timing: Food and Faith is meant to be flexible, and can be used in a variety of settings. Ideally, this course would be held in group members' homes with enough time (about 1½ to 2 hours) to experience and go through the material fully. Such an informal setting contributes to a more relaxed, community-building atmosphere.

The material is also well suited for a Sunday School hour or adult education forum. Unlike other curricula which often specifically state how many minutes should be spent on each section, allow the group to make such decisions based upon the flow of the discussion and interest of the group. However, the facilitator should have a general idea of how time might be spent during the meeting.

For those using the course in a 45-60 minute time slot, you may not have time to consider each of the suggested questions. Feel free to modify meetings as you see fit; the facilitator could choose which questions to highlight. Some groups have chosen to take two weeks to cover all the material in each chapter.

Group Size: Ideal group size is between six and eight participants. If your group is larger, remain together for the opening prayer/meditation as well as the closing prayer, but break into appropriately sized groups for the discussion periods.

Book Sharing: Of course, it's best if everyone has a copy of *Food and Faith.* On the other hand, and in the spirit of this book, if sharing works out well, great. It is important that the people facilitating the next meeting have a copy of the book the week prior to "their" meeting.

Journal: There is space within the study guide—though you may also wish to bring a journal or notebook—to take notes and jot down feelings, ideas and impressions while you are together and during the week. Your notes will become a valuable resource, charting how your thoughts and feelings may have changed over time.

A Note on the Readings: This resource as an attempt to help you form a learning community. This community will hear from a variety of "voices." Some of those voices will be your own and those of your fellow group members. Other voices will come from the readings. It is important not to treat these readings as authoritative. Think of these as the stories and ideas of other group members not able to join your discussion in person. Not all of the perspectives will be meaningful or useful to everyone. Focus on what you do find meaningful. In a learning community, different people find different things helpful. The object is not that everyone will emerge from this experience thinking, doing and believing the same things. Rather, in an open sharing of ideas and experiences, each individual's own exploration of the issues will be enhanced and supported.

Length of Readings: There are approximately 30-60 minutes of reading each week. If you think you may not have time, we suggest you read the brief introduction (found on the first page of every reading) to each essay and decide which one you would like to start with. (Since much of the learning and discussion emanates from your perceptions and thoughts on these readings, your experience will be more complete if you read the suggested articles. If not, perhaps you can read and discuss them at a later date.)

Guidelines for Participation

This course seeks to value your perspectives, life experiences and wisdom. We encourage you to interact with each other and the materials honestly and to be open about your questions, misgivings and hopes. The Seattle guru of simplicity study circles, Cecile Andrews, has a number of helpful guidelines for creating a community-oriented group. These are her suggestions:

- *No leaders. Be participatory.* This is a circle, not a pyramid, so no one can be a dictator; everyone is responsible.
- *Respond as equals.* In this course we act on the idea that we are all equal.
- *Be authentic.* We spend a lot of our lives trying to look successful. No one really gets to know us. In this group, try not to pretend. Describe what you really think or feel.
- *Focus on the heart.* Some conversations come just from the head. When you communicate from the heart you bring in the whole of yourself: emotions, imagination, spiritual insight and thoughts.
- *View conversations as barn-raising instead of battle.* Ways to do this include:
  — Listen and focus on understanding. As others speak, try to suppress the instinct to criticize or compare.
  — No attacking, dismissing or denigrating. The facilitator should be especially committed to responding to others with support, thus modeling a caring response.
  — No persuading. It is enough to state what you think—you do not have to convince people that you are right.
  — No playing devil's advocate. Although this is a common form of communication, it violates just about all of the above guidelines.
- *Question conventional wisdom and seek out alternative explanations and views.*
- *Discover wisdom through stories.* Throughout human history people have learned through story telling. Everyone can tell his or her story and there's no right or wrong interpretation. Ultimately, stories connect people; in listening to someone else's story, we often hear strains of our own.

(These guidelines are taken from Cecile Andrews, *The Simplicity Circle: Learning Voluntary Simplicity Through a Learning for Life Study Circle*, 1994; and *The Circle of Simplicity: Return to the Good Life*, HarperCollins 1997.)

Meeting Format

Each meeting has all or most of the following components:

The "Facilitator Overview" should be read by the facilitator prior to the meeting. Specific instructions for the meeting will be given in this section.

Participants should be familiar with the meeting's "Purpose."

"Read Before Next Gathering" lists the readings for the following meeting.

The "Opening Meditation and Prayer" provide a brief centering time. This time can be led by the facilitator or a member who feels comfortable doing so. Feel free to bring in prayers of your own or pray spontaneously as you are comfortable. This goes for the "Closing Prayer" as well.

The "Check-In" is a *brief* report to the group about the "Action Step" you took during the week. If you are pressed for time, you may wish to skip this section. People should also feel free to pass.

A few of the meetings include a "Group Reading" which we suggest reading aloud, cooperatively by the group.

Each meeting's discussion emanates from that week's readings. There will be time for "Group Discussion" as well as "Small Group/Pair Discussions." The themes of these latter discussions will frequently be reported back to the whole group.

Many meetings suggest an "Action Step" which would be both meaningful and "doable."

Toward the end of most meetings you will find a "Grace"—a mealtime prayer. Use these in your own home or if/when you share meals together as a group.

End with the "Closing Prayer."

One Final Important Note

Use this resource to engage with the ideas presented, not as a "course" to be "mastered." Your creative adaptation to meet your own needs is encouraged. You may find you don't have time to answer every question, or feel drawn to discuss only a few of the suggested questions, or have questions of your own. Perhaps you will want to spend two weeks on certain meeting topics. Please modify as needed.

Course Overview

Brief summaries of each meeting appear below, followed by alternatives to the full eight session course. As you read through the meeting summaries, you may find an organizing theme or length that might work well for your group. Feel free to be creative!

This Study Guide delves into fairly challenging and sometimes controversial areas. **Meeting One**, however, sets an important tone and underlying theme for your time together: the celebration of food and the communities that nourish and support life. You will also have some time to begin to reflect on the connections between food choices, faith and caring for creation.

Many people first become concerned about food through a desire to "eat well" or as a result of poor health. **Meeting Two** explores the food industry's influence on our perceptions of what is healthy, and how that industry benefits from our confusion. Finally, this meeting specifically discusses connections between diet and heart disease.

The evocative readings of **Meeting Three** speak about times when food becomes a sacrament, times when that which is holy is ushered into our lives through that which is ordinary. This meeting also includes exploration of how our worldviews (our picture of reality) influence our daily decisions, and introduces theologies that support a strong Christian ecological ethic.

Industrial agribusiness; factory farming; corporately owned, vertically integrated food systems: a variety of terms exist to describe the increasing level of corporate control of farming, farmers and the food supply. The next three meetings can be seen as sharing a common theme: "What are some of the impacts of this industrialization of agriculture?"

Meeting Four discusses some of the impacts on smaller farmers and rural communities (human and nonhuman).

Meeting Five explores certain characteristics of the "free market" system and raises significant questions about how our society measures economic well-being. Both meetings highlight steps one can take to support local/regional food economies.

Meeting Six tries to uncover some of the impacts industrial agriculture has on migrant workers and farm animals.

Meeting Seven ventures into the sometimes "murky waters" surrounding genetically modified foods. This meeting also takes time to discuss some of the underlying causes of world hunger.

Meeting Eight highlights individuals and communities developing and supporting agricultural systems independent of corporate control. The meeting concludes with a potluck and time to reflect on what you have learned from the course as a whole, and how you might feel called to respond.

If You Have Four or Six Weeks...

We understand that some congregations, organizations, and small groups may not have time available for the entire eight-session Study Guide. We recommend the following four- or six-session groupings. After that appear thematic suggestions for four or six sessions.

Six Sessions
   Meeting One—Celebrating Food and Community
   Meeting Three—Creation Theology and Food As Sacrament
   Meeting Four—Industrial Agriculture and the Family Farm
   Meeting Five—Global Markets to Backyard Gardens
   Meeting Six—The Voiceless
   Meeting Eight—Promising Directions

Four Sessions
    Meeting One—Celebrating Food and Community
    Meeting Three—Creation Theology and Food As Sacrament
    Meeting Five—Global Markets to Backyard Gardens
    Meeting Eight—Promising Directions

If your group wishes to focus on a theme, find four- and six-session themes below. Of course, feel free to design your own organizing theme or length.

Theme: *Your Health, Justice, and the Industrialization of Agriculture*
    Meeting Two—Your Health, the Western Diet and Politics
    Meeting Four—Industrial Agriculture and the Family Farm
    Meeting Five—Global Markets to Backyard Gardens
    Meeting Six—The Voiceless
    Meeting Seven—Genetically Modified Organisms—Addressing Hunger
    Meeting Eight—Promising Directions

Note: Since Meeting One is not included, your group should read "How to Use This Material" prior to the first gathering, and briefly discuss the guidelines presented in that reading.

Theme: *The Community of All Creation*
    Meeting One—Celebrating Food and Community
    Meeting Three—Creation Theology and Food As Sacrament
    Meeting Six—The Voiceless
    Meeting Eight—Promising Directions

Meeting One: **Celebrating Food and Community**

Read Before Meeting One

"How to Use This Material"   —p. 241
"A Thing Shared," MFK Fisher   —p. 21
"Coming Home to Eat," Gary Paul Nabhan —p. 28
"Food as Sacramental," Michael Schut   —p. 11

Facilitator Overview

This is an important meeting as you begin to set the tone for the course, and begin to get to know one another. As today's facilitator, please:

1. Welcome everyone, and make sure everyone has access to a copy of this book.
2. After introductions, facilitate the flow of the discussion.
3. Lead (or ask someone else to lead) the opening meditation and prayer.
4. Keep track of time, ensuring that all have adequate time to speak.
5. Read aloud the group reading.
6. Determine how the group wants to choose each meeting's facilitator and designate one for your next meeting.

Introductions

Briefly introduce yourselves. (Soon you will have a chance to say more.)

Purpose:
To introduce the course as a whole and discuss course guidelines

To introduce each other and begin to create a comfortable setting

To begin to explore connections between food and faith

Read Before Next Gathering:
"Introduction to *Food Politics*," Marion Nestle
                    —p. 37

"Healthy Heart, Healthy Life," John Robbins   —p. 44

"The Politics of Food Choice," Marion Nestle
                    —p. 51

Opening Meditation

Meaningful, hilarious, community-enriching, soul-satisfying times are so often associated with a shared meal. Close friends, candlelight, homemade bread, a prayer of thanks, a meal prepared together. Or a big party, potluck, the plates not big enough for all the variety, the second helping of those dishes you particularly liked, the familiar voices and laughter. Bread and wine, people of all races, economic and social classes, young and old, sick and healthy, walking forward, recognizing their need for reconciliation and relationship with God and others, celebrating God's presence, celebrating their unity. Your favorite meal, prepared in love by those who know you, your birthday gift! The stories and settings are endless—times when the gift of food mediates the sanctity, preciousness and joy of life.

Opening Prayer

Creator, Sustainer, Redeemer, thank you for the gift of another day and for the chance to be together. Thank you for providing our daily bread, reminding us of our day-by-day dependence on your creation. For your presence in our lives we thank you. May we learn from our own lives, from each other, and from your presence among us. *Amen.*

Group Reading

(Read the following aloud—we suggest taking turns.)

So, here you are, beginning a course on food and faith. We hope this first meeting is fun and relaxed. You'll have a chance to tell a piece of your own story, and listen to others. And you'll take time to reflect on the connections between your faith and the food you eat. At Earth Ministry (see page 284 for more on Earth Ministry), we believe there are many such connections—not the least of which emanates from the fact that "How we eat determines to a considerable extent how the world is used." (Wendell Berry)

Sharing stories—your own as well as those represented in the readings—is a significant activity at these meetings. In other words, this course begins with each of you, where you are, who you are and what brings you here.

Then Jesus declared, "I am the bread of life. He who comes to me will never go hungry and she who believes in me will never be thirsty."

—*John 6:35*

"How to Use This Material" provides a brief overview to the course and also suggests guidelines for group interaction. Those guidelines are important and should help create community as you meet together. The introduction also briefly discusses logistics. Everyone should be clear about how this course is organized, the role of the facilitator, course guidelines and so on. Take ten minutes or so to answer the following questions, or others you may have, about these guidelines and logistics.

• Are there any questions about course format, organization or leadership?
• Any questions or comments on the facilitator's role? *Please note:* Some groups have found it helpful to designate facilitators for every meeting during Meeting One rather than doing so meeting by meeting. This provides each facilitator more time to prepare. (If some are uncomfortable with facilitating, they should not feel pressured to do so.)
• Any comments or questions about the group process ("Guidelines for Participation," p. 243) for this course?

> **Eaters...must understand that eating takes place inescapably in the world, that it is inescapably an agricultural act, and that how we eat determines, to a considerable extent, how the world is used.**
>
> —*Wendell Berry*

Further Introductions

Take a couple minutes to introduce yourself more fully. Be mindful of leaving sufficient time for others. Some possible prompts:

• The obvious ones: name, where are you from, your work, your family...
• If you are not a farmer, how many years/generations do you need to go back to find a farmer in your own family? If you do farm, how long has the land been in your family?
• How did you come to be interested in this course?
• What is your favorite food?

Group Discussion

(Remember, throughout the course, these are suggested questions. If you have others you wish to pursue, feel free to so do.)

• Did any of the readings particularly "stand out" to you?

• The essays by Fisher and Nabhan celebrate memorable meals. Share your experience of a particularly joyful or meaningful meal.

• Nabhan's piece also introduces certain realities of our food choices and system which we will return to later in this Study Guide: that our food today travels an average of 1,300 miles to reach our plates, and that we worry a fair bit about our food, yet still know little about how it was produced, where it was grown, or by whom. Do you see connections between these realities and your faith; between these realities and caring for creation?

• In your own family life, are there any food/meal traditions that you particularly value? Are there connections between those and your spirituality/faith?

Closing Prayer

Loving God, our food is connected vitally to many areas of our lives: to our communities, to our spirituality, to our celebrations, to our health. Surely this is a sign of your presence among us, you "in whom we live and move and have our being" (Acts 17:28). Be with us now and throughout our time together. *Amen.*

Grace—Blessing of the Stew Pot

Use in your own home or if/when you share meals together as a group.

Blessed be the Creator
and all creative hands
which plant and harvest,
pack and haul and hand
over sustenance—
Blessed be carrot and cow,
potato and mushroom,
tomato and bean,
parsley and peas,
onion and thyme,
garlic and bay leaf,
pepper and water,
marjoram and oil,
and blessed be fire—

and blessed be the enjoyment
of nose and eye,
and blessed be color—
and blessed be the Creator
for the miracle of red potato,
for the miracle of green bean,
for the miracle of fawn mushrooms,
and blessed be God
for the miracle of earth:
ancestors, grass, bird,
deer and all gone,
wild creatures
whose bodies become
carrots, peas, and wild
flowers, who
give sustenance
to human needs, whose
agile dance of music
nourishes the ear
and soul of the dog
resting under the stove
and the woman working over
the stove and the geese
out the open window
strolling in the backyard.
And blessed be God
for all, all, all.

—*Alla Renée Bozarth*

"Blessing of the Stew Pot," by Alla Renée Bozarth, from *Water Women: Poems by Alla Renée Bozarth*, Wisdom House, 1990 audiocassette; and *Moving to the Edge of the World: A Poetry Trilogy*, by Alla Renée Bozarth, iUniverse.com, 2000.

A Great Video

The movie "Babette's Feast" beautifully and powerfully captures the power, sacramentality, joy and community that food brings to life. Your group might set aside an evening to watch it together. Highly recommended!

Meeting Two: **Your Health, the Western Diet and Politics**

Purpose:

To explore connections between what we eat, the food industry and personal and ecological health

Read Before Next Gathering:

"God's Beloved Creation," Elizabeth Johnson —p. 79

"Biblical Views of Nature: Foundations for an Environmental Ethic," Marcia Bunge —p. 84

"The Interiority of Food," Thomas Moore —p. 63

"The Work at Hand," Carol Flinders —p. 70

"The Enjoyment of God and Creation," Norman Wirzba —p. 75

Facilitator Overview

As today's facilitator:

1. Lead the opening meditation and prayer.
2. Serve as timekeeper.
3. Facilitate discussions, ensuring that all those who wish to speak have the opportunity.
4. Designate next meeting's facilitator.

Opening Meditation

> To be of the Earth is to know
> the restlessness of being a seed
> the darkness of being planted
> the struggle toward the light
> the pain of growth into the light
> the joy of bursting and bearing fruit
> the love of being food for someone
> the scattering of your seeds
> the decay of the seasons
> the mystery of death and
> the miracle of birth.
>
> *—John Soos*
>
> *Earth Prayers*, p. 288. Reprinted by permission of the author.

Few of us are aware that the act of eating can be a powerful statement of commitment to our own well-being, and at the same time the creation of a healthier habitat. Your health, happiness, and the future of life on earth are rarely so much in your own hands as when you sit down to eat.

—*John Robbins*

Opening Prayer

Creator, Sustainer, Redeemer, we gather with you and with each other in thanks for the everyday miracles sustaining life. Feed us now as we continue our time together, exploring the connections between our faith and food. *Amen.*

Group Discussion

• What particularly struck you in today's readings?

• Nestle writes of the confusion we often feel in trying to answer "what is a healthy diet?" Did you find her points clarifying, surprising?

• Nestle and Robbins emphasized the food industry's influence on our food choices. In what ways are you aware that the food industry has influenced you?

In 2000 the number of overweight people in the world for the first time matched the number of undernourished people—1.1 billion each.

—*Marion Nestle*

• What connections do you find between a diet healthy for you as an individual and a diet with lower ecological impacts?

• Nestle writes that the food industry "fiercely opposes" the idea that some foods are better for health than others. Was this surprising to you? Do you think she is right?

• What did you think of Nestle's discussion on "The Ethics of Food Choice"? What ethical dilemmas come to your mind when considering dietary changes?

Closing Prayer (*Read in unison.*)

Creator God, we offer thanks for health, a gift we often take for granted. Thank you too for the sustaining gifts of this good Earth. We pray for an ever deeper appreciation of those gifts, for a growing appreciation of the beauty around us, for a reverence for all things lovely; that we might see in them a reflection of you. *Amen.*

Action Step

Two ideas:

"Rates of obesity are now so high among American children that many exhibit metabolic abnormalities formerly seen only in adults," writes Nestle. Later she reports that "the number of hours spent watching television is one of the best predictors of overweight." Not only are we sedentary when watching television, we are exposed to advertising, some of which targets our children (as Schlosser's *Fast Food Nation* describes so well). So, one possible Action Step: turn off your TV (whether or not you have kids)!

Another idea: Is there some diet change—not as in "lose weight" but as in "what you eat"—you feel inspired to try between now and your next meeting? Whether it's something you have always wanted to try or based on something you learned in the readings or the discussion today, make that a goal this week. Share that with the group, if you like, and report back next time.

Grace

(from the Buddhist tradition)

Use in your own home or if/when you share meals together as a group.

We venerate the Three Treasures (teachers, the wild, and friends)
And are thankful for this meal
The work of many people
And the sharing of other forms of life.

Meeting Three:

Creation Theology and Food as Sacrament

Purpose:

To uncover elements of our worldviews and how they might be influenced by a Christian creation theology

To explore sacramental experiences related to food

Read Before Next Gathering:

"The Pleasures of Eating," Wendell Berry —p. 142

"Where Have All the Farmers Gone?," Brian Halweil —p. 89

"There's Farming and Then There's Farming," Donella Meadows —p. 103

Facilitator Overview

As today's facilitator:

1. Lead the opening meditation and prayer.
2. Serve as timekeeper.
3. Facilitate discussions, ensuring that all those who wish to speak have the opportunity.
4. Lead the group reading.
5. Designate next meeting's facilitator.

Opening Meditation

Begin with silence and then read aloud:

A sacrament is when something holy happens. It is transparent time, time which you can see through to something deep inside time.

Generally speaking, Protestants have two official sacraments (Communion, Baptism) and Roman Catholics these two plus five others (Confirmation, Penance, Sacrament of the Sick, Ordination, and Matrimony). In other words, at such milestone moments as seeing a baby baptized or being baptized yourself, confessing your sins, getting married, dying, you are apt to catch a glimpse of the almost unbearable preciousness and mystery of life.

Needless to say, church isn't the only place where the holy happens. Sacramental moments can occur at any moment, any place, and to anybody. Watching something get born. Making love. A high-school graduation. Somebody coming to see you when you're sick. A meal with people you love. Looking into a stranger's eyes and finding out he's not a stranger.

If we weren't blind as bats, we might see that life itself is sacramental.

—*Frederick Buechner*

"Sacrament" [pp.82-83] from *Wishful Thinking: A Theological ABC* by Frederick Buechner. © 1973 by Frederick Buechner. Reprinted by permission of HarperCollins Publishers Inc.

Opening Prayer

Creator God, thank you for another day, for a chance to gather again. May our sense of your continued presence grow in us. And may our meals be times when we recognize your provision. Thank you for food in abundance. *Amen.*

Meditation Discussion Question

• How/when have you experienced food as sacramental? Think of a specific example, then share the story.

Check In

Did you try either of the Action Steps—turning off the TV, or changing (adding or subtracting) something in your diet? Briefly share your experiences, considering how you could support one another.

To live, we must daily break the body and shed the blood of creation. The point is, when we do this knowingly, lovingly, skillfully, reverently, it is a sacrament; when we do it ignorantly, greedily, clumsily, destructively, it is a desecration...in such desecration, we condemn ourselves to spiritual and moral loneliness, and others to want.

—*Wendell Berry*

Group Reading

We suggest taking turns reading this aloud.

Today's meeting highlights two themes in the readings: creation theology, and food as a sacrament. In the opening meditation, Buechner describes a sacrament as "when something holy happens." He suggests that, in addition to those times in life formally recognized by the Church as sacramental, life itself can become a sacrament, when the holy is revealed within the ordinary. In such a view, food becomes an everyday sacrament, a sign of God's goodness and care. Food becomes a path to connection with God and the rest of creation.

In contrast to that sense of connection, educator David Orr writes that "Our alien-ation from the natural world is unprecedented." This alienation is seen—perhaps most daily, or concretely—in how little we know about the food we eat. But we also embody this alienation when we protect ourselves from the realities of the ecological devastation around us. Elizabeth Johnson enumerates some of those realities: "By a conservative estimate, in the last quarter of the 20th century, 20 percent of all living species have become extinct...we are killing birth itself." These current and ongoing extinctions—caused by humans—are the most significant since the disap-pearance of the dinosaurs. Yet most of us choose not to let this reality sink in; we alienate ourselves (and our feelings) from what is arguably one of the most signifi-cant occurrences in the natural world today, indeed in geological history.

> **Respect for life and for the dignity of the human person extends also to the rest of creation.**
>
> —*Pope John Paul II*

One significant source of this alienation is simply the way we are taught to see the world, our worldview, our particular picture of reality. Our theologies significantly affect those worldviews. Some theology seems distant, esoteric—perhaps especially those points argued about at conferences. But whether we care to, or are able to, articulate our own more internal/personal theologies, they do affect our view of reality, placing certain concerns or relationships in the foreground and others in the background. Though immensely powerful, our worldviews and theologies often go unnoticed. As Charlene Spretnak says, they are "to us as water to a fish"—so omnipresent, they disappear.

Of course, worldviews are expressed daily—in the kind of economy our society creates, in how we personally spend time and money, and in how we treat the rest of our community (human and nonhuman). Today's essays by Bunge and Johnson make a strong case for a Christian theology of creation. If such theologies began to significantly inform our culture's worldview, it is not difficult to see how some of our behaviors would be called into question. The alarming rate of species extinc-tion caused by humans would not go so unnoticed by so many of us, because our worldview would include a theology that values all of life. Bunge's and Johnson's theologies also lend themselves to a sacramental view of food, acknowledging that because our food choice determines to "a considerable extent how the world [cre-ation] is used," what and how we eat matters. Bunge's and Johnson's work supports Wendell Berry's belief that when we "break the body and shed the blood of cre-ation... knowingly, lovingly, skillfully, reverently, it is a sacrament."

For variety's sake, and to give each of you more time to speak, begin by breaking into groups of two or three to discuss the creation theology essays of Johnson and Bunge.

Small Group Discussion

Break into groups of two or three, and use the following questions to guide your conversation. Add questions of your own.

- Did anything particularly strike you in the Johnson and/or Bunge essays?
- While growing up, did you receive a worldview and language that included care for and deep connection with the natural world? Discuss your answer.
- If you are, or have been, part of a faith community, how has that community shaped your worldview? Have you learned to emphasize some of the same things these authors stress?
- Johnson discusses three possible responses to our recognition of our connections with all of life: contemplative, ascetic and prophetic. Did one of those responses particularly resonate with you?

Group Discussion

Gather together as one group again and discuss:

- Any there any "hot topics" from your small group discussions that you want to bring up here?

- Do you or your family have favorite "graces" you say before a meal? Share some of them. What do they imply about "food as sacramental"?

- Because of the relationship Wirzba's grandfather had with his chickens, his enjoyment of chicken "was a sacramental eating." When do you experience "sacramental eating"?

• The essays by Moore and Flinders are particularly evocative. Anything that you especially liked about their thoughts?

• "Food is not just for the body; it also feeds the soul," Moore writes. What are some of your favorite "soul foods"? Who prepares them for you?

• What are some of your own meaningful times around the table? What made them memorable to you? Was there something sacramental in the experience?

• How do you experience a "spirituality of food"? Do you see this as part of your faith?

For everything God created is good, and nothing is to be rejected if it is received with thanksgiving, because it is consecrated by the word of God and prayer.

—*1 Timothy 4:4-5*

Recipe Sharing

Some of you may want to share "soul-food" recipes with the group at a subsequent meeting.

Action Step

If you are a member of a faith community, perhaps you would like to see your congregation embody the ecological ethic Johnson and Bunge describe. Earth Ministry has many resources, including a *Greening Congregations Handbook,* to help you get started. Contact us at *www.earthministry.org,* or call 206-632-2426.

Another idea: Invite family and friends to dinner, prepare "soul food" for them and share "soul food" stories.

An Excellent Video

We highly recommend a Maryknoll World Productions video titled "The Global Banquet: Politics of Food." The video's themes relate closely to those discussed in Meetings Four and Five. Well-done, provocative, and timely, this video is divided into two 25 minutes sections. If your group would like to view the video, you might take extra time during either Meetings Four or Five, schedule an additional meeting or have a popcorn and video night together.

In addition to ensuring a TV and VCR are available, contact one of the resource centers listed on p. 296 and ask for "The Global Banquet." Each resource center can give you information on their policies regarding the loan of videos.

Closing Prayer

"Taste and see that the Lord is good" (Psalm 34:8).

Loving God, we taste and see your goodness every day as you provide for our physical hungers through sustaining the gift of creation. For food that is plentiful, beautiful and diverse, we thank you. May we finally turn to you as well to meet all our varied hungers. In Christ's name we pray. *Amen.*

Grace

Use in your own home or if/when you share meals together as a group.

Let the sea resound, and everything in it, the world, and all who live in it. Let the rivers clap their hands, let the mountains sing together for joy (Psalm 98:7-8).

You will go out in joy and be led forth in peace; the mountains and hills will burst into song before you, and all the trees of the field will clap their hands (Isaiah 55:12).

For your daily sustenance, grace and love, we joyfully give you thanks! This food is a reminder of our connection to all that is: to sunlight, soil, water and minerals; to farmers, gardeners, truck drivers and grocers; to birds, worms and bees. Surely reason enough to celebrate! *Amen.*

Meeting Four:

Industrial Agriculture and the Family Farm

Purpose:

To reflect on our agricultural system as it relates to personal, communal and environmental health

Read Before Next Gathering:

"The Gross Domestic Product, Well-Being, and Waistlines," *Redefining Progress* —p. 112

"The Great Hunter-Gatherer Continuum," Jim Mulligan —p. 136

"French Fries," Alan Durning and John Ryan —p. 123

"The Idea of a Local Economy," Wendell Berry —p. 125

Facilitator Overview

As today's facilitator:

1. Serve as timekeeper.
2. Facilitate discussion, making sure that everyone who wants to has the opportunity to speak.
3. Lead the opening prayer.
4. Designate next meeting's facilitator.
5. If your group has decided to view the Maryknoll video "The Global Banquet: Politics of Food," make sure someone takes responsibility for setting up the VCR/TV. See the end of Meeting Three (p. 261) for a note about this video.

Opening Meditation

Berry describes "industrial eaters" as essentially ignorant of the history of the food they consume. Reflect on your lives, your parents' lives, your grandparents' lives. How far back in your family's history do you need to go to find people who knew where most of their food came from? Tell some of these family stories.

Group Discussion

Reminder: In all these discussions, remember the group participation guidelines as presented in "How to Use This Material" (p. 243) and discussed in Meeting One. Also, feel free to choose those questions in which your group is most interested.

Both Halweil, at some length, and Meadows, briefly, write about the realities facing farmers worldwide.

• What most impressed you about what they had to say?

• What would be the values/advantages of large agribusiness farms?

• What would be the values/advantages of a smaller family farm?

In the United States, the share of the consumer's food dollar that trickles back to the farmer has plunged from nearly 40 cents in 1910 to just above 7 cents in 1997.

—*Brian Halweil*

- Halweil discusses "agrarian services" and believes that small farms have the advantage in offering these services. What are some of these agrarian services, and do you agree that smaller farms have the advantage?

> **Find the shortest, simplest way between the earth, the hands and the mouth.**
>
> —*Lanza del Vasto*

- Both authors conclude their essays describing "local foodsheds"—farmers markets, community supported agriculture, and other "direct buying arrangements between farmers and consumers." Have any in your group tried these or other direct buying arrangements? What was your experience?

- What do you see as the social and ecological benefits of such arrangements?

> **Anyone who cares about good food has a stake in good farming and in methods of food production, processing, and distribution that accord with the long term health and sustainability of farmers, farming communities, and the land upon which they, and we, depend.**
>
> —*Robert Clark*

Berry describes the industrial food economy as a trap. He suggests escape comes via "restoring one's consciousness of what is involved in eating; by reclaiming responsibility for one's part in the food economy."

• What did you think of Berry's seven suggestions for reclaiming this responsibility?

• In which of the seven do you already participate?

• Which do you find more difficult? Why?

Action Step

Take one of Berry's seven suggestions, perhaps one you find a bit difficult, but that also feels doable. Share your plan with the group and see how it goes between now and your next meeting.

Closing Prayer *(Read in unison.)*

Loving God, thank you for the gift of life. You open your hand and satisfy the desire of every living thing, giving them their food in due season. We thank you for sustaining such a rich and bountiful Earth, our home. Grant us continued gratitude at the richness you provide. *Amen.*

Grace

Use in your own home or if/when you share meals together as a group.

My friends, let us give thanks for Wonder.
Let us give thanks for the Wonder of Life
that infuses all things now and forever.

Blessed is the Source of Life, the Fountain of Being
the wellspring of goodness, compassion and kindness
from which we draw to make for justice and peace.
From the creative power of Life we derive food and harvest,
from the bounty of the earth and the yields of the heavens
we are sustained and are able to sustain others.
All Life is holy, sacred,
worthy of respect and dignity.
Let us give thanks for the power of heart
to sense the holy in the midst of the simple.

We eat not simply to satisfy our own appetites,
we eat to sustain ourselves in the tasks we have been given.
Each of us is unique,
coming into the world with a gift no other can offer: ourselves.
We eat to nourish the vehicle of giving,
we eat to sustain our task of world repair,
our quest for harmony, peace and justice.

We eat and we are revived, and we give thanks
to the lives that were ended to nourish our own.
May we merit their sacrifice, and honor their sparks of holiness
through our deeds of loving kindness.

We give thanks to the Power that makes for Meeting,
for our table has been a place of dialogue and friendship.

We give thanks to Life.
May we never lose touch with the simple joy and wonder
of sharing a meal.

—*Rabbi Rami M. Shapiro*

From *Earth Prayers*, pp. 354-355. Reprinted by permission of the author.

Meeting Five: Global Markets to Backyard Gardens

Facilitator Overview

As today's facilitator:

1. Serve as timekeeper.
2. Facilitate discussion, making sure everyone who wants to has the opportunity to speak.
3. Lead the opening meditation and prayer.
4. Read aloud the group reading.
5. Designate next meeting's facilitator.
6. If your group has decided to view the Maryknoll video "The Global Banquet: Politics of Food," make sure someone takes responsibility for setting up the VCR/TV. See the end of Meeting Three (p. 261) for a note about this video.

Opening Meditation and Prayer

Begin with silence, then pray together:

> Eternal Spirit of Justice and Love,
> At this time of Thanksgiving we would be aware
> of our dependence on the earth and on the
> sustaining presence of other human beings
> both living and gone before us.

Purpose:

To discuss externalities and local economies as they connect to food choices

To reflect on our place along the "Hunter-Gatherer Continuum"

Read Before Next Gathering:

"On the Range," Eric Schlosser
—p. 149

"The Most Dangerous Job," Eric Schlosser
—p. 157

"Farm Factories: The End of Animal Husbandry," Bernard Rollin
—p. 163

As we partake of bread and wine, may we remember that there are many for
whom sufficient bread is a luxury, or for whom wine, when attainable, is
only an escape.

Let our thanksgiving for Life's bounty include a commitment to changing the
world, that those who are now hungry may be healed and those without
hope may be given courage.

Amen.

—*Frederick E. Gillis*

"Eternal Spirit of Justice and Love" by The Congregation of
Abraxas. From *Earth Prayers*, p. 351. Reprinted by permission of the
author.

Check In

Those who decided to experiment with one of Berry's seven suggestions could
relate their experience to the group.

Group Reading

(We suggest members take turns reading aloud.)

Redefining Progress' (www.redefiningprogress.org) essay introduced certain weaknesses in using the Gross Domestic Product (GDP) as our measure of economic
well-being. They specifically pointed out how certain consequences of our eating
habits (health costs, dieting costs, obesity) actually increase the GDP and are more
accurately "costs" and should be subtracted from GDP.

Though the GDP article did not mention these, two other ideas merit brief explanations: "externalities" and "getting prices right." Both are important in understanding our food economies.

**For as the soil makes the
sprout come up and a gar-
den causes seeds to grow,
so the Sovereign Lord will
make righteousness and
praise spring up before all
nations.**

—*Isaiah 61:11*

Simply put, externalities are "spillover effects,"
those things which are seen as "external" to the
monetary accounting system. A common example
is the chemical factory whose effluent into a river
kills the fish and ruins the fishers' livelihood. The
costs of the externalities in this example are borne
by the fish themselves and the fishers' loss of work.
To return to Redefining Progress' example, obesity
could be seen as an externality, a spillover effect,
of American eating habits.

"Getting prices right" is one way to include the costs of externalities in the price
of what we buy. In our factory example, the manufacturer could be taxed for polluting the river. Money raised from those taxes could then be used to provide work
for unemployed fishers and clean up the river. The taxes would also serve as an

incentive to not pollute, as the manufacturer's taxes would decrease when they
cleaned up their emissions.

Let's take one more example. Most scientists now agree that global warming is
occurring. The United States, with 4 percent of the world's population, emits 25
percent of the world's greenhouse gasses.
Emissions from our cars and trucks are the
largest contributors to those gasses. The
price we pay for a gallon of gasoline does
not include the "externality" of global
warming. Should we pay more for gasoline
to "get the price right"? The money raised
could be used to mitigate the effects of
rising sea levels, say, in Bangladesh. In
addition, a different message (in the form
of price per gallon for gas) would travel
through our current market system: gasoline
is expensive; we can't afford to drive as much. Our contributions to global warming
would thereby decrease.

Modern agriculture, addicted to oil and to poisons, strips the landscape of farmers, wildlife, biotic integrity, community, moral value and spiritual vitality; all in an unsustainable effort to feed restless urban populations. To sustain the world we must rebuild rural communities; dense with complex systems of life —human and natural —and rich with culture, ethics, and spiritual significance. Urban communities and choices play an indispensable role in this rebuilding.

— *Dr. Richard Cartwright Austin*

Group Discussion

The readings today introduced a number of significant topics including GDP vs.
GPI, Berry's perspectives on economics and the "free market," and externalities. As
always, feel free to discuss that which most spoke to you. The following questions
may guide you, but may not seem as pertinent as questions of your own.

On "Externalities, Economics, and the Gross Domestic Product":
• Of today's readings, which most spoke to you? Why?

• How does your faith influence your perspectives on externalities? On getting
prices right?

• When reading Durning and Ryan's "French Fries" story, did you note any externalities related to the production and transportation of fries? The costs of the externalities are not covered by the price of those spuds. Who ends up paying the price?

• Wendell Berry writes, "We have an environmental crisis because we have consented to an economy in which by eating, drinking, working, resting, traveling, and enjoying ourselves we are destroying the natural, the God-given world." What do you think of his statement? Would adopting the Genuine Progress Indicator (GPI) make sense to you as one way to move toward correcting that economy?

• Our society seems to believe Margaret Thatcher's TINA—There Is No Alternative—principle when it comes to globalization. Berry's essay challenges that assumption: "There is...no necessity or inevitability requiring our government to sacrifice the livelihoods of our small farmers, small business people, and workers, along with our domestic economic independence to the global 'free market.'" He then argues that the way to disengage from the "total economy" of the free market is to develop local food economies. Do you find Berry's arguments convincing, his ideas hopeful? Why or why not? Besides developing local food economies, are there other effective ways to disengage from the total economy?

Jim Mulligan describes how and where we can begin, with small achievable steps, to support more local food economies.

• Where do you see yourself on the "Hunter-Gatherer Continuum"?

• Have you experimented at various points along the continuum? How did you find those experiments?

• Where on the continuum would you like to be eventually?

Closing Prayer (*Read in unison.*)
Loving God, our many interconnections in this increasingly global economy link us to people, creatures, and places far away. Grant us grace and wisdom to understand these connections and respond with compassion. Encourage in us our assumption of appropriate responsibility. We thank you again for your gracious provision for our needs; grant us the grace of loving community in our lives. *Amen.*

Action Step
What, for you, might be a realistic goal in moving along the food continuum? What first step can you make in that direction before the next meeting?

Meeting Six **The Voiceless**

Facilitator Overview

As today's facilitator:
1. Serve as timekeeper.
2. Facilitate discussion making sure that everyone who wants to has the opportunity to speak.
3. Lead the opening meditation and prayer.
4. Designate next meeting's facilitator.

Opening Meditation

"The spirit of the Lord is on me,
  because he has anointed me
    to preach good news to the poor.
He has sent me to proclaim freedom
    for the prisoners
    and recovery of sight for the blind,
to release the oppressed,
    to proclaim the year of the Lord's favor."
—*Luke 4:18-19*

Even a cursory reading of the gospels quickly reveals Jesus as a prophet decrying injustice, as a person with compassion for the poor. Jesus gave voice to the voiceless. Similarly, in ancient times, the Old Testament prophets spoke out on behalf of those whose voices had little say in society.

Following Jesus' example and the cries of the Old Testament prophets, the Church has long been an advocate for the poor and oppressed. What the Church has not generally recognized is that, at least in Western culture, the nonhuman natural world is also largely voiceless. Nor has it realized the many connections between care for people and care for the earth. But, as Elizabeth Johnson argues, "If we are to love our neighbor as ourselves, then the range of neighbors now includes...the entire community of life. If the common good requires solidarity with all who suffer, then our compassion extends to suffering human beings and other species."

Opening Prayer

Creator, Sustainer, Redeemer, we are grateful for your care, for your desire to free us from the ways we are oppressed. In turn use us to release the oppressed. Especially, we thank you for Jesus' witness of a life well-lived. *Amen.*

Check In

Did you have the opportunity to try moving along the "hunter-gatherer continuum?" If so, how did it go?

Group Discussion

• What most affected you in today's readings? Why?

• What did you think of Rollin's presentation of a biblical ethic for the treatment of animals? How might you as an individual, family, or community embody Rollin's ethic?

• Both Rollin and Schlosser provide some picture of how farm animals are treated inside farm factories and slaughterhouses. Were these images familiar to you? How did they affect you?

• Schlosser discusses working conditions in slaughterhouses. Were the realities he described familiar to you? How did they affect you?

Small Group Discussion (in groups of two or three)
Today's readings raised many issues, including treatment of farm animals, the difficulty small ranchers/farmers have staying in business, the anti-union/organizing pressures placed on workers within the factory farming industry, poor pay and health care for those workers, and so on. There is a common link undergirding these issues: increased consolidation, corporate control of power within the agribusiness industry. That common theme runs through the last few meetings, particularly Meetings Four and Five.

But ask the animals, and they will teach you, or the birds of the air, and they will tell you; or speak to the earth, and it will teach you;...Which of all these does not know that the hand of the Lord has done this? In [God's] hand is the life of every creature and the breath of all humankind.

—*Job 12:7-10*

• For you, what are the most significant difficulties in breaking with the status quo of corporate agribusiness?

• How does your faith interact with/inform all of today's questions?

• Do you feel inspired to respond in any particular way to today's readings and discussion?

Large Group Discussion
Do any of the small groups want to share elements of their discussions?

Action Step
The Center for a New American Dream's website (www.newdream.org) features a program called Turn the Tide. One of their nine suggested actions is: "Replace one beef meal each week. Meat production is extremely resource-intensive—livestock currently consume 70 percent of America's grain production. Feedlot beef is particularly wasteful. For every 1,000 of us who take this action, we save over 70,000 pounds of grain, 70,000 pounds of topsoil and 40 million gallons of water per year!" Turn the Tide features a web based calculator, which allows you to quantitatively track the (decreased) impacts your actions (in this case, eating less meat) have.

Closing Prayer (*Read in unison.*)
"Give us wisdom and reverence so to use the resources of nature, that no one may suffer from our abuse of them, and that generations yet to come may continue to praise you for your bounty; through Jesus Christ our Lord. *Amen.*"
—*From* The Book of Common Prayer

Another idea: Your city/town may well have an organization, market, farmer(s) that employ methods of animal husbandry, rather than factory farming. Some may also raise their animals on organic feed. Find out about those local growers; support them; find out where you can purchase their meat.

Meeting Seven: Genetically Modified Organisms— Addressing Hunger

Purpose:
To wrestle with some questions and concerns surrounding hunger and genetically modified food

Read Before Next Gathering:
"Taking Action: Voting with Forks," Marion Nestle
—p. 221

"Hungry for Change," Jennifer Bogo —p. 223

"Houses of Worship Sing Praises of Coffee for a Cause," Jake Batsell
—p. 227

"Heart Benefits of Shade Grown Coffee," Joel Sisolak
—p. 229

Facilitator Overview

As today's facilitator:
1. Lead the opening meditation and prayer.
2. Serve as timekeeper.
3. Facilitate discussions, ensuring that all those who wish to speak have the opportunity.
4. Designate next meeting's facilitator.
5. We suggest sharing a potluck together during Meeting Eight. If you decide to do so, make plans today for that potluck gathering.

Opening Meditation

Then God said, "Let us make humankind in our image, in our likeness: and let them rule over the fish of the sea, and the birds of the air, over the livestock, over all the earth, and over all the creatures that move along the ground."

— *Genesis 1:26*

"Dominion does not mean license to exploit. In ancient Hebrew thought, it means a responsibility. If a ruler...fails in this righteous rule of dominion, then that person forfeits the right to rule. That [incorrect] theological focus has isolated a good part of the faith community from the care of creation and [from] those themes you find in every major world tradition."

—Dean Freudenberger, in the Los Angeles Times, October 16, 1999.

Check In

Those who experimented with the Turn the Tide feature of the New American Dream's website or researched local meat producers, might share what they learned and/or experienced.

Opening Prayer

Creator, Sustainer, Redeemer, thank you again for our time together. We pray for wisdom and ask for humility in the face of creation's complexity; we pray that all creatures may share in Earth's bounty; we pray that all will be fed. We pray with hope, and in faith. *Amen*

Introduction to Discussion Questions

Today's readings include a number of voices on both genetically modified (GM) organisms and issues around hunger; Mittal and Trewavas' pieces included discussion of the potential hope that GM foods will allow us to eradicate hunger. Such issues raise plenty of questions. The majority of the following questions related to hunger are discussed within small groups. Of course those questions are related to the larger group's discussion of GM food. [If your group would rather not divide up into smaller groups, feel free to stay together—but make sure everyone who wants to has time to speak. *Reminder*: Continue to practice the "Guidelines for Participation," p. 243.]

Small Group Discussion (in groups of two or three)

• As you read this session's essays relating to hunger (Trewavas, Mittal and McGovern) what struck you as most important?

• As you reflect on today's readings on hunger and think about this course as a whole, how have your perspectives on hunger changed?

• "Hunger is a political condition," claims McGovern. Mittal writes, "Hunger is a social disease linked to poverty." What do you think of these comments?

• These authors have differing opinions on the role the Green Revolution played in decreasing hunger. They also disagree on the role GM foods can play in addressing hunger. What is your position on these questions?

Large Group Discussion (Gather together again as a group.)
• Many of us are rather confused about genetically modified (GM) foods and technology. What do you find particularly confusing/concerning? Alternately, have you found greater clarity about any of your concerns?

**The earth is the Lord's
and everything in it...**
        —*Psalm 24:1*

- Are you aware of more recent developments related to GM food that might add to this discussion?

- Tewolde claims that "the more influential governments are now really largely run by individuals who represent corporate interests...genetic engineering is really going wild because it is not controlled by society but by selfish individual interests." Any comments or reactions to his perspective?

- Shiva describes ecological agriculture as "nonviolent." What are some of the characteristics of a nonviolent agriculture?

- Shiva briefly contrasts a "worldview of abundance"—Indian women leaving food for ants on their doorstep—with a "worldview of scarcity"—corporate sales pitches' defining pollination as "theft by bees." What experiences and influences might lead some to operate out of abundance, and others out of scarcity?

- What are your perspectives on the precautionary principle in relationship to GM food?

• Do the tools of GM technology raise ethical questions for you? Why or why not?

Action Step

A number of the readings in this course have revealed that many of us are ignorant of our food's "history," including whether or not the food is genetically modified. Next week is your last meeting; we encourage you to share a potluck together. Consider, as an "Action Step," checking into the history of one item you use in your potluck dish (or else the history of one of your favorite foods). Where and how was it grown? How did it get to you? Was GM technology used?

Another idea: Holden Village, a Lutheran retreat center in Washington's Cascade Range, shares a weekly "Hunger Awareness Meal." A celebratory potluck is more appropriate for your next gathering, but you could share a "Hunger Awareness Meal" with your family or faith community in the future. The menu for that meal is usually rice or a baked potato, served without butter or other toppings.

Closing Prayer *(Read in unison.)*
Creator God, "We thank you for making the earth fruitful, so that it might produce what is needed for life: bless those who work in the fields; give us seasonable weather; and grant that we may all share the fruits of the earth rejoicing in your goodness; through Jesus Christ our Lord. Amen." From *The Book of Common Prayer*.

Reminder

We suggest sharing a potluck together during your next gathering. If you decide to do so, make plans today for that potluck.

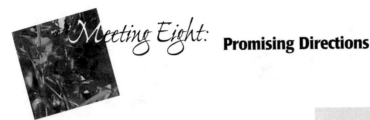

Meeting Eight: **Promising Directions**

Facilitator Overview

As today's facilitator:

1. Serve as timekeeper.
2. Facilitate discussion making sure that everyone who wants to has the opportunity to speak.
3. Lead the opening meditation and prayer.
4. Have people read aloud the in-class reading.

Opening Meditation

How many are your works, O Lord!
    In wisdom you made them all;
    the earth is full of your creatures.
There is the sea, vast and spacious,
    teeming with creatures beyond number—
    living things both large and small.
There the ships go to and fro,
    and the leviathan, which you
    formed to frolic there.
These all look to you
    to give them their food at the proper time.

Purpose:

To reflect on and share how this experience, this course may have affected your relationship to and choices about food

To discuss how those choices might relate to your faith

To enjoy a potluck meal together

Opening Prayer

Creator God, thank you for your loving sustenance of all life's creatures. We thank you that we are so often blessed with such rich abundance of food. Thank you for our time together, for the gift of life, for your ongoing work of creation in our world and for your presence in each of our lives. Be with us now and when we leave this place. *Amen.*

When you give it to them,
    they gather it up;
when you open your hand,
    they are satisfied with good things.
    —*Psalm 104:24-28*

Check In

Those who tried to discover the "secret life-history" of an item in their potluck dish should relate that story to the group. Or tell about these discoveries during the potluck.

Group Reading

This final meeting provides time for you to share with one another. Share what you have learned, new perspectives you may have gained and ways in which you have begun to express these in your daily lives. Each of our lives is a weaving, composed of interwoven and varied threads, each thread forming one strand of an autobiography. Of course, each thread is interconnected, our spiritual autobiographies affecting and affected by our familial, geographical and professional autobiographies. In a sense, this course has asked you to consider in some detail your food autobiography.

We titled this last meeting and its collection of readings, "Promising Directions." At Earth Ministry we see these examples as hopeful. They point us in promising directions. We believe they do so for many reasons. They value community health —economic viability of smaller scale farmers, the retention and building up of topsoil, clean water—rather than the bottom line profits of a few multinational corporations. Their scale is appropriate to human capacity to know and care for land, and they support and create local and regional agricultural systems, rather than agribusiness conglomerates which cannot respond to the needs of *a place.* The stories are hopeful because they show regular people making a difference.

In this meeting, take some time to reflect on this course and how it has intersected and perhaps influenced your story.

Group Discussion

• What in today's readings did you find most important?

- What has been the most meaningful part of this course for you?

- How has this experience affected your understanding of and relationship to food? of the connections between your faith, the spirituality of food and food choices?

- What actions/new directions might you take as a result of this time together? If you take this new direction/action, how would your life be or feel different?

In closing, consider the last question as a way to reflect on the whole course. Consider your answer in relationship to the following constellation of questions:

- How would this new direction relate to the perspective of food as sacramental?

Closing Prayer (*Read in unison.*)

Creator, Sustainer, Redeemer, we give you thanks for these times of sharing and learning. Help us to be of support and encouragement to one another. Nourish our hearts that we may increasingly make room for love and thereby for your transformative presence. We pray in your name. *Amen.*

—*Adapted from* The Book of Common Prayer

- How does it relate to the connections between food choices and justice?
- How does it relate to questions of health, both personal and environmental?

Celebration-Closing Potluck

Appendix A

About Earth Ministry

History

Earth Ministry is an ecumenical, Christian, environmental, eco-justice oriented, nonprofit organization based in Seattle, Washington. We began with a recognition of the underlying spiritual and moral roots of the environmental crisis and the desire to help people of faith see more clearly the connections between their faith, their daily life, the "public life" of our larger community and ecological concerns. Founded in 1992, we have become a national leader in the movement to connect faith and care for creation.

Earth Ministry recognizes that Western Christendom has at times been blamed for contributing to our environmental crisis. However, we believe that Christianity has much to offer in helping our culture live respectfully in balance with all creation, grateful for its inherent, God-given worth and integrity and nourished by its beauty and mystery. Our mission statement emanates from these understandings and vision.

Mission Statement

Earth Ministry helps connect Christian faith with care for the Earth. Our work engages individuals and congregations in knowing God more fully through deepening relationships with all of God's creation. We believe that through this experience our personal lives and our culture will be transformed. These transformations include simplified living, environmental stewardship, justice for all creation, and a worldview that sees creation as a revelation of God. Together these lead to a rediscovery of the vitality of the Christian faith.

Programs, Resources, and Opportunities for Involvement

Consistent with our mission, we design programs both for individuals and congregations. As a grassroots organization based in Seattle, we gear much of our work toward local constituents; however, a number of our programs and resources are equally applicable nationally.

National Resources

- *Simpler Living, Compassionate Life: A Christian Perspective* was awarded the 2000 second place Book Award for spirituality by the Catholic Press Association. Published by Living the Good News, it may be ordered through Earth Ministry (see contact information below) or by calling 1-800-824-1813.
- *Earth Letter,* our acclaimed mini-journal of Christian ecological spirituality for daily life, is published five times a year. Each issue features engaging, well-written articles by respected theologians, ecologists and ethicists. In addition, it

offers book reviews, poems and prayers, highlights resources for congregations and gives updates on the work of Earth Ministry and local congregations.

- *Greening Congregations Handbook,* a comprehensive and inspiring "toolbox" is chock full of articles, stories, ideas, and resources for cultivating creation awareness and care within a congregation. The Handbook provides for a process through which congregations can "green" many areas of their life together: from worship and education, to grounds care, heating and lighting, to community outreach and advocacy.
- *Ecological Healing: A Christian Vision,* a book that provides an ecologically sensitive view of Christian vocation and spirituality and an integral environmental ethic.
- Web site resources: www.earthministry.org has numerous resources that you can either download directly or order from us, by email or phone. In addition, it contains a calendar of events, help for congregational organizers, and links to other religious and environmental sites.
- Staff available for preaching, speaking, teaching, and workshop/retreat leadership both nationally and locally.

Local Resources

In addition to these national resources, people who live within the Puget Sound region can take advantage of our "Monthly Update" mailing, gatherings, lectures, field trips, resource library, annual Celebration of St. Francis and advocacy and hands-on conservation efforts. Also, our Colleague Support Program helps to strengthen the work of our volunteers who foster creation awareness and care in their congregations.

For more information on these and other programs, call or write:

Earth Ministry
6512 23rd Avenue NW
Suite 317
Seattle, WA 98117
(206) 632-2426
E-mail: emoffice@earthministry.org
Web site: www.earthministry.org

Appendix B

Organization and Resource Guide

This resource guide includes the following sections:
• Political Action and Organizing Groups
• Resources for Community Supported Agriculture (CSA) and Farmers Markets
• Educational, Action-Oriented Organizations
• Coffee Activism (Java Justice)
• Animals
• Videos

(For purposes of clarity, the organizations below are listed alphabetically under certain categories. Some organizations could be listed under more than one heading.)

Political Action and Organizing Groups

American Farmland Trust
One of the more effective groups in establishing conservation easements and other strategies to protect rural landscapes and single farms. 1200 18th Street NW, Suite 800, Washington, DC 20036; 202-331-7300; www.farmland.org.

Bread for the World
A nationwide Christian movement seeking justice for the world's hungry people by lobbying our nation's decision makers. 50 F Street, NW, Suite 500, Washington, DC 20001; 202-639-9400; 800-82-BREAD; www.bread.org.

Center for Rural Affairs
An effective group advocating for family farmers and helping them maintain their economic and ecological well-being. P.O. Box 406, Walthill, NE 68067; www.cfra.org.

Center of Concern
Their Food Security Project monitors the world food system, especially its globalization, analyzes the food system, describes its injustices, develops food security policy recommendations based on Catholic social teaching, and works with governments and non-governmental organizations to enact and implement such policy. 1225 Otis Street, NE, Washington, DC 20017; 202-635-2757; www.coc.org.

Citizens for Health
Empowers consumers to make informed health choices, especially about dietary supplements, complementary and alternative medicine, food and water safety. P. O. Box 2260, Boulder, CO 80306; www.citizens.org

Community Alliance with Family Farmers (CAFF)
Founded in 1978, a nonprofit member-activist organization. CAFF political and educational campaigns are building a coalition of rural and urban people who foster

family-scale agriculture that cares for the land, sustains local economies, and promotes social justice. For fifteen years CAFF has published the *National Organic Directory*, a national listing of organic farmers, wholesalers, suppliers, resource groups, publications, certification laws and state laws for organic farming. CAFF, PO Box 464, Davis, CA 95617; 800-852-3832, 916-756-8518; www.caff.org.

Community Food Security Coalition (CFSC)

A nonprofit, membership-based national coalition of over 600 organizations and individuals who work together to bring about lasting social change by promoting community-based solutions to hunger, poor nutrition, and the globalization of the food system. P.O. Box 209, Venice, CA 90294; 310-822-5410; www.foodsecurity.org.

Food and Water

Leads tenacious and effective public campaigns against toxic food technologies, including food irradiation, pesticides and GMOs, while stimulating efforts to build safe, sustainable alternatives; publishes the *Food and Water Journal* and *Wild Matters*. 389 Rt. 215, Walden, VT 05873; 800-EAT-SAFE; www.foodandwater.org.

The Institute for Agriculture and Trade Policy (IATP)

IATP promotes resilient family farms, rural communities and ecosystems around the world through research and education, science and technology and advocacy. For reports on U.S. trade policy and food security contact IATP at: 2105 First Avenue South, Minneapolis, MN 55404; 612-870-0453; www.iatp.org.

The International Forum on Globalization (IFG)

The International Forum on Globalization (IFG) is an alliance of sixty leading activists, scholars, economists, researchers and writers formed to stimulate new thinking, joint activity, and public education in response to economic globalization. Representing over 60 organizations in 25 countries, the IFG associates come together out of a shared concern that the world's corporate and political leadership is undertaking a restructuring of global politics and economics that may prove as historically significant as any event since the Industrial Revolution. IFG includes a focus on agriculture through their "International Forum on Food and Agriculture," 1009 General Kennedy Avenue #2, San Francisco, CA 94129; 415-561-7650; www.ifg.org

Land Stewardship Project

A private, nonprofit farm and social justice organization founded in 1982 and based in Minnesota. LSP works locally and nationally to foster an ethic of stewardship toward the land and promote sustainable communities and agriculture through grass-roots organizing, advocacy, participatory education and policy initiatives. 2200 Fourth Street, White Bear Lake, MN 55110; 612-653-0618; www.landstewardship-project.org.

National Campaign for Sustainable Agriculture

A network of diverse groups whose mission is to shape national policies fostering a sustainable food and agricultural system that is economically viable, environmentally sound, socially just and humane. P.O. Box 396, Pine Bush, NY 12566. 845-744-8448; www.sustainableagriculture.net.

National Family Farm Coalition (NFFC)

NFFC serves as a national link for grassroots organizations working on family farm issues. NFFC brings together farmers and others to organize national projects focused on preserving and strengthening family farms. Over the past fourteen years, NFFC has worked to promote the safety of the food supply and the security of those who make it possible. 110 Maryland Ave., N.E., Suite 307, Washington, DC 20002; 202-543-5675; www.nffc.net.

Pesticide Action Network

PANNA (Pesticide Action Network North America) works to replace pesticide use with ecologically sound and socially just alternatives. Links local and international consumer, labor, health, environment and agriculture groups into an international citizens' action network. It challenges the global proliferation of pesticides, defends basic rights to health and environmental quality and works to insure the transition to a just and viable society. 49 Powell St., Suite 500, San Francisco, CA 94102; 415-981-1771; www.panna.igc.org.

Resources for Community Supported Agriculture (CSA) and Farmers Markets

Biodynamic Farming and Gardening Association

Contact them for the most up-dated list of CSAs in your area. Give them your zip code and they mail you the list! They also have good information about biodynamic growing methods. PO Box 550, Kimberton, PA 19442; 800-516-7797; www.biodynamics.com.

Helpful Websites

Supporting local, small-scale agriculture ventures can be an ecologically sound and socially just activity. For a national listing of local farmers markets go to www.ams.usda.gov/farmersmarkets/. To find out more about the nationwide Community Supported Agriculture (CSA) movement, go to www.nal.usda.gov/afsic/csa. This site will help to connect you with CSA farmers near you. To do a comprehensive search in your area for CSAs, farmers markets, u-pick locations, farm stands, and sources of fresh eggs, and meat go to www.localharvest.org.

Educational, Action-Oriented Organizations

The Center for a New American Dream

The Center has an excellent website and quality resources including information on connecting food choices with greater equity and sustainability. They also highlight issues like "kids and commercialism," "simplifying the holidays" and much more. The Center's website includes a web-based calculator (see their Turn the Tide program) to help individuals and groups quantify the impacts of daily lifestyle changes (such as eating less beef, or driving fewer miles). 6930 Carroll Avenue, Suite 900, Takoma Park, MD 20912; 877-68-Dream; www.newdream.org.

Co-op America

A nonprofit linking consumers with socially and environmentally responsible businesses in a nationwide "green" marketplace. Their *National Green Pages* lists over 100 categories of products and services, including food, body care products, restaurants, socially responsible financial planning and long-distance telephone service, travel and more. It also includes contact information and descriptions of socially and environmentally responsible businesses. 1612 K Street NW, Suite 600, Washington, DC 20006; 800-584-7336; www.coopamerica.org.

EarthSave

EarthSave has chapters throughout the country (and some overseas). Many chapters hold regular vegetarian potlucks. They have some excellent food specific publications: *Our Food, Our World: Transition to Healthy Food Choices*, as well as John Robbins' books *Diet For a New America* and *May All Be Fed*. For information on the EarthSave chapter nearest you, call: 800-362-3648; www.earthsave.org.

Food First/Institute for Food and Development Policy

A high-quality, member-supported, nonprofit people's think tank and education-for-action center. For information and action suggestions: 398 60th Street, Oakland, CA 94618; 510-654-4400; www.foodfirst.org.

Heifer Project International

Heifer works around the world teaching sustainable, environmentally sound, agricultural techniques. Heifer animals offer hungry families around the world a way to feed themselves and become self-reliant. Children receive nutritious milk or eggs; families earn income for school, health care and better housing; communities go beyond meeting immediate needs to fulfilling dreams. P.O. Box 8058, Little Rock, AR 72203; 800-422-0474; www.heifer.org.

National Catholic Rural Life Conference

An organization grounded in a spiritual tradition that brings together the church, care of community, and care of creation. NCRLC serves as a prophetic voice for America's countryside, acts as a catalyst and convener for social justice and supports rural pastoral ministers. 4625 Beaver Avenue, Des Moines, IA 50310; 515-270-2634; www.ncrlc.com.

North American Vegetarian Society (NAVS)

Dedicated to promoting the vegetarian way of life by sponsoring conferences and campaigns, distributing educational materials, and publishing *Vegetarian Voice*.

Contact NAVS for a listing of vegetarian organizations in North America. P. O. Box 72, Dolgeville, NY 13329; 518-568-7970; www.navs-online.org.

Redefining Progress
They have developed an alternative measure of economic well being, the Genuine Progress Indicator. Unlike the Gross Domestic Product, the GPI subtracts for social and ecological costs. 1904 Franklin Street, 6th Floor, Oakland, CA 94612; 510-444-3041; ww.redefiningprogress.org.

Seed Savers Exchange
The oldest and most active group in preserving heirloom vegetables, fruits, flowers and rare breeds throughout the world. 3076 North Winn Road, Decorah, IA 52101; 319-382-5590; www.seedsavers.com.

Slow Food USA
A gastronomic movement ideologically and sensually engaged with regional, traditional foods. PO Box 1737, New York, NY 10021; www.slowfood.com.

Sustainable Agriculture Research and Education (SARE)
To find out more about sustainable agriculture, go to www.sare.org. This site includes educational items, news and events and links to organizations and individuals that support sustainable agriculture across the country.

Web of Creation
A website filled with good information, including a page entitled "Sustainable Diet," with helpful book and internet resources; see www.webofcreation.org.

Coffee Activism (Java Justice)
Coffee is the world's second most heavily traded commodity (next to oil). National programs such as Equal Exchange, The Songbird Foundation, TransFair USA and the Organic Coffee Association (see below), help to link individuals and entire congregations with coffee farmers who are guaranteed a fair price for their beans and who grow coffee in ecologically beneficial ways. A number of these organizations have programs that link congregations with Fair Trade coffee, enabling churches to buy and serve shade-grown, organic, and fair-trade coffee as an example of their commitment to protecting communities and ecosystems world-wide. Individuals can purchase such coffees at many retailers; if not, ask yours to stock it!

Equal Exchange
251 Revere Street, Canton, MA 02021; 781-830-0303, www.equalexchange.org.

Organic Coffee Association
www.orcacoffee.org

The Songbird Foundation
2367 Eastlake Ave East, Seattle, WA 98102; 206-374-3674; www.songbird.org.

TransFair USA
1611 Telegraph Ave., Suite 900, Oakland, CA 94612; 510-663-5260, www.transfairusa.org.

Animals

Center for Respect of Life and Environment
The Center was founded in 1986 to foster an ethic of compassion toward all sentient beings and respect for the integrity of nature. This ethic urges each of us to expand our moral concern to future generations; to poor, oppressed and disenfranchised human beings, to animals, plants and the earth as a whole. With a particular focus on higher education and religious institutions, the Center promotes a humane and sustainable future for all members of the earth community. 2100 L St., NW, Washington, DC 20037; 202-778-6133; www.crle.org.

Farm Animal reform movement (FARM)
Promotes vegetarianism and advocates for the well-being of farm animals through national grassroots educational campaigns, massive media blitzes and participation in government decision-making processes. P.O. Box 30654, Bethesda, MD 20824; 888-FARM-USA; www.farmusa.org.

The Fund for Animals
Protects wildlife and domestic animals through education, legislation, litigation, and hands-on care at several sanctuaries. 200 West 57th St., Suite 705, New York, NY 10019; 888-405-FUND; www.fund.org.

GRACE Factory Farm Project
Helps rural communities around the country oppose the spread of new factory farms and helps close down existing ones which threaten health and well-being; addresses the impacts of industrial animal production on diet, the environment, and human and animal health. 145 Spruce St., Lititz, PA 17543; 717-627-0410; www.factoryfarm.org.

Humane Farming Association
Works to stop animal abuse in factory farming and slaughterhouses with anti-cruelty investigations and exposés, national media and ad campaigns, direct hands-on emergency care and refuge for abused farm animals, consumer awareness programs, state and federal legislation and youth humane education. P. O. Box 3577, San Rafael, CA 94912; 415-485-1495; www.hfa.org.

Tribe of Heart
Makes use of storytelling, visual media, and the arts to present a vision of a compassionate future; creators of *Witness*, a powerful documentary about the fur industry. P. O. Box 149, Ithaca, NY 14851; 607-275-0806; www.tribeofheart.org.

Videos

Affluenza: The Cost of High Living
An excellent video produced by John DeGraaf and public TV station KCTS in Seattle, which highlights environmental, social, community and spiritual costs of consumption. A significant portion of *Affluenza* focuses on a Christian response to over-consumerism. Sixty minutes, with a guide for group discussion. Call 800- 937-5387.

Beyond Organic: The Vision of Fairview Gardens
Produced by John DeGraaf (producer of *Affluenza*), this inspiring video tells the story of Fairview Gardens and its struggle to survive in the face of rapid suburban development. It draws a sharp contrast between community supported agriculture and conventional chemical farming. 33 minutes. Bullfrog Films, P.O. Box 149, Oley, PA 19547; 800-543-3764; www.bullfrogfilms.com.

The Global Banquet: The Politics of Food
One of the best videos on the globalization of the food industry! Discussion and study guide included, this video is divided into two 25 minute segments. Produced by Maryknoll World Productions, P.O. Box 308 Maryknoll, NY 10545; 800-227-8523, www.maryknoll.org. (See p. 296 for resource centers that lend this film.)

Hot Potatoes
Explores the dangers of potato blight and the chemicals used to control it. More than 150 years after Ireland's potato famine, late blight is still an immense global threat. Potatoes have gradually become one of the world's three most important sources of nutrition, especially in developing nations. But the failure to heed the warnings of an exceptional scientist in the 1950s is having dire consequences at the beginning of the 21st century. 57 minutes; Bullfrog Films, P.O. Box 149, Oley, PA 19547; 800-543-3764; www.bullfrogfilms.com.

Who's Counting? Marilyn Waring on Sex, Lies, and Global Economics
Waring challenges the myths of economics, and our tacit compliance with political agendas that masquerade as objective economic policy. 94 Minutes. Bullfrog Films, P.O. Box 149, Oley, PA 19547; 800-543-3764; www.bullfrogfilms.com.

Bibliography

Food and Agriculture

Abelman, Michael. *From the Good Earth: A Celebration of Growing Food around the World*. New York: Harry N. Abrams, Inc., 1993.

Abelman, Michael and Cynthia Wisehart. *On Good Land: The Autobiography of an Urban Farm*. San Francisco: Chronicle Books, 1998.

Berry, Wendell. *What are People For?* San Francisco: North Point Press, 1990.

————. *Home Economics*. San Francisco: North Point Press, 1987.

————. *Sex, Economy, Freedom, and Community: Eight Essays*. New York: Pantheon Books, 1993.

————. *The Unsettling of America: Culture & Agriculture*. San Francisco: Sierra Club Books, 1977.

Boucher, Douglas. *The Paradox of Plenty: Hunger in a Bountiful World*. Oakland: Food First Books, 1999.

Brower, Michael and Leon, Warren. *The Consumer's Guide to Effective Environmental Choices: Practical Advice from the Union of Concerned Scientists*. New York: Three Rivers Press, 1999.

Jackson, Wes. *Becoming Native to This Place*. New York: Counterpoint Press, 1996.

Jackson, Wes and William Vitek. *Rooted in the Land: Essays on Community and Place*. New Haven, CT: Yale University Press, 1996.

Lappe, Frances Moore. *Diet for a Small Planet*. New York: Ballantine Books, 1971.

Lappe, Frances Moore and Joseph Collins. *World Hunger: Twelve Myths*. New York: Grove Weidenfeld, 1986.

Lappe, Frances Moore and Anna Lappe. *Hope's Edge*. New York: Tarcher/Putnam, 2002.

Nabhan, Gary Paul. *Coming Home to Eat: The Pleasures and Politics of Local Foods*. New York: W.W. Norton, 2001.

Nearing, Helen. *Simple Food for the Good Life*. Walpole, NH: Stillpoint Publishing, 1980.

Nestle, Marion. *Food Politics: How the Food Industry Influences Nutrition and Health*. Berkeley: University of California Press, 2002.

Robbins, John. *Diet for a New America*. Walpole, NH: Stillpoint Publishing, 1987.

————. *The Food Revolution: How Your Diet Can Help Save Your Life and the World*. Berkeley CA: Conari Press, 2001.

Robbins, John and Jia Patton. *May All Be Fed*. New York: William Morrow and Co., 1992.

Ryan, John and Alan Durning. *Stuff: The Secret Lives of Everyday Things*. Seattle: Northwest Environment Watch, 1997.

Schlosser, Eric. *Fast Food Nation: The Dark Side of the All-American Meal*. New York: HarperCollins, 2002.

Shiva, Vandana. *Stolen Harvest: The Hijacking of the Global Food Supply*. Cambridge, MA: South End Press, 2000.

———. *Biopiracy: The Plunder of Nature and Knowledge*. Cambridge, MA: South End Press, 1997.

———. *The Violence of the Green Revolution*. London: Zed Books, 1992.

Sider, Ronald. *Rich Christians in an Age of Hunger*. Dallas: Word Publishing, 1990.

Christian Eco-Theology

Austin, Richard Cartwright. *Reclaiming America: Restoring Nature to Culture*. Abingdon, VA: Creekside Press, 1990.

———. *Hope for the Land: Nature in the Bible*. Atlanta: John Knox Press, 1988.

Berry, Thomas. *The Dream of the Earth*. San Francisco: Sierra Club Books, 1988.

Boff, Leonardo. *Ecology and Liberation: A New Paradigm*. Maryknoll, NY: Orbis Books, 1995.

Bradley, Ian. *God is Green: Ecology For Christians*. New York: Doubleday, 1992.

Brueggemann, Walter. *The Land: Place As Gift, Promise, and Challenge in Biblical Faith*. Philadelphia: Fortress Press, 1997.

DeWitt, Calvin. *Earthwise: A Biblical Response to Environmental Issues*. Grand Rapids, MI: CRC Publications,1994.

Hessel, Dieter, ed. *After Nature's Revolt: Eco-Justice and Theology*. Minneapolis: Augsburg Fortress Press, 1992.

McFague, Sallie. *Models of God*. Philadelphia: Fortress Press, 1987.

———. *Abundant Life: Rethinking Theology and Ecology from a Planet in Peril*. Minneapolis: Augsburg Fortress Press, 2001.

McKibben, Bill. *The Comforting Whirlwind: God, Job, and the Scale of Creation*. Grand Rapids, MI: WB Eerdmans Publishing, 1994.

Nash, James. *Loving Nature*. Nashville: Abingdon Press, 1991.

Radford-Ruether, Rosemary. *Gaia and God: An Ecofeminist Theology of Earth Healing*. San Francisco: HarperSanFrancisco, 1992.

———. *Women Healing Earth: Third World Women on Ecology, Feminism and Religion*. Maryknoll, NY: Orbis Books, 1996.

Rasmussen, Larry. *Earth Community, Earth Ethics*. Maryknoll, NY: Orbis Books, 1996.

Roberts, Elizabeth and Elias Amidon. *Earth Prayers From Around the World*. New York: HarperCollins, 1991.

Roth, Nancy. *Organic Prayer: Cultivating Your Relationship with God*. Cambridge, MA: Cal Publications, 1993.

Santmire, H. Paul. *The Travail of Nature: The Ambiguous Ecological Promise of Christian Theology*. Philadelphia: Fortress Press, 1985.

Sherrard, Philip. *Human Image: World Image*. Ipswich, England: Golgonooza Press,1992.

Global Economics and Simpler Living

Andrews, Cecile. *The Circle of Simplicity: Return to the Good Life*. New York: Harper-Collins, 1997.

Brandt, Barbara. *Whole Life Economics: Revaluing Daily Life*. Philadelphia: New Society Publishers, 1995.

Cobb, Clifford, Ted Halsted and Jonathan Rowe. "If the GDP Is Up, Why Is America Down?" *Atlantic Monthly*, October 1995.

Cobb, John B., Jr. *Sustainability: Economics, Ecology, and Justice*. Maryknoll, NY: Orbis Books, 1995.

———. *Sustaining the Common Good: A Christian Perspective on the Global Economy*. Cleveland: The Pilgrim Press, 1994.

Daly, Herman and John B. Cobb, Jr. *For the Common Good: Redirecting the Economy Toward Community, the Environment, and a Sustainable Future*. Boston: Beacon Press, 1989.

Dominguez, Joe and Vicki Robin. *Your Money or Your Life*. New York: Penguin Books USA Inc., 1992.

Durning, Alan. *How Much is Enough? The Consumer Society and the Future of the Earth*. New York: W.W. Norton, 1992.

Elgin, Duane. *Voluntary Simplicity: Toward a Way of Life That is Outwardly Simple, Inwardly Rich*. New York: William Morrow, 1981.

Foster, Richard. *The Freedom of Simplicity*. San Francisco: Harper & Row, 1981.

Hawken, Paul. *The Ecology of Commerce: Doing Good Business*. New York: Harper-Collins, 1993.

Hawken, Paul, Amory Lovins and L. Hunter Lovins. *Natural Capitalism: Creating the Next Industrial Revolution*. Boston: Little, Brown and Co., 1999.

Korten, David. *When Corporations Rule the World*. West Hartford, CT: Kumarian Press, 1996.

———. *The Post-Corporate World: Life after Capitalism*. West Hartford, CT: Kumarian Press, 1999.

Meadows, Donella H. *Beyond the Limits: Confronting Global Collapse, Envisioning a Sustainable Future*. Mills, VT: Chelsea Green, 1992.

Schumacher, E.F. *Small is Beautiful: Economics as if People Mattered*. New York: Harper & Row, 1973.

Schut, Michael, ed. *Simpler Living, Compassionate Life: A Christian Perspective*. Denver, CO: Living the Good News, 1999.

Simon, Arthur. *How Much Is Enough? Hungering for God in an Affluent Culture*. Grand Rapids: Baker Book House, 2003.

Video Resource Centers

Helen Scimeca
Media Resource Center
Archdiocese of Baltimore
1201 Caton Ave.
Baltimore, MD 21227
(410) 646-5102

Noreen Stevens
Eastern Minnesota Resource Center, ELCA
2481 Como Ave.
St. Paul, MN 55108
(651) 523-1607

Tovi Harris
Ministry Resource Coordinator
Diocese of Olympia
1551 Tenth Ave.
E/PO Box 12126
Seattle, WA 98102
(206) 325-4200

Janice Horkey
Rocky Mountain Synod Resource Center
4500 Wadsworth Blvd.
Wheat Ridge, CO 80033
(303) 423-5654

Jackie Fielding
Education Coordinator
Diocese of California
1055 Taylor
San Francisco, CA 94108
(415) 673-5015

Carolyn Hardin Engelhardt
Ministry Resource Center
Yale University Divinity School
409 Prospect St.
New Haven, CT 06511
(203) 432-5319